Designing Enterprise Solutions with Sun™ Cluster 3.0

Richard Elling
Tim Read

Sun Microsystems Press
A Prentice Hall Title

The publisher offers discounts on this book when ordered in bulk quantities. For more information, contact: Corporate Sales Department, Phone: 800-382-3419; Fax: 201-236-7141; E-mail: corpsales@prenhall.com; or write: Prentice Hall PTR, Corp. Sales Dept., One Lake Street, Upper Saddle River, NJ 07458.

Editorial/production superviser: *Nicholas Radhuber*
Cover design director: *Jerry Votta*
Cover designer: *Kavish & Kavish Digital Publishing & Design*
Manufacturing manager: *Alexis R. Heydt*
Marketing manager: *Debby vanDijk*
Acquisitions editor: *Gregory G. Doench*

Sun Microsystems Press
Marketing manager: *Michael Llwyd Alread*
Publisher: *Rachel Borden*

10 9 8 7 6 5 4 3 2 1

ISBN 0-13-008458-1

Sun Microsystems Press
A Prentice Hall Title

Contents

6.   Case Study 2—Database Cluster   157

Figures

Tables

Preface

Designing Enterprise Solutions with Sun Cluster 3.0 is published under the auspices of the Sun BluePrints™ program. This book is written for systems architects and engineers who design clustered systems. It describes the fundamental systems engineering concepts behind clustered computer systems and discusses solutions and trade-offs in some detail.

Systems engineering is concerned with the creation of the entire answer to some real-life problem, with the answer based on science and technology [Ramo 65]. Systems engineers deal with the people/process/technology balance and multivariate problems. They integrate huge numbers of components, unwanted modes, partial requirements, indefinite answers, probabilities of external conditions, the testing of complicated systems, and all of the natural sciences behind the technology. This book contains little detail on specific engineering solutions; instead, it focuses on the fundamental concepts that are used repeatedly in the design of clustered computer systems.

This book provides detailed examples of the effective use of clustered system technology, along with information about the features and capabilities of the Sun™ Cluster 3.0 system (hereafter referred to as Sun Cluster 3.0).

Three concepts are addressed throughout the book—failures, synchronization, and arbitration. These three concepts are examined repeatedly at all levels of the systems design.

First, complex systems tend to fail in complex ways. Implementing clustered systems can prevent some of these failures. Businesses implement clusters when the cost of implementing and maintaining a cluster is less than the cost of a service outage. While anticipating the many ways in which services hosted on clusters can fail, you must be diligent when designing clustered systems to meet business needs.

Second, clustered systems use redundancy to ensure that no single point of failure renders the data inaccessible. However, adding redundancy to a system inherently creates a synchronization problem—the multiple copies of the data must remain synchronized, or chaos ensues.

Third, redundancy and failures create arbitration problems. Given two copies of data that are potentially out of sync, which is the correct copy? Similarly, any data service operating on the data must do so with the expectation that no other data service is operating on the same data without its knowledge. These arbitration problems are solved with services supplied by the cluster infrastructure.

Sun BluePrints Program

The mission of the Sun BluePrints™ program is to empower Sun's customers with the technical knowledge required to implement reliable, extensible, and secure information systems within the data center using Sun products. This program provides a framework to identify, develop, and distribute best practices information that applies across the Sun product lines. Experts in technical subjects in various areas contribute to the program and focus on the scope and advantages of the information.

The Sun BluePrints program includes books, guides, and online articles. Through these vehicles, Sun can provide guidance, installation and implementation experiences, real-life scenarios, and late-breaking technical information.

The monthly electronic magazine, Sun BluePrints OnLine, is located on the web at `http://www.sun.com/blueprints`. To be notified about updates to the Sun BluePrints Program, please register on this site.

Who Should Use This Book

This book is primarily intended for readers with varying degrees of experience with or knowledge of clustered system technology. Detailed examples of using this technology effectively are provided in combination with the features and capabilities of the Sun Cluster 3.0 software.

Before You Read This Book

You should be familiar with the basic system architecture and design principles, as well as the administration and maintenance functions of the Solaris™ operating environment. You should also have an understanding of standard network protocols and topologies.

How This Book Is Organized

This book has six chapters and four appendixes:

- Cluster and Complex System Design Issues
- Enterprise Cluster Computing Building Blocks
- Sun Cluster 3.0 Architecture
- Management Server
- Case Study 1—File Server Cluster
- Case Study 2—Database Cluster
- Sun Cluster 3.0 Design Checklists
- Sun Cluster Technology History and Perspective
- Data Center Guidelines
- Tools

Chapter 1 introduces the problems that clustered systems try to solve. Emphasis is placed on failures, synchronization, and arbitration. Complex systems tend to fail in complex ways, so thinking about the impact of failures on systems should be foremost in the mind of the systems engineer. Synchronization is key to making two or more things look like one thing, which is very important for redundant systems. Arbitration is the decision-making process—what the system does when an event occurs or does not occur.

Chapter 2 reviews infrastructure business component building blocks—file, database, and name services, application services, and web services—and examines how clustering technology can make them highly available and scalable.

Chapter 3 describes the Sun Cluster 3.0 product architecture. This is the cornerstone of building continuously available services using Sun products. Sun Cluster 3.0 software includes many advanced features that enable the systems architect to design from the services perspective, rather than the software perspective.

Chapter 4 covers a Sun Cluster 3.0 management server example. This chapter describes the basic infrastructure services and a management server that provides these services first. This management server is used in the clustered systems solutions described in subsequent chapters.

Chapters 5 and 6 contain two hypothetical case studies—a low-cost file service and online database services. Each case study describes the business case and defines th requirements of the customer. These solutions are used to derive the design priorities that provide direction to the systems architect when design trade-offs mus be made. Next, these chapters describe the system design, discussing the systems design methodology, and exploring in detail some of the design trade-offs that fac the systems architect.

Appendix A contains a series of design checklists for the new Sun Cluster 3.0 product.

Appendix B provides an insight into the genesis of the new Sun Cluster 3.0 produc and contrasts the features of Sun Cluster 2.2 with those of Sun Cluster 3.0.

Appendix C contains guidelines for data center design that supports highly available services.

Appendix D is a brief survey of tools that systems architects and engineers find useful when designing or analyzing highly available systems.

Ordering Sun Documents

The SunDocs[SM] program provides more than 250 manuals from Sun Microsystems, Inc. If you live in the United States, Canada, Europe, or Japan, you can purchase documentation sets or individual manuals through this program.

Accessing Sun Documentation Online

The docs.sun.com web site enables you to access Sun technical documentation online. You can browse the docs.sun.com archive or search for a specific book titl or subject. The URL is http://docs.sun.com/.

Related Books

The following table lists books that provide additional useful information.

Title	Author and Publisher	ISBN Number/Part Number/URL
Sun Cluster Environment Sun Cluster 2.2	Enrique Vargas, Joseph Bianco, and David Deeths Sun Microsystems Press/Prentice Hall, Inc. (2001)	0-13-041870-6
Backup and Restore Practices for Sun Enterprise Servers	Stan Stringfellow, Miroslav Klivansky, and Michael Barto Sun Microsystems Press/Prentice Hall, Inc. (2000)	0-13-089401-X
System Interface Guide	Sun Microsystems	806-4750-10
Multithreaded Programming Guide	Sun Microsystems	806-5257-10
Sun Cluster 3.0 7/01 Collection	Sun Microsystems	`http://www.sun.docs` and AnswerBook2™
Building a JumpStart Infrastructure	Alex Noordergraaf Sun Microsystems	`http://www.sun.com/blueprints`
Cluster Platform 220/1000 Architecture—A Product from the SunTone Platforms Portfolio	Enrique Vargas Sun Microsystems	Sun BluePrints OnLine article `http://www.sun.com/blueprints`

Typographic Style

Typeface	Meaning	Examples

AaBbCc123	Names of commands, files, and directories, and URLs	Edit your `.login` file.
		Use `ls -a` to list all files.
		`machine_name % You have mail.`
		`http://www.sun.com`

AaBbCc123	Text entered into the system (**bold**)	`machine_name % ` **`su`** `Password:`
AaBbCc123	Text displayed on the monitor	`Text varies with output`
AaBbCc123	Book titles, new words or terms, words to be emphasized	Read Chapter 6 in the *User's Guide*. These are called *class* options. You *must* be superuser to do this.
	Command-line variable; replace with a real name or value	To delete a file, type `rm` *filename*.

Shell Prompts in Command Examples

The following table identifies the default system prompt and superuser prompt for the C shell, Bourne shell, and Korn shell.

Shell	Prompt
C shell	*machine_name*%
C shell superuser	*machine_name*#
Bourne shell and Korn shell	$
Bourne shell and Korn shell superuser	#

Acknowledgements

The authors would especially like to thank Chuck Alexander whose vision and drive behind the Sun BluePrints program has made it so successful; Shuroma Herekar and Barbara Jugo for supporting the writers, editors, and illustrators who made it all possible; and of course Gary Rush, for managing the Blueprints projects.

This book was conceived, written, reviewed, edited, produced, and printed in less than six months. Publication would not have been possible without the collaboration and cooperation of the subject matter experts, writer, reviewers, editors, and artist, who gave its development top priority, while continuing to perform their usual duties.

We would like to acknowledge and thank the cluster experts and reviewers who helped shape the technical content of this book, all of them—Mike Arwood, Joseph Bianco, Michael Byrne, Ralph Campbell, Al Clepper, David Deeths, Tom Cox, Steven Docy, Andrew Hisgen, Mark Kampe, Yousef Khalidi, Peter Lees, James MacFarlane, James McPherson, Kim Merriman, Hossein Moiin, Declan Murphy, Sohrab Modi, David Nelson-Gal, Dan Orbach, Shankar Pasupathy, Ted Persky, Ira Pramanick, Marty Rattner, Nicolas Solter, Ronnie Townsend, Nancy Tu, and Enrique Vargas—for their input and support. And, to the entire Sun Cluster engineering team, well done!

A special thanks to Dany Galgani, who is one of the most responsive and talented illustrators at Sun Microsystems, for creating and revising more than 50 illustrations in less than 15 days; and Rashmi Shah, who helped input the editorial comments in the deadline crunch.

Thanks to George Wood, our mostly patient, tenacious, and tireless technical writer and editor for blending the diverse writing styles of the subject matter experts, authors, and reviewers from several different countries into the finished product.

We would also like to acknowledge and thank Regina Elling, Rex Casey, Billie Markim, Linda Wiesner, and Mary Lou Nohr, for editing the book and providing invaluable developmental, organizational, trademark, and glossary contributions; and Cathy Miller for creating a superb index.

Richard Elling

I'd like to specially thank Regina, who always makes sure my writing is clear and puts up with my long hours at the keyboard. Thanks to Boca, who contributed much to the early conversations about this book. And, of course, Rusty, who is always along for the ride. I'd also like to thank Enrique Vargas and Ted Persky for their contributions to the book.

Tim Read

I would like to start by thanking Hazel for the love, support, and cups of tea provided as the deadlines approached. I would also like to thank my manager, Keith Glancey, for allowing me time to write this book. I am eternally grateful to my parents (all of them!), without whose support I would never have made it this far. And finally, I would like to return the compliment to Brian, Cindy and Shaun.

CHAPTER 1

Cluster and Complex System Design Issues

This chapter addresses the following topics:

- The need for a business to have a highly available, clustered system
- System failures that influence business decisions
- Factors to consider when designing a clustered system
- Failure modes specific to clusters, synchronization, and arbitration

To understand why you are designing a clustered system, you must first understand the business need for such a system. Your understanding of the complex system failures that can occur in such systems will influence the decision to use a clustered system and will also help you design a system to handle such failures. You must also consider issues such as data synchronization, arbitration, caching, timing, and clustered system failures—split brain, multiple instances, and amnesia—as you design your clustered system.

Once you are familiar with all the building blocks, issues and features that enable you to design an entire clustered system, you can analyze the solutions that the Sun Cluster 3.0 software offers to see how it meets your enterprise business needs and backup, restore, and recovery requirements.

The sections in this chapter are:

- Business Reasons for Clustered Systems
- Failures in Complex Systems
- Data Synchronization
- Arbitration Schemes
- Data Caches
- Timeouts
- Failures in Clustered Systems
- Summary

Business Reasons for Clustered Systems

Businesses build clusters of computers to improve performance or availability. Some products and technologies can improve both. However, much clustering activity driving the computer industry today is focused on improving service availability.

Downtime is a critical problem for an increasing number of computer users. Computers have not become less reliable, but users now insist on greater degrees of availability. As more businesses depend on computing as the backbone of their operation, around-the-clock availability of services becomes more critical.

Downtime can translate into lost money for businesses, potentially large amounts of money. Large enterprise customers are not the only ones to feel this pinch. The demands for mission-critical computing have reached the workgroup, and even the desktop. No one today can afford downtime. Even the downtime required to perform maintenance on systems is under pressure. Computer users want the systems to remain operational while the system administrators perform system maintenance tasks.

Businesses implement clusters for availability when the potential cost of downtime is greater than the incremental cost of the cluster. The potential cost of downtime can be difficult to predict accurately. To help predict this cost, you can use risk assessment.

Risk Assessment

Risk assessment is the process of determining what results when an event occurs. For many businesses, the business processes themselves are as complex as the computer systems they rely on. This significantly complicates the systems architect's risk assessment. It may be easier to make some sort of generic risk assessment in which the business risk can be indicted as cost. Nevertheless, justifying the costs of a clustered system is often difficult unless one can show that the costs of implementing and supporting a cluster can reduce the costs of downtime. Since the former can be measured in real dollars and the latter is based on a multivariate situation with many probability functions, many people find it easier to relate to some percentage of "uptime."

Clusters attempt to decrease the probability that a fault will cause a service outage, but they cannot prevent it. They do, however, limit the maximum service outage time by providing a host on which to recover from the fault.

Computations justifying the costs of a cluster must not assume zero possibility of a system outage. Prospect theory is useful to communicate this to end users in such a situation. To say the system has "a 99 percent chance of no loss" is preferable to "a 1 percent chance of loss." However, for design purposes, the systems architect must consider carefully the case where there is 1 percent chance of loss. You must always consider the 1 percent chance of loss in your design analysis. After you access the risks of downtime, you can do a more realistic cost estimate.

Cost Estimation

Ultimately, everything done by businesses can be attributed to cost. Given infinite funds and time ("time is money)" perfect systems can be built and operated. Unfortunately, most real systems have both funding and time constraints.

Nonrecurring expenses include hardware and software acquisition costs, operator training, software development, and so forth. Normally, these costs are not expected to recur. The nonrecurring hardware costs of purchasing a cluster are obviously greater than an equivalent, single system. Software costs vary somewhat. There is the cost of the cluster software and any agents required. An additional cost may be incurred as a result of the software licensing agreement for any other software. In some cases, a software vendor may require the purchase of a software license for each node in the cluster. Other software vendors may have more flexible licensing, such as per-user licenses.

Recurring costs include ongoing maintenance contracts, consumable goods, power, network connection fees, environmental conditioning, support personnel, and floor space costs.

Almost all system designs must be justified in economic terms. Simply put, is the profit generated by the system greater than its cost? For systems that do not consider downtime, economic justification tends to be a fairly straightforward calculation.

$$Plifetime = Rlifetime - Cdowntime - Cnonrecurring - \Sigma Crecurring$$

where:

$P_{lifetime}$ is the profit over the lifetime of the system.

$R_{lifetime}$ is the revenue generated by the system over its lifetime.

$C_{downtime}$ is the cost of any downtime.

$C_{nonrecurring}$ is the cost of nonrecurring expenses.

$C_{recurring}$ is the cost of any recurring expenses.

During system design these costs tend to be difficult to predict accurately. However, they tend to be readily measurable on well-designed systems.

The cost of downtime is often described in terms of the profit of uptime.

$$Cdowntime(t) = tdown \times \frac{Puptime}{tup}$$

where:

$C_{downtime}$ is the cost of downtime.

t_{down} is the duration of the outage.

P_{uptime} is the profit made during $t_{up.}$

t_{up} is the time the system had been up.

For most purposes, this equation suffices. What is not accounted for in this equation is the opportunity cost. If a web site has competitors and is down, a customer is likely to go to one of the competing web sites. This defection represents an opportunity loss that is difficult to quantify.

The pitfall in using such an equation is that the P_{uptime} is likely to be a function of time. For example, a factory that operates using one shift makes a profit only during the shift hours. During the hours that the factory is not operating, the P_{uptime} is zero, and consequently the $C_{downtime}$ is zero.

$$Cdowntime(t) = tdown \times \frac{Puptime(t)}{tup}$$

where:

$P_{uptime(t)} = P_{nominal}$, when t is during the work hours

$= 0$, all other times

Another way to show the real cost of system downtime is to weight the cost according to the impact on the business. For example, a system that supports a call center might choose impacted user minutes (IUM), instead of a dollar value, to represent the cost of downtime. If 1,000 users are affected by an outage for 5 minutes, the IUM value is 1,000 users times 5 minutes, or 5,000 IUMs. This approach has the advantage of being an easily measured metric. The number of logged-in users and the duration of any outage are readily measurable quantities. A service level agreement (SLA) that specifies the service level as IUMs can be negotiated. IUMs can then be translated into a dollar value by the accountants.

Another advantage of using IUMs is that the service provided to the users is measured, rather than the availability of the system components. SLAs can also be negotiated on the basis of service availability, but it becomes difficult to account for the transfer of the service to a secondary site. IUMs can be readily transferred to secondary sites because the measurement is not based in any way on the system components.

Failures in Complex Systems

This section discusses failure modes and effects in complex systems. From this discussion you can gain an appreciation of how complex systems can fail in complex ways. Before you can design a system to recover from failures, you must understand how systems fail.

Failures are the primary focus of the systems architect designing highly available (HA) systems. Understanding the probability, causes, effects, detection, and recovery of failures is critical to building successful HA systems. The professional HA expert has many years of study and experience with a large variety of esoteric systems and tools that are used to design HA systems. The average systems architect is not likely to have such tools or experience but will be required to design such systems. Fortunately, much of the detailed engineering work is already done by vendors, such as Sun Microsystems, who offer integrated HA systems.

A typical systems design project is initially concerned with defining "what the system is supposed to do." The systems architect designing highly available clusters must also be able to concentrate on "what the system is not supposed to do." This is known as testing for unwanted modes, which can occur as a result of integrating components that individually perform properly but may not perform together as expected. The latter can be much more difficult and time consuming than the former, especially during functional testing. Typical functional tests attempt to show that a system does what it is supposed to do. However, it is just as important, and more difficult, to attempt to show that a system does not do what it is not supposed to do.

A *defect* is anything that, when exercised, prevents something from functioning in the manner in which it was intended. The defect can, for example, be due to design, manufacture, or misuse and can take the form of a badly designed, incorrectly manufactured, or damaged hardware or software component. An *error* usually results from the *defect* being exercised, and if not corrected, may result in a *failure.*

Examples of *defects* include:

- Hardware factory defect—A pin in a connector is not soldered to a wire correctly, resulting in data loss when exercised.
- Hardware field defect—A damaged pin no longer provides a connection, resulting in data loss when exercised.
- Software field defect—An inadvertently corrupted executable file can cause an application to crash.

An *error* occurs when a component exhibits unintended behavior and can be a consequence of:

- A defect being exercised
- A component being used outside of its intended operational parameters
- Some other cause, for example a random, though anticipated, environmental effect

A *fault* is usually a defect, but possibly an imprecise error, and should be qualified. "Fault" may be synonymous with bug in the context of software faults [Lyu95], but need not be, as in the case of a page fault.

Highly available computer systems are not systems that never fail. They experience, more or less, the same failure rates on a per component basis as any other systems. The difference between these types of systems is how they respond to failures. You can divide the basic process of responding to failures into five phases.

FIGURE 1-1 shows the five phases of failure response:

1. Fault detection

2. Fault isolation to determine the source of the fault and the component or field-replaceable unit (FRU) that must be repaired

3. Fault correction, if possible, in the case of automatically recoverable components, such as error checking and correction (ECC) memory

4. Failure containment so that the fault does not propagate to other components

5. System reconfiguration so you can repair the faulty component

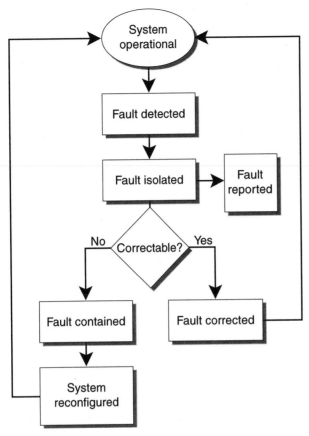

FIGURE 1-1   HA System Failure Response

Fault Detection

Fault detection is an important part of highly available systems. Although it may seem simple and straightforward, it is perhaps the most complex part of a cluster. The problem of fault detection in a cluster is an open problem—one for which not all solutions are known. The Sun Cluster strategy for solving this problem is to rely on industry-standard interfaces between cluster components. These interfaces have built-in fault detection and error reporting. However, it is unlikely that all failure modes of all components and their interactions are known.

While this may sound serious, it is not so bad when understood in the context of the cluster. For example, consider unshielded twisted pair (UTP), 10BASE-T Ethernet interfaces. Two classes of failures can affect the interface—physical and logical.

These errors can be further classified or assigned according to the four layers of the TCP/IP stack, but for the purpose of this discussion, the classification of physical and logical is sufficient. Physical failures are a bounded set. They are often detected by the network interface card (NIC). However, not all physical failures can be detected by a single NIC, nor can all physical failures be simulated by simply removing a cable.

Knowing how the system software detects and handles error conditions as they occur is important to a systems architect. If the network fails in some way, the software should be able to isolate the failure to a specific component.

For example, TABLE 1-1 lists some common 10BASE-T Ethernet failure modes. As you can see from this example, there are many potential failure modes. Some of these failure modes are not easily detected.

TABLE 1-1   Common 10BASE-T Ethernet Failure Modes

Description	Type	Detected by	Detectability
Cable unplugged	Physical	NIC	Yes, unless Software Query Enable (SQE) is enabled
Cable shorted	Physical	NIC	Yes
Cable wired in reverse polarity	Physical	NIC	Yes
Cable too long	Physical	NIC (in some cases only)	Difficult because the error may range from no link (with SQE disabled) to high bit error rate (BER) that must be detected by logical tests
Cable receive pair wiring failure	Physical	NIC	Yes, unless SQE is enabled
Cable transmit pair wiring failure	Physical	Remote device	Yes, unless SQE is enabled
Electromagnetic interference (EMI)	Physical	NIC (in some cases only)	Difficult, because the errors may be intermittent with the only detection being changes in the BER
Duplicate medium access control address (MAC)	Logical	Solaris operating environment	Yes

TABLE 1-1   Common 10BASE-T Ethernet Failure Modes *(Continued)*

Description	Type	Detected by	Detectability
Duplicate IP address	Logical	Solaris operating environment	Yes
Incorrect IP network address	Logical		Not automatically detectable for the general case
No response from remote host	Logical	Sun Cluster software	Sun Cluster software uses a series of progressive tests to try to establish connection to the remote host

Note – You may be tempted to simulate physical or even logical network errors by disconnecting cables, but this does not simulate all possible failure modes of the physical network interface. Full physical fault simulation for networks can be a complicated endeavor.

Probes

Probes are tools or software that you can use to detect most system faults and to detect latent faults. You can also use probes to gather information and improve the fault detection. Hardware designs use probes for measuring environmental conditions such as temperature and power. Software probes query service response or act like end users completing transactions.

You must put probes at the end points to effectively measure end-to-end service level. For example, if a user community at a remote site requires access to a service, a probe system must installed at the remote site to measure the service and its connection to the end users. It is not uncommon for a large number of probes to exist in an enterprise that provides mission-critical services to a geographically distributed user base. Collecting the probe status at the operations control center that supports the system is desirable. However, if the communications link between the probe and operations control center is down, the probe must be able to collect and store status information for later retrieval. For more information on probes, see "Failure Detection" on page 91.

Complex services require complex probes to inquire about all capabilities of the service. This complexity produces opportunity for defects in the probe itself. You cannot rely on a faulty probe to deliver an accurate status of the service.

Latent Faults

To detect latent faults in hardware, you can use special test software such as the Sun Management Center Hardware Diagnostic Suite (HWDS) software. The HWDS allows you to perform tests that exercise the hardware components of a system at scheduled intervals. Because these tests consume some system resources, they are done infrequently. Detected errors are treated as normal errors and reported to the system by the normal error reporting mechanisms.

The most obvious types of latent faults are those that exist but are not detected during the testing process. These include software bugs that are not simulated by software testing, and hardware tests that do not provide adequate coverage of possible faults.

Fault Isolation

Fault isolation is the process of determining, from the available data, which component caused a failure. Once the faulty component is identified or isolated, it can be reset or replaced with a functioning component.

The term fault isolation is sometimes used as a synonym for fault containment, which is the process of preventing the spread of a failure from one component to others.

For analysis of potential modes of failure, it is common to divide a system into a set of disjointed *fault isolation zones*. Each error or failure must be attributed to one of these zones. For example, a FRU or an application process can represent a fault isolation zone.

When recovering from a failure, the system can reset or replace numerous components with a single action. For example, a Sun Quad FastEthernet™ card has four network interfaces located on one physical card. Because recovery work is performed on all components in a *fault recovery zone*, replacing the Sun Quad FastEthernet card affects all four network interfaces on the card.

Fault Reporting

Fault reporting notifies components and humans that a fault has occurred. Good fault reporting with clear, unambiguous, and concise information goes a long way toward improving system serviceability.

Berkeley Standard Distribution (BSD) introduced the `syslogd` daemon as a general-purpose message logging service. This daemon is very flexible and network aware, making it a popular interface for logging messages. Typically, the default `syslogd` configuration is not sufficient for complex systems or reporting structures. However, correctly configured, `syslogd` can efficiently distribute messages from a number of systems to centralized monitoring systems. The `logger` command provides a user level interface for generating `syslogd` messages and is very useful for systems administration shell scripts.

Not all fault reports should be presented to system operators with the same priority. To do so would make appropriate prioritized responses difficult, particularly if the operator was inexperienced. For example, media defects in magnetic tape are common and expected. A tape drive reports all media defects it encounters, but may only send a message to the operator when a tape has exceeded a threshold of errors that says that the tape must be replaced. The tape drive continues to accumulate the faults to compare with the threshold, but not every fault generates a message for the operator.

Faults can be classified in terms of correctability and detectability. Correctable faults are faults that can be corrected internally by a component and that are transparent to other components (faults inside the black box). Recoverable faults, a superset of correctable faults, include faults that can be recovered through some other method such as retrying transactions, rerouting through an alternate path, or using an alternate primary. Regardless of the recovery method, correctable faults are faults that do not result in unavailability or loss of data. Uncorrectable errors do result in unavailability or data loss. Unavailability is usually measured over a discrete time period and can vary widely depending on the SLAs with the end users.

Reported correctable (RC) errors are of little consequence to the operator. Ideally, all RC errors should have soft-error rate discrimination algorithms applied to determine whether the rate is excessive. An excessive rate may require the system to be serviced.

Error correction is the action taken by a component to correct an error condition without exposing other components to the error. Error correction is often done at the hardware level by ECC memory or data path correction, tape write operation retries, magnetic disk defect management, and so forth. The difference between a correctable error and a fault that requires reconfiguration is that other components in the system are shielded from the error and are not involved in its correction.

Reported uncorrectable (RU) errors notify the operators that something is wrong and give the service organization some idea of what to fix.

Silent correctable (SC) errors cannot have rate-discrimination algorithms applied because the system receives no report of the event. If the rate of an SC error is excessive because something has broken, no one ever finds out.

Silent uncorrectable (SU) errors are neither reported nor recoverable. Such errors are typically detected some time after they occur. For example, a bank customer discovers a mistake while verifying a checking account balance at the end of the month. The error occurred some time before its eventual discovery. Fortunately, most banks have extensive auditing capabilities and processes ultimately to account for such errors.

TABLE 1-2 shows some examples of reported and correctable errors.

TABLE 1-2 Reported and Correctable Errors

	Correctable	Uncorrectable
Reported	RC DRAM ECC error, dropped TCP/IP packet	RU Kernel panic, serial port parity error
Silent	SC Processor branch prediction table error	SU Undetected data corruption

For additional details on detectable faults, see "Fault Detection" on page 7 and "Failure Detection" on page 91.

Fault Containment

Fault containment is the ability to contain the effects and prevent the propagation of an error or failure, usually due to some boundary. For clusters, computing nodes are often the fault containment boundary. The assumption is that the node halts, as a direct consequence of the failure or by a *failfast* or *failstop*, before it has a chance to do significant I/O and propagate the fault.

Fault containment can also be undertaken proactively, for example, through failure fencing. The concept of failure fencing is closely related to failstop. One way to ensure that a faulty component cannot propagate errors is to prevent it from accessing other components or data. "Disk Fencing" on page 112 describes the details of how the Sun Cluster software products use this failure fencing technique.

Fault propagation occurs when a fault in one component causes a fault in another component. This propagation can occur when two components share a common component; it is a common mode fault. For example, a SCSI-2 bus is often used for low-cost, shared storage in clusters. The SCSI-2 bus represents a shared component that can propagate faults. If a disk or host failure hangs the SCSI-2 bus (interferes with the bus arbitration), the fault is propagated to all targets and hosts on the bus. Similarly, before the development of unshielded twisted pair (UTP) Ethernet (10BASE-T, 100BASE-T), many implementations of Ethernet networks used coaxial cable (10BASE-2). The network is subject to node faults, which interfere with the arbitration or transmission of data on the network, and can propagate to all nodes on the network through the shared coaxial cable.

Another form of fault propagation occurs when incorrect data is stored and replicated. For example, mirrored disks are synchronized closely. Bad data written to one disk is likely to be propagated to the mirror. Sources of bad data may include operator error, undetected read faults in a read-modify-write operation, and undetected synchronization faults.

Operator error can be difficult to predict and prevent. You can prevent operator errors from propagating throughout the system by implementing a time delay between the application of changes on the primary and remote site. If this time delay is large enough to ensure detection of operator error, changes on the remote site can be prevented so that the fault is contained at the primary site. This containment prevents the fault from propagating to the remote site. For details, see "High Availability Versus Disaster Recovery" on page 53.

Reconfiguration Around Faults

Reconfiguring the system around faults is a technique commonly employed in clusters. A faulty cluster node causes reconfiguration of the cluster to remove the faulty node from the cluster. Any cluster-aware services that were resident on the faulty node are started on one or more surviving nodes in the cluster. Reconfiguration around faults can be a complicated process. The paragraphs that follow examine this process in more detail.

A number of features in the Solaris operating environment allow system reconfiguration around faults without requiring clustering software. These features are:

- Dynamic reconfiguration (DR)
- Internet protocol multipathing (IPMP)
- I/O multipathing (Sun StorEdge™ Traffic Manager)
- Alternate pathing (AP)

DR attaches and detaches system components to an active Solaris operating environment system without causing an outage. Thus, DR is often used for servicing components. Note that DR does not include the fault detection, isolation, containment, or reconfiguration capabilities available in Sun Cluster software.

IPMP automatically reconfigures around failed network connections.

I/O multipathing balances loads across host bus adapters (HBAs). This feature, which is also known as MPxIO, was implemented in the Solaris 8 operating environment with kernel patch 108528-07 for SPARC®-based systems and 108529-07 for Intel-based systems.

AP reconfigures around failed network and storage paths. AP is somewhat limited in capability, and its use is discouraged in favor of IPMP and the Sun StorEdge Traffic Manager.

Future plans include tighter alignment and integration between these Solaris operating environment features and Sun Cluster software.

Fault Prediction

Fault prediction is the process of observing a component over time to predict when a fault is likely. Fault prediction works best when the component includes a consumable subcomponent or a subcomponent that has known decay properties. For example, an automobile computer knows the amount of fuel in the fuel tank and the instantaneous consumption rate. The computer can predict when the fuel tank will be empty—a state that would cause a fault condition. This information is displayed to the driver, who can take corrective action.

Practical fault prediction in computer systems today focuses primarily on storage media. Magnetic media, in particular, has behavior that can be used to predict when the ability to store and retrieve data will fall out of tolerance and result in a read failure in the future. For disks, this information is reported to the Solaris operating environment as soft errors. These errors, along with predictive failure information, can be examined using the iostat(1M) or kstat(1M) command.

Unfortunately, a large number of unpredictable faults can occur in computer systems. Software bugs make software prone to unpredictable faults.

Data Synchronization

More than one copy of data is a data synchronization problem. This section describes data synchronization issues.

Throughout this book, the concept of *ownership of data* is important. Ownership is a way to describe the authoritative owner of the single view of the data. Using a single, authoritative owner of data is useful for understanding the intricacies of modern clustered systems. In the event of failures, the ownership can migrate to another entity. "Synchronization" on page 99 describes how the Sun Cluster 3.0 architecture handles the complex synchronization problems and issues that the following sections describe.

Data Uniqueness

Data uniqueness poses a problem for computer system architectures or clusters that use duplication of data to enhance availability. The representation of the data to people requires uniqueness. Yet there are multiple copies of the data that are identical and represent a single view of the data, which must remain synchronized.

Complexity and Reliability

Since the first vacuum tube computers were built, the reliability of computing machinery has improved significantly. The increase in reliability resulted from technology improvements in the design and manufacturing of the devices themselves. But increases in individual component reliability also increase complexity. In general, the more complex the system is, the less reliable it is. Increasing complexity to satisfy the desire for new features causes a dilemma because it works against the desire for reliability (perfection of existing systems).

As you increase the number of components in the system, the reliability of the system tends to decrease. Another way to look at the problem of clusters is to realize that a fully redundant cluster has more than twice as many components as a single system. Thus, the cost of a clustered system is almost twice the cost of a single system. However, the reliability of a cluster system is less than half the reliability of a single system. Though this may seem discouraging, it is important to understand that the reliability of a system is not the same as the availability of the service provided by the system. The difference between reliability and availability is that the former only deals with one event, a failure, whereas the latter also takes recovery into account. The key is to build a system in which components fail at normal rates, but which recovers from these failures quickly.

An important technique for recovering from failures in data storage is data duplication. Data duplication occurs often in modern computer systems. The most obvious examples are backups, disk mirroring, and hierarchical storage management solutions. In general, data is duplicated to increase its availability. At the same time, duplication uses more components, thus reducing the overall system reliability. Also, duplication introduces synchronization fault opportunities. Fortunately, for most cases, the management of duplicate copies of data can be reliably implemented as processes. For example, the storage and management of backup tapes is well understood in modern data centers.

A special case of the use of duplicate data occurs in disk mirrors. Most disk mirroring software or hardware implements a policy in which writes are committed to both sides of the mirror before returning an acknowledgement of the write operation. Read operations only occur from one side of the mirror. This increases the efficiency of the system because twice as many read operations can occur for a given data set size. This duplication also introduces a synchronization failure mode, in which one side of the mirror might not actually contain the same data as the other side. This is not a problem for write operations because the data will be overwritten, but it is a serious problem for read operations.

Depending on the read policy, the side of the mirror that satisfies a given read operation may not be predictable. Two solutions are possible—periodically check the synchronization and always check the synchronization. Using the former solution maintains the performance improvements of read operations while periodic synchronization occurs in the background, preferably during times of low utilization. The latter solution does not offer any performance benefit but ensures that all read operations are satisfied by synchronized data. This solution is more common in fault tolerant systems.

RAID 5 protection of data also represents a special case of duplication in which the copy is virtual. There is no direct, bit-for-bit copy of the original data. However, there is enough information to re-create the original data. This information is spread across the other data disks and a parity disk. The original data can be re-created by a mathematical manipulation of the other data and parity.

Synchronization Techniques

Modern computer systems use synchronization extensively. Fortunately, only a few synchronization techniques are used commonly. Thus, the topic is researched and written about extensively, and once you understand the techniques, you begin to understand how they function when components fail.

Microprocessor Cache Coherency

Microprocessors designed for multiprocessor computers must maintain a consistent view of the memory among themselves. Because these microprocessors often have caches, the synchronization is done through a *cache-coherency* protocol. The term coherence describes the values returned by a read operation to the same memory location. Consistency describes the congruity of a read operation returning a written value. Coherency and consistency are complementary—coherence defines the behavior of reads and writes to the same memory location and consistency defines the behavior of reads and writes with respect to accesses to other memory locations. In terms of failures, loss of either coherency or consistency is a major problem that can corrupt data and increase recovery time.

UltraSPARC™ processors use two primary types of cache-coherency protocols—*snooping* and *distributed directory-based coherency.*

- *Snooping protocol* is used by all multiprocessor SPARC implementations. No centralized state is kept. Every processor cache maintains metadata tags that describe the shared status of each cache line along with the data in the cache line. All of the caches share one or more common address buses. Each cache *snoops* the address bus to see which processors might need a copy of the data owned by the cache.

- *Distributed directory-based coherency protocol* is used in the UltraSPARC III processor. The status of each cache line is kept in a directory that has a known location. This technique releases the restriction of the snooping protocol that requires all caches to see all address bus transactions. The distributed directory protocol scales to larger numbers of processors than the snooping protocol and allows large, multiprocessor UltraSPARC III systems to be built. The Oracle *9i* Real Application Cluster (Oracle *9i* RAC) database implements a distributed directory protocol for its cache synchronization. "Synchronization" on page 99 describes this protocol in more detail.

As demonstrated in the Sun Fire™ server, both protocols can be used concurrently. The Sun Fire server uses snooping protocol when there are four processors on board and uses directory-based coherency protocol between boards. Regardless of the cache coherency protocol, UltraSPARC processors have an atomic test-and-set operation, ldstub, which is used by the kernel. Atomic operations must be guaranteed to complete successfully or not at all. The test-and-set operation implements simple locks, including spin locks.

Kernel-Level Synchronization

The Solaris operating environment kernel is re-entrant [Vahalia96], which means that many threads can execute kernel code at the same time. The kernel uses a number of lock primitives that are built on the test-and-set operation [JMRM00]:

- *Mutual exclusion (mutex) locks* provide exclusive access semantics. Mutex locks are one of the simplest locking primitives.

- *Reader/writer locks* are used when multiple threads can read a memory location concurrently, but only one thread can write.

- *Kernel semaphores* are based on Dijkstra's [Dijkstra65] implementation in which the semaphore is a positive integer that can be incremented or decremented by an atomic operation. If the value is zero after a decrement, the thread blocks until another thread increments the semaphore. Semaphores are used sparingly in the kernel.

- *Dispatcher locks* allow synchronization that is protected from interrupts and is primarily used by the kernel dispatcher.

Higher level synchronization facilities, such as *condition variables* (also called *queuing locks*), that are used to implement the traditional UNIX® sleep/wake-up facility are built on these primitives.

Application-Level Synchronization

The Solaris operating environment offers several application program interfaces (APIs) that you can use to build synchronization into multithreaded and multiprocessing programs.

The *System Interface Guide* [SunSIG99] introduces the API concept and describes the process control, scheduling control, file input and output, interprocess communication (IPC™), memory management, and real-time interfaces. POSIX and System V IPC APIs are described; these include message queues, semaphores, and shared memory. The System V IPC API is popular, being widely implemented on many operating systems. However, the System V IPC semaphore facility used for synchronization has more overhead than the techniques available in multithreaded programs.

The *Multithreaded Programming Guide* [SunMPG99] describes POSIX and Solaris threads APIs, programming with synchronization objects, compiling multithreaded programs, and finding analysis tools for multithreaded programs. The threads-level synchronization primitives are very similar to those used by the kernel. This guide also discusses the use of shared memory for synchronizing multiple multithreaded processes.

Synchronization Consistency Failures

Condition variables offer an economical method of protecting data structures being shared by multiple threads. The data structure has an added condition variable, which is used as a lock. However, broken software may indiscriminately alter the data structure without checking the condition variables, thereby ignoring the consistency protection. This represents a software fault that may be latent and difficult to detect at runtime.

Two-Phase Commit

The two-phase commit protocol ensures an atomic write of a single datum to two or more different memories. This solves a problem similar to the consistency problem described previously, but applied slightly differently. Instead of multiple processors or threads synchronizing access to a single memory location, the two-phase commit protocol replicates a single memory location to another memory. These memories have different, independent processors operating on them. However, the copies must remain synchronized.

In phase one, the memories confirm their ability to perform the write operation. Once all of the memories have confirmed, phase two begins and the writes are committed. If a failure occurs, phase one does not complete and some type of error handling may be required. For example, the write may be discarded and an error message returned to the requestor.

The two-phase commit is one of the simplest synchronization protocols and is used widely. However, it has scalability problems. The time to complete the confirmation is based on the latency between the memories. For many systems, this is not a problem, but in a wide area network (WAN), the latency between memories may be significant. Also, as the number of memories increases, the time required to complete the confirmation tends to increase. Attempts to relax these restrictions are available in some software products, but this relaxation introduces the risk of loss of synchronization, and thus the potential for data corruption. Recovery from such a problem may be difficult and time consuming, so you must carefully consider the long-term risks and impact of relaxing these restrictions. For details on how Sun Cluster 3.0 uses the two-phase commit protocol, see "Mini-Transactions" on page 60.

Systems also use the two-phase commit for three functions—disk mirroring (RAID 1), mirrored cache such as in the Sun StorEdge™ T3 array and Sun StorEdge™ Network Data Replicator (SNDR software), and the Sun Cluster cluster configuration repository (CCR.)

Locks and Lock Management

Locks that are used to ensure consistency require lock management and recovery when failures occur. For node failures, the system must store the information about the locks and their current state in shared, persistent memory or communicate it through the interconnect to a shadow agent on another node.

Storing the state information in persistent memory can lead to performance and scalability issues because the latency to perform the store can affect performance negatively. These locks work best when the state of the lock does not change often. For example, locking a file tends to cause much less lock activity than locking records in the file. Similarly, locking a database table creates less lock activity than locking rows in the table. In either case, the underlying support and management of the locks does not change, but the utilization of the locks can change. High lock utilization is an indication that the service or application will have difficulty scaling.

An alternative to storing the state information in persistent memory is to use shadow agents—processes that receive updates on lock information from the owner of the locks. This state information is kept in volatile, main memory, which has much lower latency than shared, persistent storage. If the lock owner fails, the shadow agent already knows the state of the locks and can begin to take over the lock ownership very quickly.

Lock Performance

Most locking software and synchronization software provide a method for monitoring their utilization. For example, databases provide performance tables for monitoring lock utilization and contention. The mpstat(1m), vmstat(1m), and iostat(1m) processes give some indications of lock or synchronization activity, though this is not their specialty. The lockstat(1m) process provides detailed information on kernel lock activity, monitors lock contention events, gathers frequency and timing data on the events, and presents the data.

Arbitration Schemes

Arbitration is the act of deciding. Many forms of arbitration occur in computer systems. I/O devices arbitrate for access to an I/O bus. CPUs arbitrate for access to a multiprocessor interconnect. Network nodes arbitrate for the right to transmit on the network. In clusters, arbitration determines which nodes are part of the cluster. Once they are part of the cluster, arbitration determines how the nodes host the services. To accurately predict the behavior of the cluster and services in the event of a failure, you must understand the arbitration schemes used in the cluster.

Asymmetric Arbitration

Asymmetric arbitration is a technique commonly used when the priority of competing candidates can be established clearly and does not change. An example of this is the SCSI-2 protocol. In SCSI-2, the target address specifies the priority. If multiple targets attempt to gain control of the bus at the same time, the SCSI-2 protocol uses the target address to arbitrate the winner.

By default, the Solaris operating environment sets the host SCSI target address to 7, the highest priority. This helps ensure the stability of the bus because the host has priority over all of the I/O slave devices. Additional stability in the system is ensured by placing slow devices at a higher priority than fast devices. This is why the default CD-ROM target address is 6 and the default disk drive target addresses begin with 0.

SCSI priority arbitration creates an interesting problem for clusters using the SCSI bus for shared storage. Each address on the bus can be owned by only one target on the bus. Duplicate SCSI target addresses cause a fault condition that is difficult to detect and yields unpredictable behavior. For simple SCSI disks, each node of the cluster must have direct access to the bus. Therefore, one node must have a higher priority than the other node. In practice, this requirement rarely results in a problem, because the disks themselves are the unit of ownership and both nodes have higher priority than the disks.

Asymmetric arbitration is also used for Fibre Channel Arbitrated Loop (FC-AL). FC-AL is often used instead of the SCSI bus as a storage interconnect because of its electrical isolation (electrical faults are not propagated by fiber), its long distance characteristics (components can be separated by many kilometers), and its ability to be managed as a network. The priority of FC-AL nodes or ports is based on the physical loop address. Each candidate that wants to send data must first send an arbitration request around the loop to all other candidates. Once the port that is receiving the arbitration request approves and detects it, the candidate can send data. An obvious consequence is that greater numbers of candidates increase the arbitration time. Also, the candidates can be separated by several kilometers, resulting in additional latency, and the time required to arbitrate may significantly impact the amount of actual throughput of the channel.

Symmetric Arbitration

Symmetric arbitration is used when the candidates are peers and a priority-based arbitration is not used. This case is commonly found in symmetric multiprocessor (SMP) systems and networks. Arbitration is required so that all candidates can be assured that only one candidate has ownership of the shared component.

10BASE-T and 100BASE-T Ethernet networks use a carrier sense, multiple access, with collision detection (CSMA/CD) arbitration scheme. This scheme allows two or more nodes to share a common bus transmission medium [Madron89]. The node listens for the network to become idle, then begins transmitting. The node continues to listen while transmitting to detect collisions, which happen when two or more nodes are transmitting simultaneously. If a collision is detected, the node will stop transmitting, wait a random period of time, listen for idle, and retransmit. Stability on the network is assured by changing the random wait time to increase according to an algorithm called *truncated binary exponential backoff*. With this method it is difficult to predict when a clean transmission will be possible, which makes 10BASE-T or 100BASE-T Ethernet unsuitable for isochronous workloads on networks with many nodes. Also, many busy nodes can result in low bandwidth utilization.

The faster versions of Ethernet, 1000BASE-SX and 1000BASE-T (also known as Gigabit Ethernet), are only available as full duplex, switched technologies, thereby eliminating the CSMA/CD arbitration issues on the common medium. For larger networks, the arbitration role is moved into the network switch. Direct, node-to-node connections are full duplex, requiring no arbitration.

Voting and Quorum

Voting is perhaps the most universally accepted method of arbitration. It has been time tested for many centuries in many forms—popularity contests, selecting members of government, and so forth. This is the method used by Sun Cluster software for arbitration of cluster membership (see "Majority Voting and Quorum Principles" on page 108).

One problem with voting is plurality—the leading candidate gains more votes than the other candidates, but not more than half of the total votes cast. Many different techniques can be used during these special cases—run-off elections, special vote by a normally nonvoting member, and so forth. Another problem with voting is that ties can occur.

A further problem with voting is that it can be time consuming. The act of voting as well as the process of counting votes is time consuming. This may not scale well for large populations.

Occasionally, voting is confused with a quorum. They are similar but distinct. A vote is usually a formal expression of opinion or will in response to a proposed decision. A quorum is defined as the number, usually a majority of officers or members of a body, that, when duly assembled, is legally competent to transact business [Webster87]. Both concepts are important; the only vote that should ratify a decision is the vote of a quorum of members. For clusters, the quorum defines a viable cluster. If a node or group of nodes cannot achieve a quorum, they should not start services because they risk conflicting with an established quorum.

Data Caches

Data caching is a special form of data duplication. Caches make copies of data to improve performance. This is in contrast to mirroring disks, in which the copies of data are made primarily to improve availability. Although the two have different goals, the architecture of the implementations is surprisingly similar.

Caches are a popular method of improving performance in computer systems. The Solaris operating environment essentially uses all available main memory, RAM, as a cache to the file system. Relational database management systems (RDBMS) manage their own cache of data. Modern microprocessors have many caches, in addition to the typical one to three levels of data cache. Hardware RAID arrays have caches that increase the performance of complex redundant arrays of independent disks (RAID) algorithms. Hard drives have caches to store the data read from the medium. The use of these forms of caching can be explained by examination of the cost and latency of the technology.

Cost and Latency Trade-Off

All memories are based on just a few physical phenomena and organizational principles [Hayes98]. The features that enable you to differentiate between memory technologies are cost and latency. Unfortunately, the desire for low cost and low latency are mutually exclusive. For example, a dynamic RAM (DRAM) storage cell has a single transistor and a capacitor. A static RAM (SRAM) storage cell has four to six transistors (a speed/power trade-off is possible here). The physical size of the design has a first-order impact on the cost of building integrated circuits. Therefore, the cost of building N bits of DRAM memory is less than SRAM memory, given the same manufacturing technology. However, DRAM latency is on the order of 50 nanoseconds versus 5 nanoseconds for SRAM.

The cost/latency trade-off can be described graphically. FIGURE 1-2 shows the latency versus cost for a wide variety of technologies used in computer systems design. From this analysis, it is clear that use of memory technologies in computer system design is a cost versus latency trade-off. Any technology above the shaded area is not likely to survive because of costs. Any technology below the shaded area is likely to spawn radical, positive changes in computer system design.

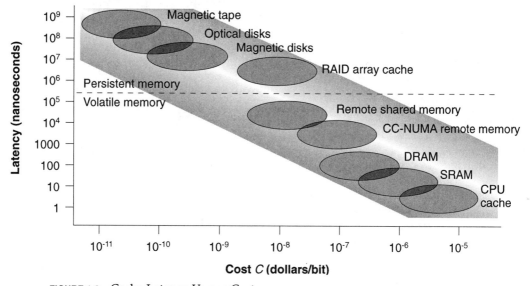

FIGURE 1-2 Cache Latency Versus Cost

The preceding graph also shows when caches can be beneficial. The memory technologies to the left, above the dashed line, tend to be persistent, while the memory technologies to the right, below the dashed line, tend to be volatile. Important data that needs to survive an outage must be placed in persistent memory. Caches are used to keep copies of the persistent data in low-latency memory, thus offering fast access for data that is reused. Fortunately, many applications tend to reuse data—especially if the "data" are really "instructions." A given technology can be effectively cached by another technology having lower latency, such as those to the right.

Cache Types

CPU caches are what most computer architects think about when they use the term *cache*. While CPU caches are an active source of development in computer architectures, they are only one of the caches in a modern SMP system. CPU caches are well understood and exhibit many of the advances in computer architecture.

Metadata caches store information about information. On disk, the metadata is duplicated in multiple locations across the disk. In the Solaris operating environment UNIX file system (UFS), metadata is cached in main memory. The kernel periodically flushes the UFS metadata to disk. This metadata cache is stored in volatile main memory. If a crash occurs, the metadata on disk may not be current. This situation results in a file system check, `fsck`, which reconciles the metadata for the file system. The logging option introduced with UFS in the Solaris 7 operating environment stores changes in the metadata, the log of metadata changes, on the disk. This dramatically speeds up the file system check because the metadata can be regenerated completely from the log.

File system read caches are used in the Solaris operating environment to store parts (pages) of files that have been read. The default behavior for the Solaris operating environment is to use available RAM as a file system cache. When the Solaris 8 operating environment system gets low on available memory, the system discards file system cached pages in preference to executable files or text pages. Similar behavior can be activated in the Solaris 2.6 or Solaris 7 operating environment by enabling `priority_paging` in the `/etc/system` file.

Buffer caches provide an interface between a fast data source and a slow data sink. This type of cache is quite common, especially in I/O subsystem design. A buffer design is commonly used to implement I/O subsystems. For instance, modern SCSI or FC-AL disk drives have 8 to 16 megabytes of track cache. Track cache is really a read buffer cache designed to contain the data on at least one track of the disk media. This design allows significant improvements in performance of read operations that occur in the same track because the media require only one physical read. The latency for physically reading data from disk media depends on the rotation speed of the media, and is often in the 5 to 10 millisecond range. Once the whole track is in the buffer, the data can be read in the latency of a DRAM access, which is on the order of 200 nanoseconds.

File systems often have a buffer cache in main memory for writing the data portion of files. These write buffers are distinguished from the file system read caches in that the write cache pages cannot be discarded when available memory is low. UFS implements a high-water mark for the size of its write buffer cache on a per file basis that can be tuned in the /etc/system file with the *ufs:ufs_HW* variable. The memory used for write buffer caches can cause resource contention for memory when the available RAM is low. For low memory situations, the use of write buffer cache should be examined closely.

Cache Synchronization

What all caches have in common is that the data must be synchronized between the copy in the low-latency memory and the higher latency memory. Sequential access caches, such as the buffer cache, have relatively simple synchronization—whatever comes in, goes out in the same order. Random access caches such as CPU, metadata, and file system read caches can have very complex synchronization mechanisms.

Random access caches typically have different policies for read and write. Since the cost per bit of caches is higher than that of higher latency memories, the caches tend to be smaller. All of the data that can be stored in the higher latency memory cannot fit in the cache. The cache policy for reading data is to discard the data, if needed, because it can be read again in the future. The cache policy for writing cannot simply discard data. Write policies tend to belong to two categories—*write-through* and *write-behind*. A write-through policy writes the data to the lower-latency memory, immediately ensuring that the data can be safely discarded if necessary. A write-behind policy does not immediately write the data to the higher latency memory, thus improving performance if the data is to be written again soon. Obviously, the write-behind policy is considerably more complicated. For this, the hardware or software must maintain information about the state of the data, that is, whether or not the data has been stored in the higher-latency memory. If not, then the data must be written before it can be discarded to make room for other data.

If the persistence requirement of the cache and its higher-latency memory is the same, either both are persistent or not, write-behind cache policies make good sense. If the cache is not persistent and the higher latency memory is persistent, write-through policies provide better safety.

As can be expected, the increasing complexity in cache designs increases the number of failure modes that can affect a system. At a minimum, caches add hardware to the system, thereby reducing overall system reliability. Alternatively, caches use existing storage resources that are shared with other tasks, potentially introducing unwanted modes. For every synchronization mechanism added, an arbitration mechanism must also be added to handle conflicts and failures. A good rule of thumb is to limit the dependence on caches when possible. This trade-off decision must often be made while taking into account the benefits of caching. You should have a firm understanding of the various caches used in a system. To help with the decision making process, you can use the example in FIGURE 1-2, which shows the caching hierarchy of the system.

Timeouts

Computer systems use timeouts to help maintain state information. Since digital computers are discrete systems, you must use some mechanism to create an event and to verify that an event was not completed. You can use timeouts for cluster heartbeats, arbitration cycles to determine if a processor has hung, and so forth.

Caution – Reducing the size of timeouts in an effort to improve the ability to detect component failures is tempting. You must avoid destabilizing conditions in which the timeout values are too small. Ensuring that the system remains stable when timeouts are changed requires due diligence and detailed engineering analysis.

Timeouts are also opportunities for defects. In particular, the stability of a system can be undermined if you design a series of nested timeouts incorrectly. FIGURE 1-3 is a nested timing diagram example.

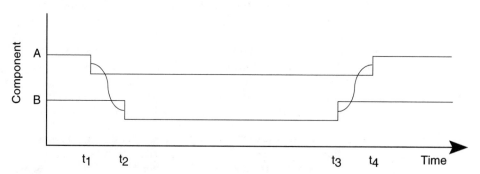

FIGURE 1-3 Nested Timing Diagram—Example

In this example, component A has a state change at time t_1 that causes a state change in component B at time t_2. Component B then has a state change at time t_3 that causes a state change in component A at t_4. This timing diagram example is analogous to a host, A, issuing a read data command to a disk drive, B. This system has deterministic, sequential behavior. However, if a failure occurs in component B between t_2 and t_3, the state change of component A at t_4 will never occur.

Component A will hang. If a timeout is implemented, component A can detect the failure of component B. FIGURE 1-4 shows the failure of B and the point at which A times out.

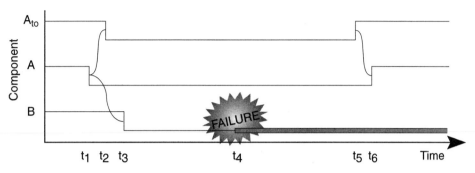

FIGURE 1-4   Nested Timing Diagram With Timeout

In this case, A implements an internal timeout, A_{to}. At time t_1, component A starts the timeout counter, A_{to}, at t_2 and causes a state change in B at t_3. At time t_4, component B fails, never to recover. At time t_5, the A_{to} timeout expires, causing A to change its state. Since both A and A_{to} are part of component A, A knows an error condition occurred in component B.

Stable System

FIGURE 1-5 shows a stable system implementing timeouts. In this case, the component timeout of A is greater than the service time of component B.

Timeout for $Ato = (t6 - t2) > (t4 - t3)$

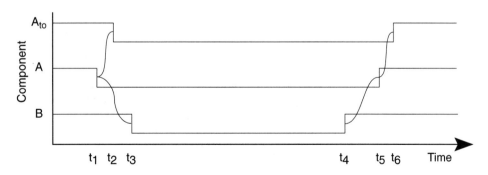

FIGURE 1-5   Stable System With Timeout

Unstable System

FIGURE 1-6 shows an unstable system implementing timeouts. In this case, the timeout value component A is less than the service time of component B.

Timeout for $Ato = (t4 - t2) > (t6 - t3)$

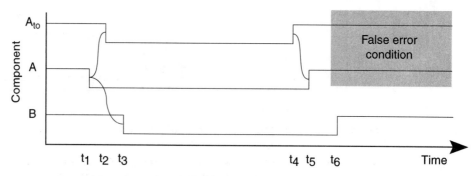

FIGURE 1-6   Unstable System With Timeout

The system is unstable because it detects false errors. The action taken by component A, because of the presumed failure of component B, determines the stability of the overall system.

Stability Problems

The *stability problems* inherent in complex computer systems using timeouts are difficult to predict or prove mathematically because of the multivariate and nonlinear nature of these systems.

Timeouts that are too long increase the time to detect errors. Timeouts that are too short generate false error conditions. False error conditions cause unnecessary failovers.

Timeouts are a source of systems integration errors. For components that use timeouts, the default timeout values are set according to their expected uses. When combined to build a larger system, the timeouts can cause system instability. You must understand the component timeouts and their effect on event detection.

Failures in Clustered Systems

A number of faults are specific to clustered systems. These faults affect synchronization between nodes, arbitration of conflicts regarding shared components, or the presentation of a single view of data or services to external users and systems. "Cluster Failures" on page 91 describes how Sun Cluster 3.0 avoids and handles these faults. The sections that follow describe the split brain, multiple instance, and amnesia faults.

Split Brain

Split-brain failure occurs when a single cluster has a failure that results in reconfiguration into multiple partitions, with each partition forming without knowledge of the existence of any other. If each new cluster does not know of the existence of the others, there could be a collision in shared resources. Network addresses can be duplicated because each of the new clusters thinks it should own the shared network address. Shared storage could also be affected, because each cluster believes that it owns the shared storage. The result is *severe data corruption*.

"Amnesia and Temporally Split Configurations" on page 90 explains how Sun Cluster 3.0 avoids the split-brain condition.

Multiple Instances

A multiple instance failure occurs when an application is designed to operate on data assuming it has *exclusive access* to the data and more than one instance of the application is started. For a single system there are many ways to prevent this failure, such as semaphores, checking the process list, creating lock files, and so forth. In a clustered environment, this prevention becomes more difficult. Using semaphores and checking the process list only applies to the local node. Creating lock files works, but only if the lock files are on shared storage. Even then, a simple lock file will not suffice, because the application must have a mechanism to correctly query each node in the cluster to ensure that another instance of the application is actually running, since the application may have failed without releasing the lock.

Amnesia

Amnesia is a failure mode in which a node starts with stale cluster configuration information. This is a synchronization error because the cluster configuration information is not propagated to all of the nodes. For example, if a node fails and the cluster is then reconfigured, cluster configuration information of the node is now stale. If the node tries to rejoin the cluster, the node must resynchronize its cluster configuration information.

A more difficult situation occurs when the node fails, the cluster is reconfigured, the cluster is brought down, and then the failed node is brought back up. In this case, the stale cluster configuration information is presumed to be correct, and a new cluster is built with the stale configuration information.

Summary

Many businesses implement highly available clusters when the risk of the costs of downtime exceeds the costs of the cluster. This can be quantified in business terms and measured by well designed systems.

We examined how failures occur in complex systems and showed methods that contain, isolate, report, and repair failures. Synchronization is used by any component or system that creates copies of data, including redundant storage, caches, and cluster components. Arbitration is important in clustered systems for deciding which of many components is the appropriate configuration to provide services.

Finally, we examined special considerations for clustered systems. Many systems use caches to improve performance. Caches introduce synchronization problems because they represent duplication of data. Timeouts are used to try to determine if a component has failed, but care must be taken to ensure that timeouts are properly tuned.

A number of failure modes are specific to clusters—split brain, amnesia, and multiple instances. Clusters use special techniques to help prevent such failures.

CHAPTER 2

Enterprise Cluster Computing Building Blocks

When building a highly available and scalable enterprise architecture, you must consider the resilience and growth potential of every component in the network and systems path between the client and data. There is little value in investing in a clustered database solution if the network between the users and the database is unreliable or insecure. From a client perspective, the end-to-end reliability and availability of a solution is the product of the values for each subcomponent.

This chapter reviews the business infrastructure components—file, database and name services, and application and web servers—and examines how clustering technology can make them highly available and scalable. The descriptions in this chapter follow the flow of data through an organization, starting with the back-end data repositories and working through to the user-access layer provided by the web servers. The descriptions assume that these components are connected by a reliable, available, and scalable network infrastructure; this infrastructure is not explicitly described since it is beyond the scope of this book. This chapter describes other common computational clustering requirements, and highlights some of the technologies available to write distributed and clustered applications.

This chapter contains the following sections:

- Data Repositories and Infrastructure Services
- Business Logic and Application Service
- User Access Services: Web Farms
- Compute Clusters
- Technologies for Building Distributed Applications

Data Repositories and Infrastructure Services

All but the smallest businesses rely on computers to store and retrieve the data that flows through their organizations. For rapid retrieval, this data usually resides on high-performance magnetic storage, rather than tape. Normally, mirroring or RAID 5 protects the data to prevent a disk failure leading to data loss. However, a server outage renders the data unavailable until the server is fixed. As a result, other information-processing tiers within a corporation cannot function until the data is available again. A Sun Cluster solution provides an insurance policy by limiting the maximum service outage of vital data to the time it takes to recover and restart the service.

Within most organizations, corporate data is held, accessed, and used in a variety of ways, including flat files and relational database management systems (RDBMSs). Often, email and name services play a crucial role too. The sections that follow describe these services and the benefits they realize from being hosted on a cluster.

File Services

File servers proliferate in many organizations, hosting a wide variety of data types ranging from text documents and web pages to multimedia data, such as audio and video files. Client workstations and PCs commonly share these files, using the Network File System (NFS) or Common Internet File System (CIFS) protocol. A file server may support many hundreds of users, so an outage can prevent large numbers of staff from working. For example, when an NFS server centralizes web farm data or stores archived log files from a database, a failure can impact several other critical servers too. For details, see the impacted user minutes (IUM) example in "Cost Estimation" on page 3.

NFS

The NFS is commonly deployed as a way of centralizing the provision of home and data directories, thereby simplifying corporate backup and space management tasks. Similarly, many large web farm installations use NFS servers as a central repository for web pages, common gateway interface (CGI) scripts, and servlets, rather than replicating updates to multiple web servers. The majority of corporations that use NFS this way can use the Sun Cluster 3.0 software to ensure the availability of these resources.

NFS is a stateless protocol, which means that it is capable of surviving a server failure without losing data or requiring users to restart their applications. Deploying an NFS service on a cluster reduces the possibility that a server outage results in a prolonged period of downtime, while continuing to make any failure transparent to the users.

SAMBA

SAMBA provides a UNIX SMB/CIFS file and print service that enables Microsoft Windows interoperability, without additional software on the client machine. Features include—Microsoft Windows NT 4.0 primary domain controller (PDC) and backup domain controller (BDC) capability and Microsoft Windows NT file system (NTFS) and printing support for Microsoft Windows clients. (For details on the features SAMBA supports, see http://www.samba.org). SAMBA data services can be written with the Sun Cluster 3.0 APIs described in "Agent Application Program Interfaces" on page 100, which, when deployed on a Sun Cluster, create highly available PC file and print services.

Most Microsoft Windows NT services are connection oriented and not stateless like NFS. However, if a network problem occurs, the underlying Microsoft Windows operating system services try to reestablish a connection and state, so most Microsoft Windows applications using file access services from SAMBA are unaffected by a switchover. Other Microsoft Windows NT services, such as graphical user interface (GUI) management tools, server administration tools, and printing, notice the failure and must be restarted.

Database Services

Most business applications, including enterprise resource planning (ERP) solutions from the SAP AG and Siebel Systems, Inc. customer relationship management (CRM) products, rely on an RDBMS to store data. These applications are often implemented on clustered hardware because of the key role the applications play in day-to-day business functions. Without access to the database, middle-tier applications and dependent processes within the organization stall or fail. This high degree of interdependency makes a strong case for putting a critical database on a clustered system.

Businesses use a variety of applications that rely on databases to hold data. Broadly speaking, these applications are in two categories—online transaction processing (OLTP) and decision support systems (DSS). The role that clustering plays in supporting these application types depends not only on the financial and customer satisfaction penalties of an outage, but also on the way in which database technology combines the computer hardware resources of two or more servers into a single, more powerful entity. The suitability of an application, such as

Oracle 8*i* Parallel Server (Oracle 8*i* OPS) or Oracle 9*i* Real Application Cluster (Oracle 9*i* RAC), to parallel database technology determines whether Sun Cluster 3.0 can offer the desired combination of increased availability and enhanced scalability.

Sun Cluster 3.0 data services provide failover support for IBM DB2, Informix, ORACLE®, and Sybase products. In addition, these data services enable parallel database support for IBM DB 2 7.2 Extended Enterprise Edition (EEE) and Oracle 8*i* OPS and Oracle 9*i* RAC.

Sun Cluster 3.0 supports both simple failover of the Oracle server, through the HA-Oracle data service, and the parallel capabilities of Oracle 8*i* OPS and Oracle 9*i* RAC.

HA-Oracle

The start, stop, and monitoring scripts in the Sun HA-Oracle data service make an individual, standard Oracle server instance highly available. A Sun Cluster system can host multiple HA-Oracle instances distributed across the entire cluster, even when the same node hosts several instances. However, unlike Oracle 8*i* OPS or Oracle 9*i* RAC, each instance uses only the resources available to it on the node that is executing the instance. The paragraphs that follow outline the benefits and disadvantages that govern the business decision to use one or the other of these products.

When an HA-Oracle cluster is deployed, data files are laid out on the file system or on raw devices, in exactly the same manner as they are on a standalone server. The addition of the Sun HA-Oracle agent makes the database highly available. This approach has the advantage of requiring minimal additional database administrator training, since all the tuning and other day-to-day tasks are identical. After a failure, the database recovers its consistency, using its log files in the normal way. The time taken to recover depends entirely on the volume and type of transactions being processed at the time of the failure.

Oracle 8*i* OPS and Oracle 9*i* RAC

The Oracle 8*i* OPS and Oracle 9*i* RAC parallel packages are designed to run in a clustered environment. Unlike HA-Oracle, these packages require the data be placed on raw devices, under the control of the Cluster Volume Manager (a licensable component of VxVM) if the devices are not hardware RAID devices, rather than on the file system. This scheme enables concurrently physical I/O to a single device from multiple nodes. The UNIX distributed lock manager (UDLM) protects data from corruption. See "Locks and Lock Management" on page 19 and "Lock Mastering" on page 170. In contrast to an HA-Oracle system, instances for that specific database are already running on a second cluster node, ready to accept user connections and transactions. As a result, users can reconnect to the database service almost immediately after a failure, enabling the Oracle 8*i* OPS and Oracle 9*i* RAC implementations to offer and meet higher service levels. The consequent trade-off comes in increased license and staff training costs; the latter is due to the increased product complexity.

Deploying a parallel database does not guarantee that an application automatically scales or performs well. In particular, applications in which tables and indexes suffer high contention rates for specific data blocks may result in lower than expected, or even negative, scalability. Lower scalability occurs because the data blocks may move back and forth across the cluster interconnect to fulfill cache coherency requirements. Even though faster interconnects are being developed, there is no substitute for rearchitecting the application to be more cluster friendly. Programmers writing a distributed computing application should first optimize its internode communication before demanding a faster interconnect.

Both Oracle 8*i* OPS and Oracle 9*i* RAC can run in one of two modes— *active/ passive* or *active/active* mode.

When you deploy the active/passive mode, user connections are made to one node only, thus eliminating the overhead of lock contention, because all of the locks are owned by one node. If the node that is hosting the users fails, all connections are lost and must be reestablished. In addition, only the resources on the active node are being fully used.

In contrast, active/active deployment distributes users across every node, thereby fully utilizing the available hardware resources. A node failure affects only the users connected to that node, requiring them to re-establish their connections. The failure of a node in a two-node cluster, for example, results in only half the users losing their connection and consequently only half the number of transactions require recovery.

Regardless of whether you use an HA or parallel Oracle implementation, the failure of the database disconnects the users from the system. Typically, users get an ORA-3113 or similar error message. The loss of connection is not easy to mask and requires the use of transaction monitors like suitably written Enterprise JavaBeans™ (EJB™), Tuxedo from BEA systems, or CICS from IBM, that can plug into an application server. See "Application Servers" on page 39. The decision to invest in the additional integration work needed to mask these interruptions depends on the benefits it brings versus the higher development and maintenance costs.

Messaging Services

Scalable mail services are particularly important for Internet service providers (ISPs), application service providers (ASPs), and large corporations that want to consolidate their email. The message storage area is usually implemented as a set of index files, enabling it to sustain higher throughput than that achievable through standard sendmail(1M) implementations.

Sun Cluster 3.0 supports iPlanet™ Messaging Server 5.1 through the SUNW.ims resource type [iMS51]; messages are stored on the cluster file system. The SUNW.ims agent can start, stop, and monitor the message transfer agent (MTA) that is central to the process of sending and receiving messages. MTA, in turn, depends on a highly available Lightweight Directory Access Protocol (LDAP) service. See "LDAP" on page 37.

Name Services

Name services provide central repositories for a range of system and user data. Traditionally, services like domain name service (DNS) and network information service (NIS) were used for storage and retrieval of Internet Protocol (IP) address to host name mappings. Also, NIS enabled a number of other mappings to be stored—usernames to passwords, services to port number, and so forth. More recently, LDAP has extended this role to include storage of application configuration and user profile data. As a result, many enterprise applications are highly dependent on its services.

DNS

DNS is an important service for any organization with a large network infrastructure and any corporation connected to the Internet. Through DNS, client systems can resolve the host names of other servers, both on the intranet and on the Internet. Similarly, web servers can use reverse name lookup to track the usage of their web site, though this impacts the performance of high-throughput web servers.

The DNS implementation for a particular zone uses *primary, secondary,* and possibly *cache-only* servers. The primary server is the authoritative source for all queries to its zone, and it is where your system administrator makes all necessary updates to the files that in.named(1M) loads. Secondary servers can provide additional resilience and throughput when the primary is overloaded or unavailable; however, secondary servers are not the central point of control for the zone. All of the updates to the secondary server come from the primary. Therefore, making the primary server highly available is still substantially beneficial.

Cache-only DNS servers are used to reduce the amount of DNS traffic over slow networks or wide area networks (WAN.) The DNS caching algorithm is simple and based on a serial number and expiration time for the DNS data. When the timeout expires and a new request arrives, the caching server reloads the data from the primary or secondary server. The serial number is used to indicate that the data has been changed by the primary. This simple cache synchronization method works well for the Internet because the primary does not know or care how many cache-only servers exist.

The Sun DNS data service is a failover rather than a scalable service. The DNS data files are stored in the global file system, rather than on the root disk. This method allows the in.named(1M) process to read them in, regardless of which node is hosting the service. Because the system creates and destroys the connections for each lookup performed, requests fail if they are being processed when a DNS outage occurs.

LDAP

The LDAP protocol is gaining popularity as the standard way to store user profile and application configuration data. Products like the iPlanet™ Portal Server and iPlanet Messaging Server, for example, use it extensively to hold user preferences.

Sun Cluster 3.0 supports the Netscape Directory Server (NDS) through its SUNW.nsldap agent. For accessibility from every node, all LDAP data must reside in the global file service. As with DNS connections, requests fail if they are being processed when an LDAP outage occurs.

NIS and NIS+

Currently, Sun Cluster 3.0 does not support NIS or NIS+ as data services. However, both data services can provide resilience through configuration of appropriate slave servers.

Business Logic and Application Service

Business application architecture has changed over the past two decades from monolithic, centrally hosted applications to a multitiered, distributed model. Data, business logic, presentation, and user access are divided into separate components. This division increases manageability, but it does not remove the need to make each component highly available. End-to-end application availability depends on the product of the availability metrics for each component.

Two types of application servers are commonly found in an enterprise. The first type is application servers that are built into packages like SAP and Oracle applications; the second type is the more general-purpose application servers, such as the iPlanet Application Server.

Packaged Business Solutions

Business application suites, such as those sold by SAP AG or ORACLE, employ a multitiered architecture to separate business logic and data storage from the user presentation layer. As you scale up deployments, the business logic components are often replicated across multiple servers to increase throughput and resilience. The application may still require the services of a cluster framework to make parts of the application, which otherwise might be a single point of failure (SPOF), highly available.

Some applications may allow a load balancer to distribute user requests to multiple servers that host identical application services. Cisco Systems, Inc., Alteon, and Extreme Switches all offer this kind of session-aware, IP load-balancing capability. Siebel eBusiness 2000 6.3.x, for example, uses Resonate Central Dispatch 3.1 to load-balance requests.

SAP R/3 uses a group of processes called the central instance to control the distribution of users among the application server instances. These, in turn, host the application processing modules, such as sales and distribution, finance, human resources, and so on. FIGURE 2-1 shows the SAP R/3 application architecture.

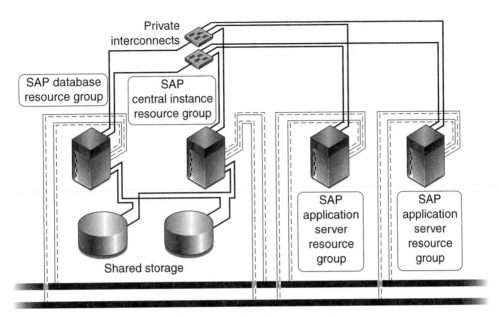

FIGURE 2-1 SAP R/3 Application Architecture

Application Servers

Application servers, like iPlanet™ Application Server and BEA System WebLogic, provide a platform that complies with the certified Java™ 2 Platform, Enterprise Edition (J2EE™). J2EE software consists of a number of components and APIs including Enterprise JavaBeans (EJB) 1.1, used for business logic; JavaServer Pages™ (JSP™) 1.1, used for page layout; and Java Servlets 2.2, used for presentation logic. FIGURE 2-2 shows this multitiered model.

When used in conjunction with the iPlanet™ Web Server, J2EE software ties together users and the persistent data storage. J2EE software also helps integrate legacy mainframe data stores, through Java Database Connectivity™ (JDBC™), into a modern information architecture, encapsulating the data they hold in object wrappers.

Because business, presentation, and page layout logic can be encapsulated in a Write Once, Run Anywhere™ language, you can defer the choice of delivery platform until the point of deployment. The object-oriented programming model enables faster assembly of applications from previously tested components. Strong interfaces hide implementation detail, enabling you to replace components with new versions as they are developed.

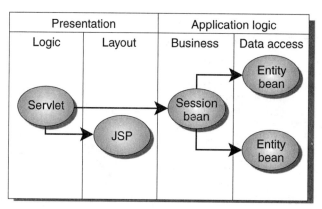

FIGURE 2-2 Multitiered Model

The iPlanet Application Server 6.0 software is a prime example of an application that does not rely on an underlying cluster platform to make its services highly available. By not relying on such a specific cluster product, iPlanet Application Server software is both available and scalable more readily on a wide range of platforms—the Solaris operating environment, Microsoft Windows NT, HP-UX, and AIX. FIGURE 2-3 shows the iPlanet Application Server overview.

The iPlanet Application Server software uses the following techniques to achieve high scalability—database connection pooling and caching, data streaming, application partitioning, and a multithreading, multiprocess architecture. User connections can be load-balanced across the installed servers through a range of policies that include server load, response time, and weighted round-robin.

Replicating distributed user session and application state information across all iPlanet application servers in a cluster achieves high availability. Session bean states enable the state of an application to be failed over in a server crash, without program modification. For rich clients that use the Internet Inter-Orb Protocol (IIOP), the CORBA executive service (CXS) bridge provides a similar level of transparent application failover.

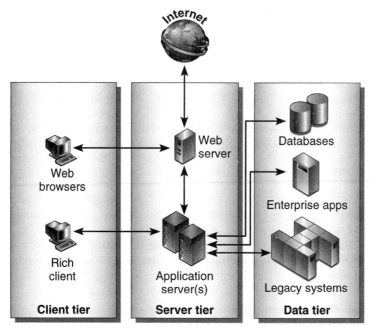

FIGURE 2-3   iPlanet Application Server Overview

The processes that make up an iPlanet application server show how to achieve high availability features without the aid of an underlying clustering product. This architecture has three main processes—the executive server (KXS), the administrative server (KAS), and the Java server (KJS). A C++ server (XCS) is provided for backward compatibility. FIGURE 2-4 shows how these processes interact.

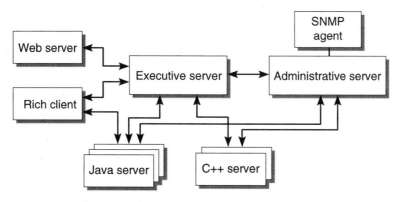

FIGURE 2-4   iPlanet Application Server Processes

The KXS forwards incoming web requests to one of the configured Java servers to process. On completion of the request, the results are sent back to the client. If an XJS process fails, the KXS process restarts it. In turn, if the XKS process fails, the XAS restarts it. Further monitoring within the iPlanet Application Server software ensures that the XAS server is always running.

If an entire iPlanet Application Server host system, running in a clustered environment, crashes, another server picks up the workload. The constituent KXS servers, hosted on the physical systems, achieve this failover by running as primary sync, backup sync, or alternate sync servers. The primary sync server communicates the latest distributed data to all of the backup sync servers so that it can take over if the primary fails. If the primary sync server fails, the alternate sync server is promoted to a backup sync server.

Transparent failover between primary and backup sync servers is achieved by distributed data synchronization (Dsync) messages passed between the iPlanet Application Server software sync servers. This action replicates the necessary state data. In many ways the Dsync mechanism mirrors the HA replica management framework within Sun Cluster 3.0, at the user level rather than the kernel level.

User Access Services: Web Farms

Web servers provide the link between the presentation and business logic and the client user. The omnipresence of the browser makes application access available to anyone, anywhere, anytime, and on virtually any device. However, a web server represents a SPOF in the enterprise architecture unless measures are taken to ensure its continued availability. The following paragraphs describe how web farms can guarantee continuous availability and massive scalability for user connectivity.

Web services such as Hypertext Transfer Protocol (HTTP), Java, Active Server Pages (jsp and asps), and common gateway interface (CGI) are often implemented with the "rack and stack" approach. Large ISPs deploy hundreds, or even thousands, of identical, low-cost servers installed in data center racks to provide a reliable and scalable service. This approach works because most browser sessions are stateless; clients request a web page, with its various subcomponents, and then close their connection. Another host can then service subsequent requests without any knowledge of the previous connection. Only state-based connections, like HTTPS, require special consideration. These connections must be routed to the same host until the session is complete.

Smaller ISPs often use a simple DNS round-robin approach to load-share `http` requests between the configured nodes. Client nodes attempt to connect to a host name, such as `www.sun.com`, that is dynamically resolved to one of multiple physical IP addresses. Most clients will try to connect to the first physical IP address in the list, so the DNS server uses the round-robin approach to place different IP addresses at the head of the list.

Since this method has no concept of session state, however, it does not work for connections that are dropped and remade, because they may be directed to a separate machine. This approach also has no concept of target machine load or the operational status of the node.

Larger deployments are more likely to use the sophisticated load-balancing facilities built into common network switches (FIGURE 2-5). These facilities overcome the limitations inherent in the DNS round-robin approach by maintaining both session state and target availability as well as response time metrics, using test probes programmed into the switches. Note that later versions of `in.named` such as the version in Solaris 8 automatically do the simple round-robin.

This architecture benefits from a low systems management overhead and simple replacement and scaling model. The failure of a single node results in a reduction in overall web server capacity, but service continues to be available. The failed server can then be quickly replaced by installation of a predefined, hardened Solaris operating environment implementation.

To learn more about the architectural details of a JumpStart™ environment, review the Sun BluePrints Online article *Building a JumpStart Infrastructure* [ANOL01]. This article is located at `http://www.sun.com/blueprints/online.html`. Select "Archives By Subject" and "JumpStart."

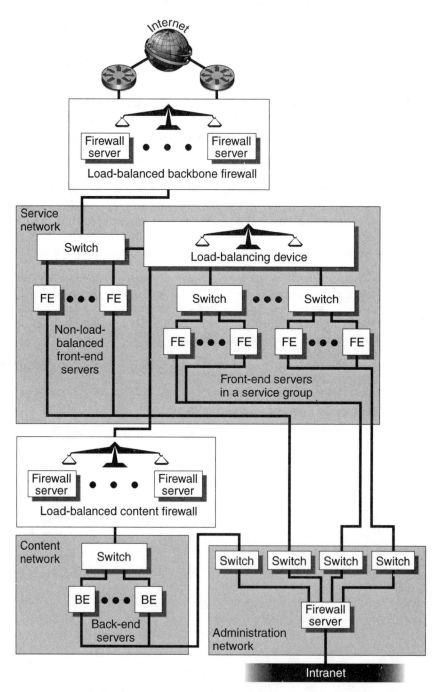

FIGURE 2-5   Web Hosting Service Ladder Approach—Load Balanced and Load Balancing

Compute Clusters

Many industry sectors harness the power of multiple computer systems to perform tasks that could not otherwise be accomplished on a single server. Moreover, some tasks can be achieved more cost effectively by a collection of smaller, lower-cost systems. Typical of this class of user tasks are computer animation in the entertainment industry and circuit simulation to verify chip design in the Electronic Design Automation (EDA) industry.

Scalability rather than availability is usually the foremost concern for applications in this sector. Task complexity rather than criticality warrants a cluster approach. If an arbitrary cluster node failure occurs, unfinished jobs can be resubmitted to the system for processing. Although there may be a chain of dependency within the jobs submitted, it is unusual for external systems to depend directly on the results of the computation. A few hybrid situations exist. These situations often involve business processes that batch process, data mine, or otherwise transform data held in corporate repositories through a series of stages.

Distributed Clusters

Distributed clusters differ from the tightly coupled solution that Sun Cluster 3.0 offers by providing more loosely coupled facilities. A cluster of distributed servers brings together the CPU, memory, and I/O resources from multiple systems without the accompanying membership monitor or extensive suite of fault probes in Sun Cluster. In contrast, distributed clusters often add a high-performance parallel file system and batch-queuing systems to schedule jobs across the available resources. One common component that both architectures rely on is a high-throughput, low-latency system area interconnect.

Parallel Processing

Applications to use parallel processing can be written two ways—*function partitioning* and *data partitioning*. Function partitioning uses different threads of execution to process data in different ways, concurrently. Data partitioning simultaneously processes multiple, independent portions of the data set in the same way. The amenability of the algorithm to parallel techniques and the volume of data that must be transferred between nodes are among the factors that govern the scalability of such clusters.

High-Performance Computing

High-performance computing (HPC) application implementation can use one of two basic approaches: *single process*, which limits the computation to the resources of a single server; or *multiprocess*, which utilizes the resources of multiple servers. Both approaches enhance performance if the application can be threaded in one of the ways described previously. Single-process programs can be made multithreaded in two ways—with parallelization directives (for example, OpenMP and the Sun parallelizing compilers) or through explicit use of the Solaris operating environment or POSIX threads in the program. Similarly, multiprocess applications can be written with the message passing interface (MPI) API or the rival parallel virtual machine (PVM) API to enable execution both within and across servers. You can also combine both approaches and use threading and MPI in a single implementation.

Often HPC clusters use a job scheduling system to distribute the workload across the available resources within a cluster. Using job scheduling maximizes utilization of the underlying hardware so that you do not waste precious CPU cycles. Combining the job scheduler, a homogeneous view of file space, and uniform access to application binaries creates the illusion of a single, seamless computing resource.

Sun HPC Clusters

Typically, high performance computing (HPC) environments are computation intensive. Often they are technical applications that require powerful or high performance systems to solve computations in a timely fashion. The Sun HPC ClusterTools™ package provides a software development environment to aid the creation, debugging, and tuning of MPI applications. These tools can be deployed subsequently, either on a single, large SMP server or on a cluster of SMP servers, depending on the resources available at the point of execution. This package also provides tools to manage the workload across the cluster. The majority of the Sun HPC ClusterTools toolkit is also available through the Sun Community Source License (SCSL) mechanism.

The SunHPC ClusterTools software has the following components:

- Sun™ Cluster Runtime Environment
- Sun MPI Communications Library
- Sun™ Parallel File System
- Sun™ Scalable Scientific Subroutine Library (Sun S3L)
- Prism™ Parallel Development Environment

Sun Cluster Runtime Environment

The Sun Cluster Runtime Environment software enables you to specify the resource requirements of an MPI application and then launch, monitor, and control it throughout its execution. You can also start applications under the control of the Prism debugger. Additionally, the Sun Cluster runtime environment interfaces with distributed resource managers (DRMs), such as the Sun™ Grid Engine software (see "Sun Grid Engine Software" on page 49) and the Platform Computing load-sharing facility (LSF), that enable you to schedule jobs across multiple systems.

Sun MPI Communications Library

The highly optimized, native MPI implementation conforms to the majority of the MPI-2 standard. It also includes full support for MPI I/O, which gives applications direct access to the Sun Parallel File System (PFS). Using the Sun RAID MPI-API, applications can take advantage of up to 64 nodes and use 1,024 processors in a single cluster. As with Sun Cluster 3.0 systems, communication between HPC cluster nodes can use standard TCP/IP interfaces, such as Gigabit Ethernet, but you can achieve high performance by using the lower latency, higher bandwidth available through the RSM™ protocol over PCI-SCI. Alternative, high-performance interconnects, such as Myricom Myrinet2000, are available as protocol modules developed through the SCSL initiative that can be loaded.

Sun Parallel File System

HPC applications often make substantial demands on the I/O subsystem of a platform. The Sun PFS, coupled with the MPI I/O routines, provides a mechanism for achieving scalable, parallel I/O. A clear and obvious distinction exists between the goals of the Sun HPC ClusterTools software PFS and the Sun Cluster 3.0 software global file system (GFS). PFS trades off availability for performance, whereas GFS makes availability paramount. Striping data across the I/O systems of multiple nodes concomitantly decreases the mean time between failure (MTBF). FIGURE 2-6 shows a high-level overview of the Sun PFS.

Sun Scalable Scientific Subroutine Library

S3L is a set of parallel and scalable tools that are commonly used in science and engineering. S3L enables you to take advantage of multiprocessor and cluster technology without writing your own parallel code. For example, parallel, multiprocessor-optimized matrix operations can be used in an otherwise single threaded program with a function call to the S3L library.

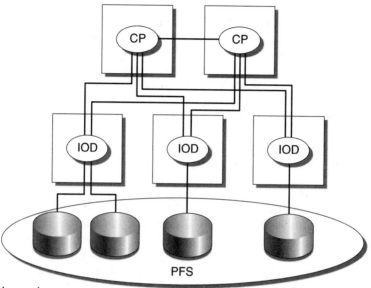

Legends
IOD: I/O daemon
CP: Compute process

FIGURE 2-6 Sun Parallel File System, High-Level View

Prism Parallel Development Environment

The Prism™ debugging tools provide a wide range of facilities for debugging multithreaded, distributed programs and visualizing their data structures. Debugging multithreaded programs has been possible for many years using products such as the Forte™ development tools and debugger. The synchronization required between the threads being debugged and the debugger is accomplished with the Solaris kernel tracing facilities. However, debugging distributed programs requires a higher level distributed debugging environment. Prism provides this environment and manages the synchronization of distributed programs and the debugger. The Prism debugging tools are invaluable for developing distributed HPC programs.

Sun Grid Engine Software

The Sun Grid Engine 5.2 software is a full-featured distributed resource manager (DRM). Its features include load-balancing and batch scheduling facilities to enable you to schedule batch, parallel, and interactive jobs across a diverse range of distributed computer resources. Using the Sun Grid Engine software can raise hardware utilization levels from their typical 20 to 30 percent range, to as high as 98 percent. Primary markets include EDA, MCAE, geosciences, and software development.

Installing the Sun Grid Engine software on a collection of workstations or servers makes the collection a single, virtual pool of computational resources. Within this virtual entity, work queues can be defined and given owners, and resource limits can be imposed; you can subsequently enable and disable these items, as required. Similarly, users can be created with priorities and job limits to constrain the resource consumption of users. All of these features can be configured from the management command line and GUI interfaces.

The Sun Grid Engine software consists of four daemon processes—execd, commd, schedd, and qmaster. These daemon processes coordinate the scheduling, dispatch, and execution of batch jobs, monitor job and machine status, report on the systems, and manage communications among components.

The Sun Grid Engine software is ported to a variety of operating environments, including the Solaris operating environment and Linux. The source code is available under the Sun Industry Standards Source License. For details, see http://www.sun.com/software/gridware.

Technologies for Building Distributed Applications

Many technologies exist for building cluster environments or creating distributed applications. The sections that follow describe examples of two such technologies.

CORBA

Probably the best known technology for building distributed applications is the Object Management Group Common Object Request Broker Architecture (CORBA). First released in October 1991, CORBA 1.0 defined an open, vendor-independent architecture and infrastructure and not a specific product. This architecture and infrastructure enables companies to compete on implementation of the specification but remain compatible and interoperable. Object request brokers (ORBs) are currently available from Inprise, Iona Technologies Ltd., IBM, and BEA Systems, among others [ORBimpl]. The latest CORBA 3.0 release includes standardization for fault-tolerant redundant software configurations through entity redundancy at the object level.

CORBA also defines an interface definition language (IDL) for specifying the parameters to be passed to and from an object when a particular method is invoked on it. The strong interface definitions of IDL form a contract between the client and the server-side object implementation. Relying on these definitions shields users and consumers of the interfaces from the actual implementation of the object. This shielding enables users to replace the object with newer or better implementations without affecting the applications that rely on it. It also means that objects can be written in any programming language that has IDL mapping, for example, C/C++, Java, COBOL, and so forth. In turn, these languages can reside on a wide range of hardware platforms and operating environments.

Programs locate the object they want to use through a name service. Once the particular target object is found, communication between them is independent of their location. The Internet Inter-Orb Protocol (IIOP) facilitates communication between ORBs.

For more information on the Object Management Group, see `http://www.omg.com`. For more information on CORBA, see [CORBAhist].

JXTA

Started as a research project by Bill Joy and Mike Clary, JXTA (pronounced "Juxta") was released by Sun in the spring of 2001. JXTA is a set of open, generalized peer-to-peer protocols. These peer-to-peer protocols enable any connected device on the network (for example, cell phone to PDA or PC to server) to communicate and collaborate. JXTA is independent of programming language, communication protocol, hardware platform, and operating environment, giving it the widest possible developer audience.

Applications like Napster and AOL Instant Messaging have their own infrastructure and protocols for communication and service location. JXTA can provide a common framework for both of them, enabling a higher degree of integration.

For more information on JXTA, read [JXTAover] and see `http://www.jxta.org`.

CHAPTER 3

Sun Cluster 3.0 Architecture

This chapter describes the Sun Cluster 3.0 product architecture. The chapter discusses the kernel infrastructure and highlights important features of the software that enable you to design from the services perspective, rather than from the software perspective.

The first half of this chapter positions Sun Cluster 3.0 in the modern enterprise Information Technology (IT) infrastructure. It demonstrates how Sun Cluster 3.0 fits in with the Sun™ Service Point Architecture vision and describes failure handling and outage time. This half of the chapter also discusses how you must clearly differentiate high availability from disaster recovery and fault tolerant solutions.

The second half of the chapter examines the technical details of the product that provide new features and functions. This part of the chapter includes examples of the use of these features and functions in a practical implementation to simplify management and application functionality. It also highlights the fact that not all applications are suitable for this environment and provides a list of suitable applications and application agents available from Sun and independent software vendors. See "Data Services and Application Agents" on page 99.

This chapter contains the following sections:

- System Architecture
- Kernel Infrastructure
- System Features
- Cluster Failures
- Synchronization
- Arbitration

System Architecture

Sun Cluster 3.0, released in December 2000, is the result of nearly six years of research, development, and testing work. This work stems from the Solaris Multicomputer (Solaris MC) project started by Sun Labs in early 1995. New global features—global disks, tapes, CD-ROMs, a global file service, and global networking—augment the Sun Cluster 3.0 support for highly available (HA) applications. These new global features enable Sun Cluster 3.0 to provide all the functionality of its predecessor, Sun Cluster 2.2, and to support a new class of scalable applications. Some examples of HA applications are the Network File System (NFS), the industry-standard relational database management systems (RDBMSs), and parallel applications such as the Oracle 8*i* Parallel Server (Oracle 8*i* OPS) and Oracle 9*i* Real Application Cluster (Oracle 9*i* RAC).

Enterprise Infrastructure

You should never consider deployment of a Sun Cluster system in isolation. The well known cliché that "a chain is only as strong as its weakest link" applies equally well to the infrastructure within an enterprise. A cluster provides a platform to host highly available services. These services, in turn, must communicate with other components within the organization and be accessible to the users who interact with it. It is important, therefore, to ensure that the surrounding infrastructure is reliable and available too. Networks that link various architectural tiers within the organization should have alternative paths so that data can flow unimpeded between the various components. Similarly, power and cooling are needed to ensure that systems continue to run and do not overheat. All of this must occur in an environment secure from malicious damage or unauthorized observation. A secure environment ensures that the data is safe from unauthorized manipulation or inadvertent corruption.

A Sun Cluster must be run by trained system administrators who understand the technology. The system administrators must also understand the need to clearly define and carefully follow change management procedures. Through the SunUP™ Network program and by focusing on the people and process in addition to the product, IT departments can ensure that Sun Cluster 3.0 systems deliver the expected level of availability. The SunUP organization, which is part of the Sun Worldwide Quality organization, works with customers and third-party partners to develop products and services that enhance availability in Sun computer systems. The Sun BluePrints program works in alliance with the SunUP program to produce best practice documentation for use by the system administrators.

Service Point Architecture

The Sun™ Service Point architecture is the Sun Microsystems vision of how modern data centers can meet the challenges placed on them. These challenges are tightened IT budgets, the Internet, all of the facets of e-business, and the demand for highly available services that are as reliable and available as the dial tone on a telephone. Sun Cluster 3.0 forms a key part of this architecture, which brings together the concepts of resource consolidation and service-level management. Sun terms this a SunPlex™. This environment is administered through a common set of tools, such as the Sun™ Management Center 3.0 software. The Service Point Architecture enables IT departments to get the most out of their resources and contain provisioning, implementation, change, and on-going management costs. The case studies in Chapters 5 and 6 implement the Sun Service Point Architecture and embody the SunUP configuration best practices.

Fault Tolerant Systems

Although Sun Cluster 3.0 makes applications highly available, you should make a clear distinction between Sun Cluster 3.0 and fault tolerant solutions like the Netra ft™ server. If an unrecoverable hardware component failure, such as a processor failure or an uncorrectable ECC memory error occurs, the server panics. Depending on the type of service, you, the system administrator, may need to restart the services running on that node on another node within the cluster. Consequently, users of the service may experience a pause in the service or an outage that requires reconnection to the service. The advantages of a Sun Cluster solution over a fault tolerant solution are threefold. A Sun Cluster solution is considerably less expensive because it is based on general-purpose Solaris servers. Therefore, this solution can be used on a wider range of server platforms, thus enabling greater application scalability. And they can recover from software faults (bugs) that would otherwise be a single point of failure in a fault tolerant system.

High Availability Versus Disaster Recovery

Because the primary goal of Sun Cluster 3.0 is to provide a platform for highly available and scalable applications, you must clearly distinguish the goals of the Sun Cluster product and the goals of a disaster recovery strategy. Disaster recovery policies often trigger strong business processes that involve a large number of staff in a "firefighting" mode. A simple software failure that causes an application failover to a second node should not provoke such a complex response.

A genuine disaster recovery policy must take into account failures other than those outlined previously. These failures include data corruption and deletion, both accidental and malicious, plus the occasions that require rapid rollback of data or application changes.

When combined with the Sun StorEdge Network Data Replicator (SNDR software), Sun Cluster 3.0 provides a suitable combination of availability and disaster recovery solutions.

Sun Cluster 3.0 relies heavily on the private interconnects between its nodes for communication of "heartbeat" messages and the data required for the new global functionality. Increasing the node separation to afford protection from local disasters such as floods, fires, or power failures introduces latency into the internode communication. This results in potential performance penalties for applications that make any substantial use of internode communication for synchronization of data or state. Given that almost all applications have some data that must be read from a cluster file system or written to it, the node separation will inevitably affect system performance.

Separating cluster nodes over a long distance also requires substantial additional costs for the associated dedicated fiber communications networks needed to support the disk mirroring and the related public and private network infrastructure needed. Because the data must be mirrored across sites to ensure the survival of a site failure, all write transactions must be completed on both halves of the mirror before any disk write returns. FIGURE 3-1 shows the I/O overhead of campus clustering versus replication.

This action not only increases latency, but puts a substantial demand on bandwidth, because whole disk blocks must be transmitted across the public network to the remote site regardless of the size of change. The extended interconnects impact system performance, even if the system uses the HAStorage data service. See "Application Performance" on page 78. The extended node separation also adds latency to the internal Sun Cluster 3.0 coherency traffic. See "File and Attribute Caches" on page 73. Consequently, Sun Cluster 3.0 currently limits internode separation of campus clusters to 500 meters.

You should also consider failures that result in all or part of a disk mirror requiring synchronization again. The additional latency impacts the performance of the system and the completion time of the resynchronization. When dark fiber is used for intersite links, the links must be tested to ensure that they can sustain full bandwidth to minimize the period of disruption.

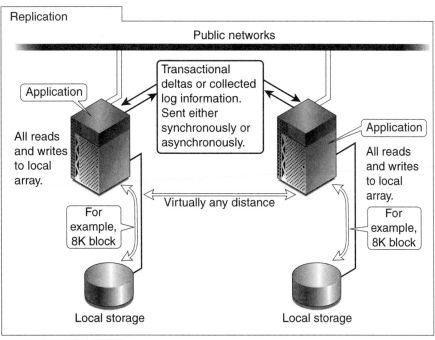

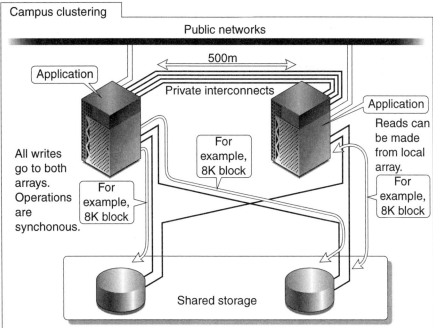

FIGURE 3-1 I/O Overhead of Campus Clustering Versus Replication

Data Deletion and Corruption Recovery

A genuine disaster recovery policy must account for failures other than those outlined previously, including data corruption and deletion, both accidental and malicious, plus the occasional need to rapidly roll back data or application changes. A Sun Cluster 3.0 system, even with mirrored storage, cannot recover from such errors. A corrupted or deleted file, by definition, is corrupted or deleted on all subcluster mirrors. The only way to recover data integrity is to restore the file from tape or from a locally held file system snapshot. In an RDBMS system, you may subsequently have to apply transactions to the recovered file or files.

You can use a number of technologies to facilitate recovery from data corruption or deletion, the most basic being a tape backup and recovery system. Other alternatives include:

- The fssnap(1M) feature in Solaris 8 update 3 operating environment, which enables you to take snapshots of the file system. The fssnap(1M) snapshots are a point-in-time copy of data created on storage attached locally.

- Sun StorEdge™ Instant Image 3.0 software, which enables you to take snapshots of data from both raw devices and file systems. This feature cannot be used with Oracle 8*i* OPS or Oracle 9*i* RAC systems. In contrast to the SNDR software, the Sun StorEdge Instant Image snapshots are a point-in-time copy of data created on storage attached locally. You can quickly update these snapshots by copying over only the changed disk blocks.

- Sun StorEdge Network Data Replicator 3.0 software, which enables you to replicate raw devices or file systems synchronously or asynchronously, to remote sites continuously. This feature cannot be used with Oracle 8*i* OPS or Oracle 9*i* RAC systems. In contrast to the Sun StorEdge Instant Image, the SNDR software replicates data continuously to storage connected to a host on a remote site.

Most relational database management systems (RDBMS) have built-in replication technology. Oracle 9*i* RAC, for example, has Oracle Data Guard, which enables you to copy complete archive log files to one or more remote sites and then replay the log files at a suitable time. This feature enables you to replay transactions up to a specific error, thus avoiding a corruption or deletion. This feature can also replicate changes to one or more tables to tables in remote databases.

A suitable disaster recovery architecture should, therefore, include Sun StorEdge Instant Image 3.0, Sun StorEdge Network Data Replicator 3.0 software products, and application-level replication, plus Sun Cluster 3.0 software to provide high availability.

Kernel Infrastructure

Most traditional clusters, such as Sun Cluster 2.2 and other competing clustering products, relied on layering collections of compiled programs and shell scripts on top of a plain operating system. Sun Cluster 3.0 offers enhanced functionality because it is tightly integrated with the Solaris 8 operating environment and the system interconnects. The following sections highlight the problems the Sun hardware engineers and software developers had to overcome and extols the benefits of their solutions. These sections contain an overview of how participating cluster nodes interact, an overview of the supporting kernel framework, and a description of replica management. FIGURE 3-2 shows a basic Sun Cluster 3.0 system hardware configuration.

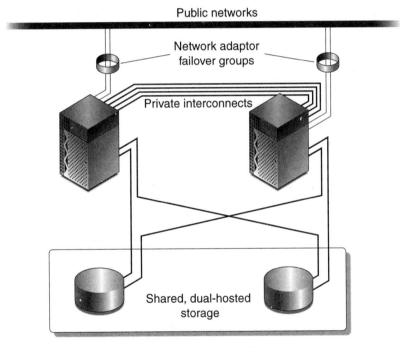

FIGURE 3-2 Sun Cluster 3.0 System Hardware Diagram

Subject to certain configuration guidelines, participating nodes can be individual physical servers or system domains within Sun Enterprise™ 10000 and Sun Fire systems. Multiple private interconnect networks connect every node with the other nodes and one or more of the public network subnets to provide resilient user connectivity. Each server in the cluster runs a separate copy of the Solaris 8 operating environment.

Depending on the storage topology used, one or more pairs of nodes can support dual-hosted disk subsystems. You can use standard disk management products, such as Solaris Volume Manager (SVM), formerly known as Solstice DiskSuite™, or VERITAS Volume Manager (VxVM) to manage the disk space. Currently, Sun Cluster 3.0 supports only the Solaris UNIX File System (UFS). Support for the VERITAS File System (VxFS) is expected at a later date.

Installing the Sun Cluster 3.0 software makes available the global features—global file service, global devices, and global networking. These features enable the cluster to provide highly available, scalable, and parallel services.

Kernel Framework

The Sun Cluster 3.0 software extends the Solaris 8 operating environment into a cluster operating system through a number of kernel components that work together to overcome the technical problems of cluster computing described in Chapter 1. FIGURE 3-3 shows the relationship between these components and their user interfaces.

The ps(1) command lists the processes:

- cluster—This process is the user-level representation of the cluster kernel processes, similar in concept to the sched or pageout processes. These processes control all the cluster kernel threads and the object request broker (ORB).

- clexecd—This process performs some user-level file system tasks on behalf of the cluster framework, for example, file system checking of the VxFS file systems when Sun Cluster 3.0 supports VxFS.

Subsequent paragraphs in this chapter cover other cluster-related processes.

The design basis of the cluster kernel framework is the ORB model. The distributed object invocation service is similar to the Common Object Request Broker Architecture (CORBA) model. Interfaces used by the cluster kernel components are described with the CORBA Interface Definition Language (IDL); components interact with one another by making requests on the interfaces of a component. The same node or another node then executes these requests regardless of the location of the object. When object invocation is on the local node, the system executes the call as a virtual function call and accesses objects hosted on a remote node by remote object invocation over the private interconnects of the cluster.

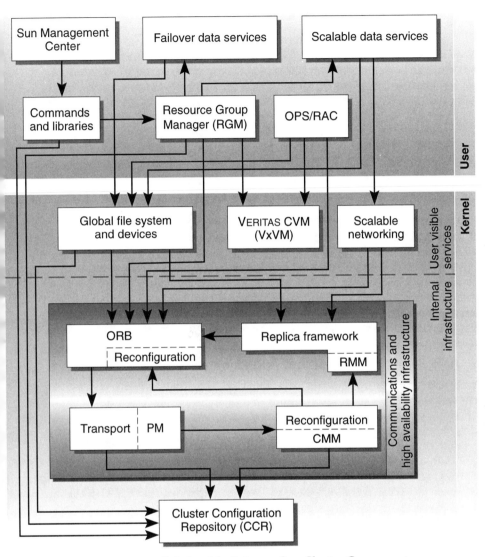

FIGURE 3-3 Relationship Between Sun Cluster Components

Replica Management

One of the main problems that Sun Cluster 3.0 overcomes is the maintenance of the distributed state of a number of its fundamental kernel components. The system achieves this by using a combination of replica managers (RM), replica manager agents (RMA), and a single replica manager (RMM).

Components within the cluster kernels interact with each other on a client/server basis. The global file service (GFS) is two separate pieces, each of which can reside on a separate node. For a client caller to receive a highly available service from a server object, an alternative server, or secondary server, located on another node must back up that object. The system also uses the concept of a standby object that can be promoted to the status of a secondary object if a secondary server must take over from a primary server. This mechanism ensures the continued availability of the object, even if a subsequent failure occurs, without the overhead of continuously updating multiple secondaries. However, this immediately leads to all of the associated clustered computing synchronization and arbitration problems described in Chapter 1. The standard Solaris operating environment has no kernel transactional facilities to support this requirement, so Sun Cluster 3.0 provides these facilities.

Mini-Transactions

A series of mini-transactions that implement a two-phase commit protocol synchronize the primary servers with one or more secondary servers. This protocol is similar to that found in modern distributed database systems. Using this protocol ensures that synchronous writes to two different memories are consistent, as described in "Microprocessor Cache Coherency" on page 16 and "Two-Phase Commit" on page 18.

FIGURE 3-4 shows the sequence of operations on a typical replicated object. The mini-transaction framework ensures "exactly once" semantics. Exactly once semantics ensure that an operation is not duplicated or repeated. In comparison, atomic operations ensure only that an operation either succeeds or does not succeed. Not only do exactly once semantics make kernel services highly available, but they mask a range of failures from user applications. The replica object handler of a service communicates with its replicas to atomically execute the request of the client object. The primary replica is then responsible for sending checkpoint messages to the secondary replica. These messages are service dependent but the effect is identical. The secondary replies with a commit message, and the primary logs the operation before replying to the client object. When the client completes the call successfully, it replies asynchronously to the primary replica to notify this replica to forget the operation.

An example of file creation on a cluster file system demonstrates how replicas work in practice and clarifies their work and benefit to user applications. A cluster file system is mounted concurrently on all of the current member nodes within a cluster. The underlying disk subsystem hosting the file system is connected to both cluster nodes simultaneously, but the I/O to the file system passes through only one controlling node (see "Storage Topologies" on page 62), the primary path, at any one time. For the file system to appear continuously available to client applications, all I/O operations that modify the state of the file system need the services of the replica manager.

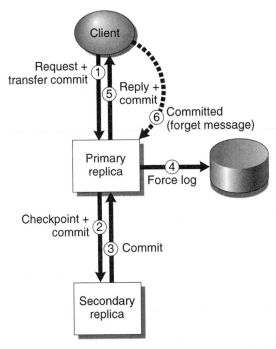

FIGURE 3-4 Mini-Transaction Replicated Object Sequence

Consider the operation of file creation on a file system. This operation must first check for the existence of the file, its permissions, and the permissions of the directory containing the file. If the file does not exist and the permissions settings allow, the system can then create the file, along with appropriate updates associated with file creation before the call returns to the user. The operation also returns the appropriate UNIX success or error return code.

System Features

This section discusses the topologies available for various business requirements and applications, global features (global devices, global file service, global networking service), cluster private interconnects, and cluster configuration control.

Storage Topologies

Currently, Sun Cluster 3.0 supports three types of storage topology—clustered pairs (FIGURE 3-5), N+1 (FIGURE 3-6), and pair+M (FIGURE 3-7). These are equivalent when only two nodes are considered. The following sections describe these topologies and their advantages and disadvantages for application deployment.

Regardless of the topology, you must configure cluster nodes with sufficient resources—CPU, memory, and I/O bandwidth—to ensure that applications can continue to meet their service level agreements even when failover to a backup node occurs. Failure to do so can result in poor performance, such that users believe the application is unavailable. Using the Solaris Resource Manager™ on a Sun Cluster 3.0 system can help prioritize resource usage and help ensure that service levels are met.

Clustered Pair Topology

A clustered pair topology (FIGURE 3-5) creates a single cluster of up to eight servers, from pairs of nodes that dual-host storage.

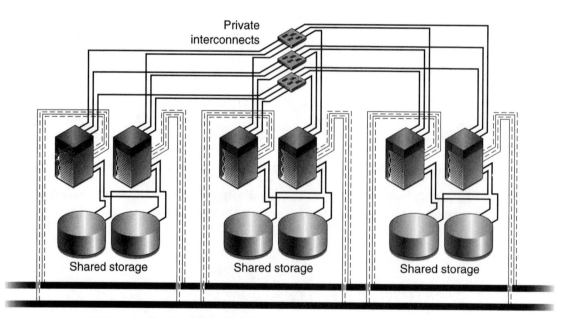

FIGURE 3-5 Clustered Pair Topology

Unlike the N+1 topology, this configuration does not demand excessive SBus or PCI slots on a single node. Instead, each node requires only sufficient I/O slots to hold the host bus adapters (HBAs) for the dual-hosted storage in the pair.

So, before you consider alternative hosts, be aware that by running one or more HA data service per node, you can achieve maximum usage of the cluster resources. This method allows every data service the option of two nodes with direct connection to the storage and, hence, higher performance.

N+1 Topology

Clusters that employ an N+1 topology (FIGURE 3-6) allow a single "backup" node to dual-host storage with up to three other nodes. The benefit of this topology is that it provides you with a single insurance policy for several other nodes, potentially lowering the cost of an HA solution. The disadvantage is that the backup node requires enough I/O slots to hold the HBAs for all of the dual-hosted storage.

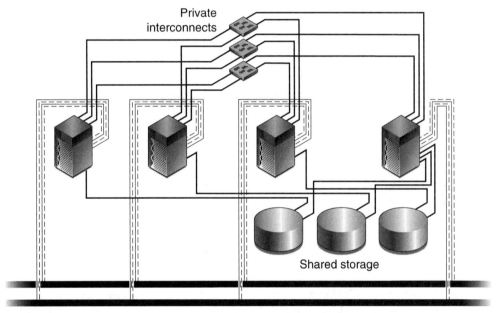

FIGURE 3-6 N+1 Topology

By configuring one or more data services to each of the N "primary" nodes and leaving the backup node idle, the failure of a single server causes failover of its applications to the backup node. Provided the backup node is equal in power to the largest primary node, the migrated applications perform to the same level as before, assuming no other node fails over its workload, too. This approach enables you to meet service level agreements (SLAs) even in the event of a cluster node failure. The alternative is to run additional data services on the backup node and experience some level of service degradation in the event that a primary node fails over its workload.

As with the clustered pair topology, you can run data services anywhere within the cluster, thanks to the global features, but they perform best when you colocate them with their storage.

Pair+*M* Topology

The new global features within Sun Cluster 3.0 make an additional pair+*M* storage topology (FIGURE 3-7) possible. Using this option, you can provide storage facilities to further *M* nodes that are also part of the cluster with a single clustered pair. You could consider this as network attached storage (NAS) for the sole use of the other nodes in the cluster.

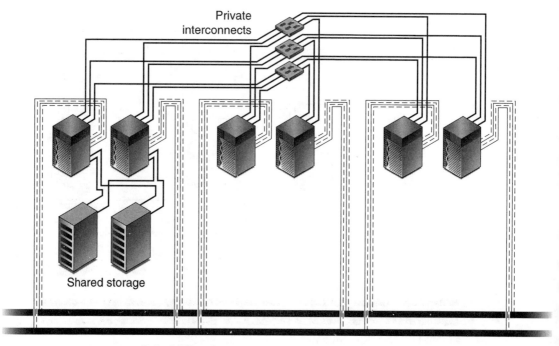

FIGURE 3-7   Pair+*M* Topology

The benefit of this architecture is to minimize the I/O slot demands on the remaining *M* nodes, but at a cost of making these nodes send all their disk I/O requests to the node hosting the storage. *M* nodes are only required to have public and private interconnect networks.

This approach is ideal if you want to consolidate a combination of back-end databases, application, and web servers. Your implementation would use the nodes with local storage as primary hosts for the back-end database, and the *M* nodes to support the web and application servers. Because, in general, the web and application servers perform a limited number of writes, remote storage does not significantly impact these servers. The system caches any data these servers read in the local Solaris page cache, thus maintaining the overall performance of the servers.

Cluster Device Connectivity

A cluster consisting of two or more nodes has a number of I/O devices—disks, tapes, and CD-ROMs—connected to its constituent nodes. You cannot attach tapes and CD-ROMs to two hosts at the same time, but you can connect disks to a single node or dual-host them between two nodes.

Sun Cluster 3.0 is SCSI-3 PGR ready. The availability of persistent group reservation (PGR) ioctls enables Sun Cluster 3.0 to support storage topologies in which more than two nodes are connected to a given disk device. See "SCSI-2 and SCSI-3 Command Set Support" on page 110.

FIGURE 3-8 is an example of local and dual-hosted devices.

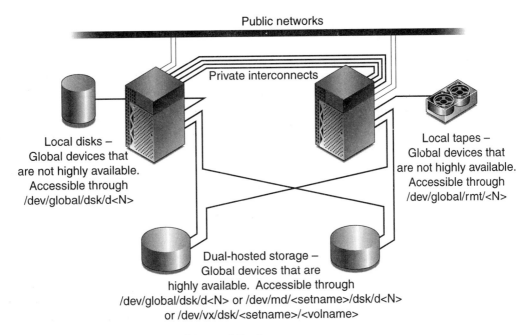

FIGURE 3-8 Local and Dual-Hosted Devices

Global Devices

The tight integration of the Sun Cluster 3.0 software and the Solaris kernel allows the cluster nodes to seamlessly share devices across the cluster. The ubiquity of the global services implemented at the operating environment level allows all cluster nodes to share devices and network interfaces. A global namespace allows devices to be uniquely identified and accessed. The result is a consistent, highly available environment upon which you can easily implement data services. The following paragraphs and sections describe these feature in more detail.

Sun Cluster 3.0 introduces the concept of a global device in which a specific device has a consistent name and a unique minor device number across the entire cluster. Using this name, a global device is accessible from all nodes. All disk, SVM disk sets, VxVM disk groups, tape, and CD-ROM devices are global, regardless of whether they are single or dual-hosted devices, and regardless of the node to which you connect them. Applications access them the same way they would in a normal single server environment, that is, through open(2), close(2), read(2), and write(2) system calls. This namespace consistency enables your system administrator to move applications from node to node within the cluster, without changing paths to data files or configuration information.

Primary and Secondary I/O Paths

When a device is connected to two cluster nodes, the cluster framework designates one connection as an active primary I/O path and the other as a passive secondary path. (This is in addition to any active and passive I/O path designations associated with a device that is attached to a single node through multiple connections and that uses Sun StorEdge Traffic Manager software functionality.) A secondary path can, transparently, become the active primary path in response to the failure of the node that hosts the primary path or by the cluster administrator manually migrating control with the scswitch(1M) command. The mini-transaction mechanism described previously replicates a significant state in the primary path to the secondary. As subsequent paragraphs describe, applications attain the best performance when they are colocated with the node that hosts the primary I/O path.

Sun Cluster 3.0 manages primary and secondary path control at the Solaris Volume Manager (SVM) disk set, or VxVM disk group level, rather than for individual disks. A collection of disks, such as this, is known as a *device group*. Therefore, dual-ported devices are available to an application continuously, even if the primary path fails. Applications are unaware of the failure until the final path becomes unavailable. When a device is connected only to one node, the failure of that node makes the device unavailable, and the system returns an EIO error to the application.

The number of nodes to which you can connect storage will increase over time. See "SCSI-2 and SCSI-3 Command Set Support" on page 110.

Device ID

To provide the required uniformity of namespace, every node in the cluster must be able to refer to a single device by a common unique name and a minor number. Sun Cluster 3.0 implements a device ID (DID) pseudodriver. On installation or under the system administrator's control, this driver searches for devices attached to any of the cluster nodes and assigns them unique DID numbers. Sun Cluster 3.0 assigns a single common number to a dual-hosted device, even if it is hosted on different controllers in the two nodes. FIGURE 3-9 is an example of the DID numbering for a three-node cluster.

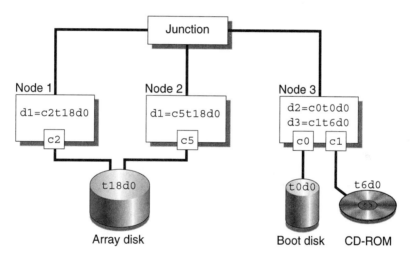

FIGURE 3-9   DID Numbering for a Three-Node Cluster

The system can access device slices locally, through a /dev/did/{r}dsk/dXsY entry, or globally, through a /dev/global/{r}dsk/dXsY entry. X and Y indicate the DID and slice numbers, respectively. The two entries differ subtly because the local entry is a symbolic link to an entry in the /devices/pseudo directory, but the global entry links into the /global/.devices/node@X/devices/pseudo hierarchy. The global entry properties differ from those of the local entry.

When a global device is accessed for the first time through a /dev/global name, the device group is put online. The device group is assigned primary and secondary nodes by the Sun Cluster framework. You can use the scstat -Dvv command to check this. The system then routes all I/O through the primary node, providing some degree of synchronization.

In contrast, the device group is not put online when a device is accessed through the /dev/did device name, and no primary or secondary I/O paths are assigned. Thus, when multiple nodes access a single device through the /dev/did names, the accesses are not synchronized. Oracle 8*i* OPS and Oracle 9*i* RAC are the only supported applications capable of coordinating concurrent access to these shared devices. In practice, they are more often part of a shared CVM device group anyway.

Attempting to access a /dev/did device that is not attached to the local machine generates an error. However, the device can be accessed by its /dev/global name.

SVM metasets and VxVM disk groups are initialized by different disk device names. SVM metaset devices are constructed with the DID device names (see "Device ID" on page 67), whereas the standard control, target, device references (c2t5d4, for example) are used when disks are put under VxVM control. Regardless of the volume management product used, the SVM metaset devices or VxVM disk group volumes have unique name and minor number combinations across the cluster. Therefore, whatever type of disk object an application uses—raw disk or a file system, SVM or VxVM—every node can access it with a consistent naming scheme.

Namespace

For applications to operate on the global devices (see "Global Devices" on page 66 and "Device ID" on page 67), they must be located in a directory somewhere under the normal UNIX hierarchy. Sun Cluster 3.0 implements a /global/.devices/node@*X* structure, where *X* represents a node number within the cluster, currently 1 to 8. Sun Cluster 3.0 design supports 64 nodes, so this could ultimately be 1 to 64. All individual disks represented in /dev/global, as well as all SVM /dev/md metadevices and VxVM /dev/vx disk group volumes are, ultimately, symbolically linked to a /global/.devices/node@*X*/devices/ pseudo entry. This differs from the /devices/pseudo because the file system on which it resides, and which the system allocates specifically at install time, is mounted globally.

Because the /global/.devices/node@*X* directory hierarchies are mounted globally, the devices within them that are opened by an application inherit the highly available semantics that the *global* mount(1M) option confers on the file system.

The global namespace is not a committed interface and is subject to change. The information given in the previous paragraphs illustrates how the namespace is constructed for Sun Cluster 3.0 update 1.

Practical Uses

You can use global devices in a number of ways within a clustered system. The most common way is to deploy an RDBMS system, such as Oracle, Sybase, Informix, or DB2. Instead of building the database on standard raw devices, you can use the global equivalents in their place. This ensures that the database not only benefits from the shortest code path to disk as a result of the use of raw devices (compared to going through a file system) but benefits from uniform naming conventions across the entire cluster. In a node failure, the database can restart on an alternative node and still gain access to the raw devices it needs. As described in "Pair+M Topology" on page 64, Sun Cluster 3.0 offers some storage topologies in which an application might not have any local path to disks. Under these circumstances, I/O requests are sent to and satisfied by the node that hosts the primary I/O path. "Private Interconnects" on page 85 describes how this communication transpires over the private interconnects.

Another simple and effective use for global devices is derived from the ability to mount a High Sierra File System (HSFS) globally. This simplifies the installation of software or updates by enabling you to mount CD-ROMs concurrently on every cluster node.

Access to global tape devices reduces the administrative effort of making simple backups or copies of data. Tapes can be accessed directly with standard UNIX commands, such as tar(1), cpio(1), ufsdump(1), dd(1), and so forth, using their /dev/global/rmt/ device name. The system blocks any attempt to simultaneously open a tape device for reading or writing until the first process has closed the device. These global semantics do not, however, extend to robot tape controllers, so tape libraries can only be accessed sequentially. Also, global devices cannot be locked directly with the fcntl(2) system call.

Global File Service

The global file service, also known as the cluster file system (CFS), is a highly available, distributed, cache-coherent file system that enables access to standard UFS or HSFS file systems from multiple cluster nodes. The CFS architecture (FIGURE 3-10) is a kernel-based client/server architecture built on the vnode/VFS interface [JMRM00]. This means that UFS and HSFS need only minimal changes, thus simplifying the work required to support other file systems in the future. Cluster file systems are built on the global devices previously described.

FIGURE 3-10 shows the global file service architecture.

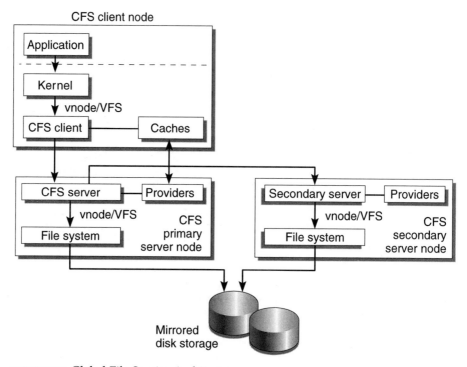

FIGURE 3-10 Global File Service Architecture

Note – The Virtual File System (VFS) vnode/VFS layer is the kernel representation of a file in a file system. It contains information regarding that file, as well as pointers to the specific implementations of the open(2), close(2), read(2), and write(2) system calls.

Although it is possible to create a CFS on a single disk, its use within a cluster would be inadvisable for anything other than temporary data because it lacks the protection of the data that a mirrored device affords. In general, you build clustered file systems on device groups that contain mirrored and protected data volumes.

Application Access

User applications, such as Oracle, NFS, or iPlanet™ Unified Web Services, normally communicate with the underlying file system, for example UFS, by making the appropriate open(2), close(2), read(2), and write(2) system calls.

One of the design goals for Sun Cluster 3.0 is to ensure that no changes are needed for an application to access the CFS. Therefore, it must present an identical vnode/VFS interface to calling applications. So, in a nonclustered environment, in which the vnode/VFS layer calls the underlying volume managers and ultimately the disk driver, the CFS interposes itself between the application and the standard file system. You can mount a file system globally by using the -g option to the mount(1M) command or by including the global flag in the relevant /etc/vfstab entry.

Client/Server Model

When an application operates on a file in a globally mounted file system or on a global device (FIGURE 3-10), it initially communicates with the CFS client object represented in the CFS vnode (the application and the CFS client are always colocated). If the requested data page or attributes are not in cache, the CFS client calls the CFS server objects on the node that is designated as the primary node for the file system. The CFS server calls the appropriate UFS vnode operations to satisfy the original request. When the call completes, the CFS server returns the data or file attributes to the CFS client, which subsequently passes them back to the calling application. The CFS client subsequently caches the data and file attributes. If the CFS client and server are colocated, special interfaces ensure that the data pages and file attributes are not double cached. As expected, introducing a cache implies the introduction of a synchronization mechanism. "File and Attribute Caches" on page 73 describes this mechanism.

The CFS client and server that operate within the kernel need not be colocated on a cluster node. The actual location of the file or device is hidden by the object invocation used to call the server methods. When the CFS client and server are colocated, the ORB optimizes the IDL invocations to local procedure calls. The implementation of CFS is also transport independent, enabling the cluster to support new interconnects as they become available.

Read and Write Implementation

When an application writes data to a CFS, the local CFS client issues a write request to the CFS server. The CFS server in turn issues a read request to the CFS client when sufficient kernel buffer space is available to receive the data to be written. This adds an extra TCP/IP message to the overall cost of a write.

Depending on their initial size, the kernel drivers might fragment large individual write requests or read replies into smaller requests. The system implements fragmented write operations as multiple asynchronous I/O that can be issued in parallel and thus benefit from having multiple interconnects. Similarly, the read operation implementation uses a read-ahead mechanism, allowing the CFS client to issue multiple smaller read requests, in parallel, over multiple interconnects. The decision to issue parallel read requests depends on the particular I/O pattern and the heuristics in the CFS drivers. For example, if an application issues a sequence of 1-megabyte reads, the CFS client can divide the 1-megabyte requests into a single 64-kilobyte read followed by the remaining 64-kilobyte reads in parallel. Using multiple interconnects can improve the performance of large I/O requests. However, the main benefit of multiple interconnects is an increase in overall I/O throughput.

When considering write operations, note that allocating extra space for a write operation that appends to a file, rather than one that updates a block that was already allocated, has additional overhead. See "Application Performance" on page 78.

FIGURE 3-11 shows the CFS read mechanism and FIGURE 3-12 shows the CFS write mechanism.

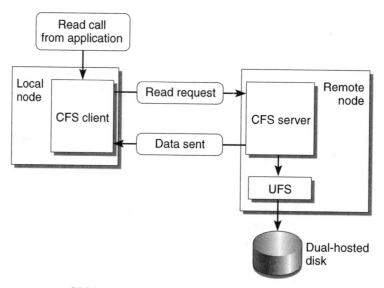

FIGURE 3-11 CFS Read Mechanism

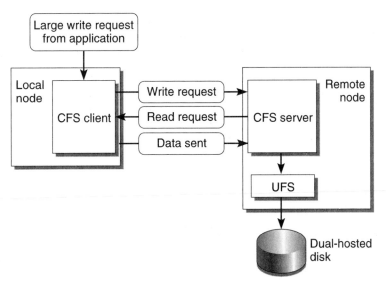

FIGURE 3-12 CFS Write Mechanism

I/O Parallelism

Certain cluster storage topologies locate the primary I/O path for a particular globally mounted file system of some applications on a remote node. Consequently, the system sends individual I/O requests over one of the private interconnects described previously. A single, small I/O request (2-kilobyte writes, for example), might not benefit from these multiple private interconnects. However, multiple I/O requests benefit from increased throughput by being load-balanced, in parallel, over all of the available connections, which leaves individual I/O latency unchanged.

All modern commercial databases have a multiprocess or multithreaded architecture that can take advantage of I/O parallelism.

File and Attribute Caches

The following description of the caching implementation is for illustration only and is correct for Sun Cluster 3.0 update 1. This implementation is subject to change in future. Caching file system data pages and file attributes is critical to overall cluster performance. When an application requests data or attributes from a file on the CFS, the system may be able to satisfy the request from a cache (FIGURE 3-10) instead of performing a physical disk I/O. The CFS server directs the necessary physical I/Os from the underlying file system, and drives the coherency management of the Solaris page and file attribute caches in the CFS client layer.

Mounting a file system globally links pairs of cached and "cacher" objects on the client and server. Among these linked pairs are pairs for the attributes and data pages of a file for every active file in the CFS. The client-side caches are synonymous with the standard Solaris caches so that the data is not cached twice.

Concurrently holding cached copies of file system data pages and attributes on multiple nodes requires three additional kernel structures. These structures manage the tags required to track the state of the particular items. These tags are analogous to the cache metadata described in "Microprocessor Cache Coherency" on page 16. Thus, compared to their local counterparts, files from the global file system use more kernel memory.

For CFS cache synchronization, Sun Cluster 3.0 uses a system of tokens to control access to and invalidation of cached objects that can be held concurrently on multiple cluster nodes. Multiple nodes can hold read tokens for data pages or file attributes. When the system reads a data page from a file or checks its attributes, the CFS client must first obtain the data or attribute read token for the specific file from the appropriate CFS server. Once the CFS client acquires the token, the data can be read in. If the system is transferring the dirty data from another node, it first flushes the data to stable storage to avoid losing updates if unrelated nodes crash. For subsequent references to the same data or the attribute while the token is still valid, the CFS client can read data from the local cache rather than the CFS server.

If a CFS client wants to change the attributes of a file or wants to write data to it, the client must first obtain or own the corresponding write token. Unlike the case with read tokens, only one node can hold the write token for the contents or attributes of a file. Before this token is granted, the CFS server invalidates all read tokens currently held and the associated cached data. The system must reread the data from the CFS server in subsequent requests for these invalidated pages or attributes. This CFS cache coherency mechanism is similar to those used in other components—microprocessors, RDBMS, and so forth.

Little can be done, from a configuration standpoint, to take advantage of these ramifications or avoid them. However, you must understand these issues to recognize workloads that are likely to perform well on the CFS. Workloads involving a significant number of writes to shared files from multiple nodes are unlikely to perform well on a CFS. However, applications that do very few writes, such as web servers, are likely to scale extremely well in this environment because of the high degree of caching that can be achieved across the cluster nodes. This issue is similar to the issues affecting multithreaded software development on symmetric multiprocessors (SMPs).

The situation will improve over time as Sun further optimizes Sun Cluster 3.0 software and develops and supports new, faster interconnects.

When transports that support the Remote Shared Memory (RSM) protocol (see "Protocols" on page 87) are available, for example Peripheral Component Interconnect-Scalable Coherent Interface (PCI-SCI), applications written to take advantage of the RSM-API will benefit from the lower latency, higher bandwidth communication. The ability of RSM to transfer data directly into the memory of a remote server removes the communication overhead that Data Link Provider Interface (DLPI) transports incur by encapsulating a message in one or more TCP/IP packets. Before the messages sent over the private interconnect by the cluster framework can benefit from RSM-capable interconnects, further developments must occur.

CFS Mounting

Cluster file systems are mounted with the standard UNIX mount(1M) command. The global nature of the mount is distinguished through the use of the *global* flag in /etc/vfstab or by entering the -g or -o global parameters on the command line. If all nodes have mount points that can accept the mount, you can issue the mount command from any node and the mount occurs on every cluster node. This feature is very powerful because you only need to initiate the process of making a file system globally available to all nodes on one node. Issuing a global flag to a UFS mount automatically implies the use of the logging flag to ensure that the system can recover file systems quickly in the event of a failover. However, it will be necessary to set it explicitly for VxFS file systems. A best practice would be to set any flags explicitly, regardless of the file system used.

The system replays all of the current active mounts to nodes that subsequently join the cluster. This allows nodes to become synchronized with the active mounts as soon as they join the cluster. If the mounts fails, for example, because a mount point does not exist, the booting node drops into single-user mode so you can correct the error. Careful change management procedures can help to ensure that the booting node does not drop into single-user mode.

You can mount the global UFS file system with or without the syncdir option. The decision to use it depends on what takes precedence—absolute performance or error semantics. The syncdir flag will not apply to a globally mounted VxFS.

The syncdir option only has an impact when the system is extending a file, either by appending data to the end or by allocating a previously unfilled page that is a hole. See mmap(2). Setting this option flushes notification of the operation directly to disk so it is not held in the in-memory logs. The write operation does not return until the system physically commits the data allocation to disk. If the file system runs out of space during this operation, the system returns an error to the write(2) call, even if a failover of the primary I/O path happens in the middle of the call. The downside is that this behavior can degrade the performance of the write(2) call substantially. For remote I/O, this degradation can be by as much as a factor of 10 because of the latency of the interconnect plus the latency of the committed write.

Without the syncdir option, CFS reserves space for the write(2) operation, but the system holds the transaction in memory and does not commit it to disk immediately. However, the write(2) call returns without an error if there was sufficient space. If a failover occurs before the in-memory log is flushed to disk, the CFS finds there is no space available when it tries to reserve space later if the file system fills up on the new primary before the CFS client flushes the dirty page. Under these circumstances, CFS returns an ENOSPC error from the close(2) call. When the application flushes data by using the sync(2) call, the call returns ENOSPC.

This behavior without the syncdir flag is similar to that of NFS but is less likely to occur because of the narrow time window in which the two events must take place. Thus, you must only use the syncdir mount option if the application cannot handle ENOSPC errors from sync(2) or close(2) and if the failure of the application to handle such errors is critical. Applications such as Oracle preallocate files and are therefore not susceptible to this problem. Oracle is capable of auto-extending its data files, but the chance of this happening in such a small time window is fairly remote.

The standard mount command supports a number of other flags or options, all of which are honored by a global mount. When an RDBMS like Oracle is running on a globally mounted UFS file system, the forcedirectio option is particularly useful.

The forcedirectio option, as its name suggests, forces the system to transfer I/O operations directly from the user address space to disk, bypassing the kernel page cache. This option is highly beneficial to applications that do their own caching, such as Oracle, in which recently used data is held in the system global area (SGA).

Note that the forcedirectio option applies to all files opened on the specified file system, so it can have a negative performance impact on other applications using the file system if those applications do not cache data themselves.

Application binaries must not be installed on cluster file systems that you mount with the forcedirectio option set. Despite this undesirable combination, because program binary text pages will not be cached in memory and may have to be reread from disk, the restriction may be lifted in a later release of the Sun Cluster 3.0 software.

Application Binaries, Data, and Logs

The CFS offers you greater flexibility in the location of application binaries, leading to simpler ongoing management. You can put application software binaries and configuration files on the local file system of each cluster node or on the cluster file system. However, there are few reasons to install any application software on individual nodes because this complicates the subsequent management of the application and its configuration files.

You must always put application data on a global file system to ensure that it continues to be available in the event of a node crash. The location of any application log files, however, depends on the type of application and whether it is a failover or a scalable service. See "Synchronization" on page 99.

When a scalable service runs on several nodes concurrently, log file placement can pose additional problems. Typically, this class of application is not designed to have multiple instances sharing the same executables and therefore has no locking mechanism to handle concurrent access to a single log file on a CFS. Under these circumstances, you can still install the application software on the global file service, but you must implement any log files mentioned in the configuration file as symbolic links to a file on the local file system. This implementation ensures that uncontrolled simultaneous access from the instances running on multiple cluster nodes does not corrupt the log files. The iPlanet Web Server is a prime example of such a setup. At a minimum, the `ErrorLog` and `PidLog` entries in `magnus.conf` should point to local files.

Applications such as Oracle 8*i* OPS or Oracle 9*i* RAC are designed as cluster applications. These applications already have the necessary controls to manage access to their raw control and log files. Therefore, you can safely install application binaries on the cluster file system without making additional changes to their configuration files. For more information on Oracle applications implementation, see "Cluster Software" on page 167.

TABLE 3-1 summarizes the pros and cons of each approach.

TABLE 3-1   Global File Service Benefits for Application Executables

Cluster File System	Local File Systems
Patches and upgrades are done only once.	Patches and upgrades are done multiple times.
Changes to configuration files are done only once.	Consistent changes must be made to multiple copies of the configuration files.
Accidental deletion of program or configuration files can stop the application from working on every cluster node.	Accidental deletion of program or configuration files can prevent the application from working on a particular node.
Upgrades that overwrite the original executables can interfere with the correct operation of the running application.	When the application is not running on that node, upgrades can overwrite local copies of application executables without affecting the original version of the application running on an alternative node.

Application Performance

Using CFS does not preclude access to any of the Solaris standard performance-enhancing features such as kernel asynchronous I/O (KAIO), aio(3HEAD), directio(3C), large pages, and so forth. The key to maximizing CFS performance is to ensure that, where possible, the running application and the primary I/O path for the particular CFS are colocated. Cluster file systems are built on device groups. At this level, Sun Cluster 3.0 controls the activation of primary and secondary I/O paths. A cluster achieves maximum flexibility, and hence performance, when it is implemented with multiple cluster file systems, each capable of having its primary I/O path migrated independently between nodes.

Sun Cluster 3.0 facilitates the primary I/O path being colocated with application execution through the use of a specialized resource type called HAStorage. See "Resource Types" on page 100. When the resource starts, the AffinityOn property ensures that the system switches its specified device groups, where possible, so that their primary path is through the local node. The system cannot start application resources that depend on HAStorage resource device groups and file systems until this initialization is complete.

Specifying which applications and workloads perform well on the CFS is difficult. However, it is possible to list the characteristics of those that are best suited to the current CFS implementation.

For simple failover applications, in which a single instance of the application executes on one node of the cluster at any one time, the primary goal is to ensure that the primary I/O path is colocated with the application. If the application has any of the following characteristics, it is likely to have less degradation from running on the CFS or on raw global devices:

- Uses Solaris KAIO or aio(3HEAD) routines

- Has read operations as most of the I/O workload

- Batches write I/O operations into a few large writes rather than preforming multiple small operations

- Preallocates data files rather than extending them on an ad hoc and regular basis

- Uses circular log files

Typically, RDBMS, OLTP, and DSS workloads, web server applications, and the majority of NFS and other file service workloads are in this category.

For scalable services, in which application instances run concurrently on several cluster nodes, it is impossible to ensure that the primary I/O path is local to all applications. Moreover, when applications have these characteristics, they are more likely to perform well on the CFS. Additionally, applications benefit when they divide the data files that they write into smaller pieces to allow greater concurrency.

With these points in mind, it is clear that a web service can benefit from running on multiple cluster nodes. This type of configuration is known as a *scalable service*.

Node Separation Performance Impact

Given the arguments for separating availability solutions from disaster recovery, most clusters should be deployed within a single data center with only meters separating the constituent nodes. However, in some circumstances you may want to place the cluster nodes in different buildings within a campus to guard against localized disasters such as fires or floods. Typically, node separation will still be under 500 meters, which is within the limits for the short wave Gigabit Interface Connector (GBIC) used by the Sun Fibre Channel-Arbitrated Loop (FC-AL) devices, such as the Sun StorEdge™ A5000 and Sun StorEdge T3 products.

As you increase node separation, internode communication latency rises. Although this increase is fairly small, on the order of 5 nanoseconds/meter, a long node separation causes this distance to become significant because of the finite speed of light in the glass of the fiber. A node separation of 10 kilometers, for example, adds 50 microseconds to each TCP/IP message sent over the private interconnects. Although this addition is small relative to typical disk I/O latency, usually on the order of 5 to 10 milliseconds, the effect on CFS performance has not yet been quantified.

CFS Versus NFS

A file system mounted globally through CFS differs from one mounted on multiple nodes using NFS in several distinct ways. TABLE 3-2 contrasts the two approaches.

TABLE 3-2   CFS and NFS Differences

CFS	NFS
Has a global namespace. Only one mount command is needed, with all nodes having equal access.	Multiple mount commands needed, one per node. Access characteristics can differ from node to node and depend on the share(1M) options. A globally consistent namespace can be implemented by using automounter (AutoFS) with the automount(1m) command and a distributed name service, but uniformity is not enforced.
Data caching is fully consistent.	Applications can read stale data for a short period of time.
Attribute caching is fully consistent.	Applications can read stale attributes for a short period of time.
File-locking semantics are maintained across failover boundaries.	Programs can get a SIGLOST error under certain circumstances.
Does not support AutoFS mounts.	Supports AutoFS mounts.
Usage is possible only within the cluster. NFS is necessary for usage outside the cluster.	Usage is possible by any machine on a network connected to this one if the security policy permits.
Writes are cached until the regular Solaris operating environment mechanisms flush out dirty pages, or until the application synchronizes data with sync(2).	Writes are written through more aggressively to the NFS server.
The CFS client caches data pages, not the underlying file system on the CFS server node.	The NFS client and the underlying file system on the NFS server node both cache data pages.
Supports seamless failover. Failover is faster.	Seamless failover in the nonclustered case is only available for read-only services.
Designed to exploit future fast private interconnects using remote DMA and zero-copy functions.	Not designed for such usage.
Provides a mechanism to support global devices.	Does not support remote devices.

Both CFS and NFS have their place in cluster deployment. The global file service provides the highly available CFS within the cluster. This, in turn, can be shared as a highly available service, through NFS, to client workstations or application servers. As a result of this combination, failure of a cluster node does not cause loss of service on the client systems, even though the service migrates from one cluster node to another, but client systems might see a pause in service during the reconfiguration process.

Global Networking Service

Another new Sun Cluster 3.0 concept is the global networking service. On a single server, you can assign IP addresses to ports on network interface cards (NICs) with the ifconfig(1M) command. A single NIC can host multiple addresses, but typically most servers present one IP address per subnet to which they are connected. Applications running on that server can then issue bind(2) system calls to bind to those addresses. Sun Cluster 3.0 extends this concept to create a global IP address visible to all nodes within the cluster hosting applications that are dependent on these specific addresses.

Global IP addresses, also known as global interfaces (GIFs), are installed on the appropriate NIC for the subnet to which the cluster is connected. The GIF is configured as a highly available, rather than scalable, resource. See "Resources" on page 102. The node hosting the GIF is known as the GIF node or GIN.

Nodes defined by the union of the resource group nodelist standard property and the resource group auxnodelist extension property have the global IP address configured on their loopback interface (lo0:2, lo0:3, and so forth), enabling local cluster applications to bind to it.

FIGURE 3-13 shows a four-node cluster with two subnets and two global IP addresses.

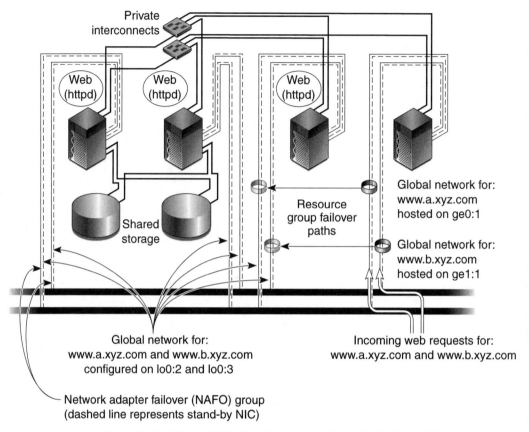

FIGURE 3-13 Four-Node Cluster With Two Subnets and Two Global IP Addresses

Hosting the global IP address on the loopback interface prevents the node from accepting incoming packets directly from the network while forcing the TCP/IP to adopt the address as local. Once the global IP packet is routed through the private interconnect to the TCP/IP stack of the node, the system acknowledges the destination address as internal and processed. The system sends a response packet (with the global IP as the source address) to the network because there is a network interface with an IP address on the same subnet on the node hosts. These services can then be brought up on these nodes and bound to the global IP address.

Scalable services, such as the iPlanet Web Server, are described in more detail throughout the following sections.

Packet Distribution Mechanisms

When the GIF accepts an incoming IP packet destined for a scalable service, the packet dispatch table (PDT) driver first examines the packet before passing it any further up the IP stack. Currently, the PDT has three policies for packet distribution—*weighted*, the system default; *ordinary sticky*, and *wildcard sticky*.

The *weighted* policy hashes incoming packets into buckets that are associated with the nodes hosting the target application, in accordance with their source IP and port number. By default, each node is given one entry in the hash array. So for three nodes, there would be three entries; each node would, statistically, get one-third of the overall traffic. The system then transfers the packets to the target node over the private interconnect to present them for consumption by the application on the loopback interface. When the application responds, the system transmits the outgoing packets using the relevant local NIC. You can change load-balancing weights dynamically at any time with the scrgadm(1M) command without shutting down dependent applications. For example, in a three-node system, the nodes A, B, and C could be given weights of 10, 30, and 40 (note that the weights do not need to add up to 100). In this case, the nodes get one-eighth, three-eighths, and one-half of the total traffic, respectively.

Under a weighted policy, packets from an individual client node that are sent from a fixed port are always hashed to the same destination server. Only a change in the weighting policy or the failure of one of the target nodes would alter the distribution by changing the result of the hash calculation. In the preceding example, if node B fails, node A would get one-fifth of the packets, and node C four-fifths of the packets.

The *ordinary sticky* policy ensures that requests from a given client IP address to a particular destination port are always directed to the same node hosting the target scalable service. This enables concurrent client connections to target nodes to share in-memory state. A good example of where this functionality is useful is an e-commerce site. The shopper can browse through the goods available and fill the shopping cart through one connection and service (HTTP on port 80) and then use a second connection and service (SSL on port 443) to pay for the goods. Having a fixed target node for packets avoids the overhead of renegotiating the SSL credentials every time a packet goes to a different host. Renegotiating the credentials every time a packet goes to a different host is a computation-expensive operation that is best minimized.

Application services that dynamically allocate ports, such as a passive mode FTP service, the initial connection on port 21 must be redirected to another port chosen by the service. This type of service must use the *wildcard sticky* policy. Under the wildcard sticky policy, all packets from a client IP address are directed to the same target node, regardless of their destination port.

Client affinity, the mapping of client traffic to a target server and service, remains in place unless the weighting distribution is changed or a target node or service becomes unavailable. If the weighting changes, existing connections can be distributed to a new target node. After a node or service failure and subsequent recovery, TCP-based applications reinstate their previous target affinity. However, this is not guaranteed to be the case with UDP-based applications.

Sun Cluster 3.0 allows both many-to-many and one-to-many relationships between services and global IP addresses. A three-node cluster, with nodes A, B, and C, can host the global IP www.xyz.com on the public network interface of node A. The system can also be configured with a scalable web service on port 80 on nodes A, B, and C and another scalable web service on port 90 on nodes A and B only. In contrast, the same cluster could host two global IP addresses: www.xyz.com and www.abc.com on node A and B respectively, both with scalable web services on port 80 running on all three nodes. Further, either of these configurations could be combined with additional failover services as required or as resources allow.

Advantages

The global networking service enables the cluster to provide scalable outbound IP traffic. This increases both throughput and response time without requiring any additional load-balancing hardware or software. Typically, inbound client network traffic is much smaller than the outbound network traffic it generates. Because of its tight integration with the cluster framework, this mechanism also ensures that the PDT driver does not distribute packets to nodes that are not currently participating in a cluster.

At first it might seem that the GIF is a system bottleneck. However, most workloads that are amenable to becoming scalable services have traffic profiles in which outbound packets outnumber inbound ones by as much as six to one. Most web servers and streaming media services are in this category.

Client Connection Recovery After a GIN Node Failure

A global IP address is defined as an instance of a SUNW.SharedAddress resource and placed in a failover resource group. See "Data Services and Application Agents" on page 99. If the node that is hosting one or more GIFs fails, the system reconfigures the address(es) onto an appropriate public network interface of another cluster node, defined in the resource group as a potential host for the GIF. IP packets reestablish their flow through the new GIN and are forwarded to the subscribing services as before. The public network monitoring (PNM) facility (see "Public Network Monitoring" on page 93) protects the GIF against NIC or network failure on the GIN.

From a client IP perspective, the global network service is available continuously. As part of the standard TCP/IP recovery mechanisms, the system retransmits packets dropped while the interface is being moved. If the application is UDP based, it retransmits lost packets. To applications on both the client and the cluster, the global IP address functions identically to IP addresses on a single server; no application changes are required. You can migrate the global IP addresses with the scswitch(1M) command.

Private Interconnects

Nodes in a Sun Cluster 3.0 system need networks over and above those required to provide client connectivity. Therefore, Sun Cluster 3.0 uses private interconnects to transmit and receive cluster heartbeat messages and a variety of other information between nodes. As with all other components in a cluster, the system requires a minimum of two private interconnects for redundancy. Although there is no inherent limitation on the number of interconnects that the system can support, Sun Cluster 3.0 imposes a practical limit of six private interconnects on cluster configurations. Bear in mind that these connections consume CPU cycles to send and receive packets. Six Gigabit Ethernet connections using the current Gigabit Ethernet cards could take as many as six 750 MHz UltraSPARC III CPUs to drive to full capacity.

Private interconnects cannot share switches or use routers because the routers would not route the DLPI heartbeat traffic. See "DLPI" on page 88.

For clusters with only two nodes, simple back-to-back (direct connection) cabling suffices. Larger clusters need multiple switches, one for each private connection. Multiple connections are particularly beneficial when the global features described previously are heavily used. FIGURE 3-14 shows back-to-back and switch-connected private interconnects.

Sun Cluster 3.0 allows you to dynamically add and remove private interconnects without taking down the cluster or stopping the applications. In addition, it supports arbitrary interconnect topologies, allowing some node pairs to have more shared interconnect bandwidth than others. For example, a three-node pair+M topology, with nodes A, B, and C, could have an additional private interconnect between B and C only, over and above the minimum dual connectivity between all the hosts. Currently, Sun Cluster 3.0 supports 100BASE-T and Gigabit Ethernet as private interconnect networks.

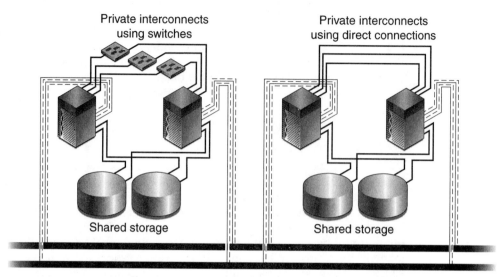

FIGURE 3-14 Switch-Connected and Back-to-Back Private Interconnects

Traffic

The cluster uses the private interconnects to transmit a variety of information. The most important communications of all are the regular cluster heartbeat messages. Each node sends a message to its cluster peers every `dlpi_heartbeat_quantum` milliseconds, as defined in the CCR. The message contains a timestamp and an echo of the last timestamp value it received from that peer. If the last echoed timestamp is older than `dlpi_heartbeat_timeout` milliseconds when a node receives a message, the path is declared down. For example, if node A receives regular heartbeats from node B but they have old timestamps (because node B has not received a message from node A recently), node A declares the path down despite receiving heartbeats. If all paths between a pair of nodes are lost, the cluster membership monitor (see "Cluster Membership" on page 107) maintains cluster integrity.

Note – Neither the `dlpi_heartbeat_quantum` interval nor the `dlpi_heartbeat_timeout` can be tuned.

To handle situations in which the nodes are receiving DLPI heartbeats but no TCP/IP messages are getting through, the private interconnect also employs a TCP/IP timeout. If the cluster cannot send a message queued for a particular path within 90 seconds, it declares that path down. The cluster then brings down the path and attempts to re-establish the path. Meanwhile, the system independently sends the message again, through an alternate path.

Applications that access global devices, such as RDBMSs implemented on raw global partitions, need these interconnect services. To ensure that primary and secondary I/O paths remain synchronized, the replica framework sends messages. If the application and the primary I/O path are not colocated, the interconnect services transfer bulk data too. Similarly, an application that relies on the CFS generates corresponding amounts of interconnect traffic.

Scalable applications, such as the iPlanet and Apache web servers, also require the private interconnect to mediate global IP traffic distribution because the system forwards packets over the interconnects once the PDT establishes the target node.

The cluster framework assigns each node a highly available, private IP address, which the system installer defines during the initial cluster setup. The loopback interface of the particular node hosts this address. Cluster-aware applications, such as Oracle 9i RAC, can use this IP connection to provide a reliable transport mechanism for distributed lock managers and other internode communication protocols.

Resiliency

A cluster can survive multiple failures of the private interconnect infrastructure. The cluster continues to function without loss of service and without requiring any node shutdowns as long as each node has a path to connect it to every other current cluster member. The cluster transport drivers load-balance the cluster framework messages, on a simple round-robin basis, across the available interconnect. Thus, multiple requests benefit transparently from the parallelism that the multiple connections offer.

Protocols

Cluster internode communication protocols depend on the transport configured. For connections based on 100BASE-T or Gigabit Ethernet, the private interconnect uses DLPI and TCP/IP messages. Future interconnects will support DLPI and be able to take advantage of the RSM protocol. Both RSM and DLPI are implemented with optimizations to enable bulk data transfer and efficient buffer allocation with respect to the underlying hardware.

TCP/IP

Despite being inexpensive, an Ethernet connection has the overhead of encapsulating each message in one or more TCP/IP packets. These packets then pass through the respective TCP/IP stacks on both the sending and receiving cluster nodes. For servers connected back to back over a distance of less than 10 meters, this process normally causes a packet latency of about 300 microseconds. Although this latency sounds insignificant, you must compare it with local memory accesses within a server. Typically, these accesses take about 200 nanoseconds. Thus, on average, messages that must be sent between servers take 1,500 times longer to arrive than if they are written directly into local memory.

Whenever the cluster framework makes an ORB call that accesses or passes data to a remote object, it uses a TCP/IP message. Each of these messages incurs the TCP/IP packet overhead.

The network interfaces that constitute the private interconnect are allocated addresses from the IP network number provided during installation. By default, the 172.16.0.0 network address is used. Additionally, the loopback interface, lo0:1, has an address from this network. Preferably, if you choose an alternative address during installation, you should select an unrouted address.

DLPI

Heartbeat messages use a low-level DLPI mechanism to determine cluster connectivity. The data is sent as raw Ethernet packets that contain the node IDs of the sender and receiver, cluster incarnation number, and two timestamps. The system generates the timestamps in the message from the current time on the sending node plus the timestamp previously received from the peer node. Because the DLPI interface uses medium access control (MAC) addresses, the heartbeat cannot be routed.

RSM

The Remote Shared Memory (RSM) protocol enables the system to transfer messages directly into a range of memory addresses that correspond to the receiving buffer on the remote server. This method avoids the overhead of putting the message in a TCP/IP packet as described previously, thus reducing the raw latency associated with sending a message between nodes to around 10 microseconds or less. However, an overhead is still associated with the Sun Cluster 3.0 protocol stacks. The potential performance improvements associated with an RSM-capable transport have not yet been characterized.

Applications written to use the RSM-API will be the first to benefit from the RSM protocol. This protocol enables applications to perform bulk data transfer, through the interconnect, without the TCP/IP overhead. The Peripheral Component Interconnect-Scalable Coherent Interface (PCI-SCI) card is the first RSM-capable card. When the PCI-SCI card becomes available, it will also support the standard DLPI protocol described previously.

Future developments will provide a mechanism to enable cluster framework messages to be sent using the RSM protocol. The potential performance improvements have yet to be characterized.

Configuration Guidelines

Despite the drawback listed previously, many workloads perform well with Ethernet-based private interconnects. A reasonable rule of thumb is to consider 100BASE-T for low-end clusters when cost is an issue or I/O expansion slots are at a premium. For midrange and some high-end clusters, Gigabit Ethernet connections are advisable. The number of connections the system requires depends on the I/O characteristics of the disk and the network workloads being supported. For larger cluster configurations running Oracle 9i RAC and using the RSM-API, you should consider PCI-SCI where and when this option is supported.

It is unlikely that the private interconnect throughput will cause I/O bottlenecks within a cluster. Tests show that interconnect throughput scales linearly as more networks are added. As a rough guide, an extra 100BASE-T adds about 7 megabytes/sec of internode throughput, whereas a Gigabit Ethernet adds around 70 megabytes/sec. Most commercial OLTP workloads are unlikely to exceed 70 megabytes/sec.

Cluster Configuration Control

To maintain an accurate and up-to-date representation of configuration information, clustered systems require configuration control. Sun Cluster 3.0 uses a cluster configuration repository (CCR) to store the most recent configuration information.

Configuration Repository

Sun Cluster 3.0 stores its configuration details in the cluster configuration repository (CCR). This repository is a set of ASCII files that resides on the root file system in the /etc/cluster/ccr directory. The storage requirement for the CCR is relatively modest. Even the largest foreseeable configuration uses less than one megabyte.

These files contain the following information:

- Cluster name
- Cluster nodes
- Node IP addresses

- Private interconnect topology
- Details of quorum devices
- Details of resource groups, resource types, and resources
- Device ID (DID) instances
- Details of device groups

By storing the CCR in multiple files, the cluster increases the failure resilience of the system. A corruption or error in one file does not preclude the consistent update of the remaining files.

The system requires some of the information in the CCR tables at boot time—for example, the node key for PGR/PGRe registration, the cluster name and transport information, and so forth.

A read-only mode enables the system to read the required information before the consistency of the tables is established. When the node successfully joins the cluster, the system puts the tables in read/write mode.

File Consistency

The cluster framework maintains the consistency of the CCR files by using a distributed two-phase commit protocol, implemented as a highly available kernel component. See "Replica Management" on page 59. This implementation reduces the susceptibility of the update procedure to resource starvation that can occur if it is implemented as a user-level process or daemon.

CCR changes can be made with the appropriate cluster commands—scrgadm(1M), scsetup(1M), and scconf(1M). Each file has its own timestamp and checksum to guarantee its integrity.

Caution – The CCR files should not be edited manually. Inconsistent manual changes can lead to a cluster-wide failure and failure of the member nodes to boot. The recovery procedure will then require one or more nodes to be booted in noncluster mode with the OBP boot command -x flag.

Amnesia and Temporally Split Configurations

A clustered system relies on the CCR for an accurate, up-to-date, representation of its configuration information. To maintain cluster integrity and assure application data integrity, the cluster nodes must not have conflicting CCR information.

Each cluster node and dual-hosted quorum disk defined within the cluster contribute one vote to the majority vote. As long as the cluster retains a majority of these votes, it continues to run. When this is true, changes can be made to the CCR. For an overview of the voting mechanism, see "Voting and Quorum" on page 22 and "Majority Voting and Quorum Principles" on page 108.

The cluster membership model governed by this majority voting mechanism ensures that only nodes that were members of the last valid cluster configuration have an up-to-date version of the CCR. The presence of emulated SCSI-3 PGR keys on the quorum disks prevents nodes that were not members of this final incarnation from completing their booting process. This action prevents the formation of a new cluster by a node with stale (out-of-date) CCR information. An amnesiac cluster cannot start the correct service, and can even corrupt user data.

Cluster Failures

This section describes how the Sun Cluster 3.0 architecture handles the complex system failures presented in "Failures in Complex Systems" on page 5 and "Failures in Clustered Systems" on page 29.

Failure Detection

No single component within the product is responsible for the detection and recovery from failures. Instead, components such as the public network infrastructure and the applications rely on their own fault probes to determine the condition of their particular service. Sun Cluster 3.0 implements a system of both local and remote fault probes, so you can distinguish connectivity problems from data service problems. Detection of failures in the disk subsystem and recovery from them lie with the volume management products."Recoverable Failures" on page 96 and "Unrecoverable Failures" on page 98 describe the failures that the cluster tolerates and does not tolerate in the disk subsystem.

A Sun Cluster 3.0 system contains completely redundant hardware components. The cluster must have two or more server nodes with the following tasks or characteristics:

- Runs separate copies of the Solaris operating environment
- Multiple disk arrays, unless the cluster uses a resilient storage unit such as the Sun StorEdge™ A3500, Sun StorEdge A3500FC arrays, or Sun StorEdge T3ES in Partner Pair mode

- Multiple private interconnects to provide a resilient framework for the cluster kernel infrastructure
- Multiple public networks to serve the client population

Sun Cluster 3.0 can survive the failure of single components and remain capable of providing a service. In some cases, Sun Cluster 3.0 can survive multiple independent failures without loss of service. For example, the cluster would be able to tolerate the loss of a disk array and a NIC with a service failover as long as that node has a standby NIC.

Failure Handling and Outage Time

A series of compiled programs and shell scripts make applications that run on a Sun Cluster 3.0 system highly available. These scripts control the start and stop functions and monitor the health of the application through a series of application-specific probes. For example, appropriate calls to the Oracle svrmgr program start and stop the Oracle database service. The health of the service can then be gauged by both the local and the peer cluster nodes. These nodes can connect to the database and perform a series of database operations—create table, insert row, delete row, drop table, and select from table. Successful completion of these operations indicates that the database is healthy. The efficiency and robustness of any probe and the heuristics it uses depend entirely on its authors and their level of application expertise.

Clustered systems make applications highly available through the combination of the application-specific probes, described previously, and the "insurance policy" of additional server nodes to host the service if a failure is detected. If a general failure occurs, a clustered system does not confer any new properties on the application other than automatic restart attempts, either on the same node or a different one. This approach produces two important results. First, the sum of the failure detection time, the cluster reconfiguration time, and the application recovery and restart time determines the outage time of an application. Second, if unrecoverable application data corruption occurs, the application will be unable to restart on any cluster node because the corruption carries over to any new host.

Accuracy Versus Speed

The time taken to detect failures is always a trade-off between two factors—the resource overhead of checking the application on a shorter interval and, more importantly, the ability to distinguish between an application that is down and one that is responding slowly. Because many applications are state based, the impact on current users and the time taken to recover and restart the application can outweigh the value of shorter timeouts.

Decisions to failover an application are always easier to take in retrospect. You should take an iterative approach to tuning fault monitor timeouts, using careful change management control procedures. When detection and recovery is fast enough to meet the service level agreements (SLAs), you should not attempt further tuning. Further tuning risks encountering the problems described in "Timeouts" on page 26.

Public Network Monitoring

Every node in a cluster is connected to one or more public networks through which client applications access the services of the cluster. Like most hardware components, though, these networks can fail; if they are the sole means by which clients access an application, any user connections are lost. To guard against this, you must connect the cluster to a resilient corporate network infrastructure and have multiple switches and routers between the client system and the cluster. Thus, the cluster requires a minimum of two network interface cards (NICs) for each public subnet connection.

With this level of resiliency built in, the cluster can survive the failure of a local NIC, switch, or hub. Then, rather than switching an entire service over from one node to another with all the delays and disruption to user connectivity that process entails, the service can continue to communicate with its clients through the alternative NIC. Sun Cluster 3.0 migrates all of the logical host IP addresses in the failed NIC to the standby NIC.

The public network monitoring (PNM) daemon process, pnmd(1M), detects the loss of connectivity. Sun Cluster 3.0 arranges public network adapters in network adapter failover (NAFO) groups, creating one NAFO group per subnet. Thus, a NAFO group consists of one or more of the NICs that are connected to the particular subnet. The rules for the NICs in a NAFO group are:

- A single NIC port can be associated only with a single NAFO group.
- NIC ports within a NAFO group must be of the same speed, for example, hme and qfe but not hme and ge.

The PNM daemon can detect the failure of a cluster NIC and the failure of the hub or switch to which it is connected. PNM monitors connectivity through the kstat(3KSTAT) kernel interface to determine whether packets have been transmitted or received by a specific NIC in the previous time interval. To minimize the use of unnecessary pings and so keep monitoring traffic to a minimum, the system uses an optimal algorithm. Thus, you cannot tune the timeouts and intervals used by the PNM daemon.

The key test that the PNM algorithm performs is to determine whether any network traffic has flowed through a particular interface in the previous time interval. If no traffic is flowing, pnmd(1M) waits a short while before first trying to reach a previously contacted host. If this attempt also fails, PNM uses a combination of ping(1M) attempts to 224.0.0.2 and 224.0.0.1 to solicit a response from any host on the particular subnet. When a response to one of these broadcasts is received, that host is used as the target for subsequent pings until it no longer responds.

If traffic was flowing originally, PNM uses a broadcast ping, for example, 192.168.200.255, to solicit a response from a host on that subnet to use as a target for future test pings.

When PNM finds that no traffic is flowing, it contacts its peers in the cluster to determine whether the failure is a localized or is a more general network problem. If a general network failure occurs, PNM takes no action because no benefit accrues by requesting the movement of the cluster services, since this action will not improve client connectivity. However, if PNM finds that the problem is localized, it marks the NAFO group as DOUBT and migrates all of the local host IP addresses to the next free adapter listed in the NAFO group until it finds one that works. If no communication is possible through any of the adapters in the NAFO group, the group is marked DOWN, and PNM requests rgmd to migrate services to a node that can provide greater client connectivity. When a successful replacement is found, PNM returns the group to the OK status.

Configuring a logical host on a NIC results in an IP and MAC address pair being broadcast on the network in question. To ensure that other systems on the network pick up the new IP-to-MAC mapping, additional gratuitous packets are broadcast. The Sun Cluster framework does not attempt to migrate MAC addresses between servers. Additionally, the *local-mac-address?* EEPROM variable must be set to false.

Native Solaris 8 IP multipathing (IPMP) will replace public network monitoring (PNM) at some future date.

Application Failure

One of the main benefits of the Sun Cluster 3.0 approach to availability, compared with that of many fault tolerant systems, is the ability to run standard off-the-shelf applications. You can make these applications highly available through the programs and shell scripts that constitute the particular resource type or agent.

The ability to distinguish between an application that actually failed and an application that is responding slowly because of excessive workload or system resource constraints governs the efficacy of an application probe. Thus, you should run all shell script fault detection tests under the hatimerun(1M) facility. This facility enables you to run the test against a tunable timeout stored in the CCR.

A probe can be as simple or as complex as the designer cares to make it. For example, the Sun Oracle database probe tries to connect to the target database and check for database activity by monitoring changes in the statistics (v$sysstat) table. If the database is idle for any reason, because of a problem, for example, the probe uses a more intrusive and expansive set of operations— create a temporary table, insert and delete a row within that table, drop the table, and a commit—to check the health of the database. If this all happens in a timely fashion without error, the database is considered to be working correctly. Traditionally, this role is fulfilled by transaction processing (TP) monitors, such as Tuxedo from BEA Systems or CICS from IBM. However, the release of the Java 2 Enterprise Edition (J2EE) standard led to the development of a number of application servers (see "Application Servers" on page 39) that could potentially meet this requirement.

A fault probe can be extended almost indefinitely to cover an increasingly esoteric problem, but such extension increases code complexity, development time and costs, and the likelihood that the fault monitor itself can fail because of program bugs.

The user perception of an application failure largely depends on the nature of the application and any intermediate software layers between it and the user. Most modern software packages implement a multitiered approach. This multitiered approach can include a database, web servers, application servers, presentation servers, and integration with legacy systems. Shielding the user from failures in any of these layers can present a considerable challenge. These approaches require middle tiers to be able to reconnect to a database after a failure. If an application server fails, you should save the state of a request to a middle tier server so it can be resubmitted.

Without any of these provisions in place, an application failure will disconnect a user from the database or state-based service and require the user to reestablish the connection. Then, when the service restarts, the user must log in to the database and re-create the state of the transaction. However, in some cases the application recovery time can be tuned to minimize the service outage, for example, by increasing the frequency of Oracle checkpoints. Because all Sun Cluster services are addressed through logical rather than physical IP addresses, users need not change the way they access or address the application.

File, DNS, and similar stateless services pose less of a problem; a user simply sees a delay while the service responds. The NFS protocol is stateless because a server failure during a write operation can result in an "NFS server not responding" message, but the write operation will complete once the server restarts. Read operations are also blocked until service is restored.

Most web interaction results in a series of HTTP requests to the web server. Each request opens and closes a session with the web server. When the web server fails in midsession, the user must resubmit the request. Failures that do not occur within a session are transparent to the user. If the user has a state-based web service, such as HTTPS, a web server failure requires the user to reestablish the transaction in a manner analogous to that of a database failure.

Process Monitoring Facility

The process monitoring facility in Sun Cluster 3.0 provides a mechanism for monitoring processes and their descendents and then restarting them on the same node if they fail, without incurring an expensive failover. The start method (see "Data Services and Application Agents" on page 99) of the data service registers a process and an associated tag, with the pmfadm(1M) command. The rpc.pmfd(1M) restarts the process if it exits unexpectedly. The daemon does this a set number of times within a particular period before the data service fault probe tries to restart the process on an alternate node. You cannot trace processes that are monitored by PMF by using the truss(1) command because truss will not trace a process that is being controlled by another process through the /proc interface.

Recoverable Failures

Sun Cluster is designed to handle single failures and some combinations of double failures. Anything that leads to a panic within a standalone Solaris operating environment results in a panic in a clustered node. These failures include software failures, such as kernel bugs, or hardware failures, such as CPU failure, hard memory errors, and backplane failures. As a result, the resource group manager migrates any applications on these nodes to a functioning node.

Data Storage

All data storage in the cluster must have some form of RAID protection. Performance and cost factors govern the choice of RAID 1 or RAID 5. You can use the Solaris Volume Manager (SVM) or the VERITAS Volume Manager (VxVM) to provide host-based mirroring capabilities within Sun Cluster 3.0. However, RAID 5 protection is usually restricted to hardware RAID controllers, such as the Sun StorEdge T3ES array (in partner pair mode), Sun StorEdge A3500, and Sun StorEdge A3500FC arrays.

When a storage device fails to successfully complete an application I/O request, the volume manager driver (md or vx) or a hardware RAID controller must contain and report the error. The volume manager should then activate a suitable hot spare disk to protect the vulnerable data from a subsequent disk failure.

Similarly, the volume manager should trap the failure of a host bus adapter or storage interconnect as long as the failure does not result in a kernel panic.

If all access paths to the user data fail, the Sun Cluster 3.0 framework does not take any action because this is considered a double failure. Generally, applications must wait until their respective fault monitors detect that they are not responding before the system attempts to restart or move them. This action only succeeds if the resource group has a SUNW.HAStorage resource that can switch control of the device group to its secondary path—assuming that alternative working I/O paths exist and that the prior failure has not compromised their termination or integrity.

Private Interconnects

The failure of a private interconnect between nodes results in a cluster reconfiguration only when the private interconnect is the last active path. If additional paths are still operating, the cluster disables the connection and routes traffic through the remaining paths. User applications are unaffected by the failure. When the final connection is lost, the CMM establishes a new cluster membership. "Cluster Membership" on page 107 describes this process in detail.

Public Networks

For public subnets, the public network monitoring daemon (see "Public Network Monitoring" on page 93) handles the failure of inbound or outbound network connectivity from a network adapter card, hub, or switch. During the adapter switchover, applications that use TCP/IP connections can drop packets, but once the system reaches the appropriate timeout, it retransmits these packets as part of the standard TCP recovery mechanism. When UDP is used instead, the application must recover the lost packets. Therefore, any application that relies on UDP must be able to handle such failures.

You should use Sun Management Center 3.0 to monitor the cluster. This software package enables you to identify network component failures and take corrective action to prevent subsequent errors from causing a service outage. For example, after a failed NIC has been replaced, you should switch any IP addresses back to the original adapter, using the pnmset(1M) command. This action prevents potential service outages when both the backup NIC on the node that is hosting the service and the potential primary NICs for the service on other cluster nodes are connected to the same hub and that hub subsequently fails. Under these circumstances, the cluster might decide that a public network is down.

Unrecoverable Failures

Regardless of the redundancy in hardware and software components within a cluster, the data, the application control of the cluster, and any system administration pertaining to it are SPOFs. Corruption and deletion of application data files render a service inoperable because the fault persists, regardless of the node on which the application resides. Similarly, all cluster nodes can mirror application bugs that result in a crash and subsequent downtime.

When you are considering how to ensure against this type of unrecoverable failure, remember that no substitute exists for a well planned and tested disaster recovery policy. At a minimum, you should implement a mechanism for rapid data restoration. This might include a high-performance tape library to bring the latest copy of the data file back from tape. Alternatively, the Sun StorEdge Instant Image 3.0 package offers a faster route to recovery, albeit at the cost of additional storage space. This program copies only the changed disk blocks rather than the entire data file. The implementation details of such an approach depend on the specific data layout.

An equivalent, but less severe, problem stems from uncontrolled, untested, or inappropriate changes to the configuration files of an application. If the cluster file system stores a single, centralized copy of the file, the problem is global and can affect all running instances. Although this problem might be faster to correct, it might take longer to diagnose, especially if the ramifications of the change are experienced only during the next major cluster reconfiguration. The alternative approach of having individual copies of the application configuration files on each cluster node simply trades off administrative convenience for protection. See TABLE 3-1 on page 78.

Failure Reporting

Sun Cluster logs all messages by issuing syslog(3) calls to the /var/adm/ messages file. Therefore, this file should be the focus for regular expression and pattern matchers that monitor the system for abnormal conditions or emerging problems. You can use the Sun Management Center 3.0 software to achieve this goal.

Other user-level cluster processes, such as the SunPlex manager, have their own log directory hierarchies in /var/cluster. Daemon processes like pnmd produce a log file only if the debug flag is set when the system restarts the process.

Also, application failure reporting is highly specific to an application. Most applications have error logs and audit files to monitor for erroneous conditions. This facility enables you to catch and remedy problems early, rather than leaving them to cause a more significant outage later.

Synchronization

This section describes how Sun Cluster 3.0 architecture handles the complex synchronization problems and issues including those presented in "Data Synchronization" on page 14.

Only applications that are crash tolerant can benefit from running on a Sun Cluster 3.0 system. Crash tolerant means the application can recover data or state consistency after a system or application crash without operator intervention. RDBMS such as Oracle, Sybase, Informix, and IBM DB2 are primary examples of applications that are crash tolerant. Their use of log files to track committed transactions enables them to synchronize the data files automatically after a server or software crash.

Applications that simply write data to a file system with the expectation that the data is guaranteed to be on disk generally do not benefit. The reason is that Sun Cluster 3.0 does not introduce any new interfaces that change the way in which an application interacts with the operating system. In fact, a primary goal of the design of Sun Cluster 3.0 is to maintain compatibility with existing Solaris operating environment and POSIX interfaces to enable applications to run unchanged, unaware that they are now running on a cluster. Therefore, if the failure of a server that is hosting such an application requires administrator intervention to recover its integrity, the same is true on a clustered system.

Data Services and Application Agents

A *data service* is an application running on a cluster and made highly available through a collection of scripts and programs that provide start, stop, and monitoring capabilities. Sun Cluster 3.0 supports three types of data service: failover, parallel, and scalable. Scalable data services rely on the new global networking and file system functions introduced in Sun Cluster 3.0.

Sun Cluster 3.0 supports a growing list of data services from Sun and independent software vendors. Currently, these data services include:

- Apache Web Server
- Apache Proxy Server
- Domain Name Service (DNS)
- IBM DB2 Enterprise Edition and Extended Enterprise Edition
- IBM Informix Dynamic Server
- iPlanet Directory Server

- iPlanet Mail Server
- iPlanet Web Server
- Netscape Directory Server (LDAP)
- Network File System (NFS)
- Oracle Server (standard and enterprise editions)
- Oracle 8*i* OPS
- Oracle 9*i* RAC
- SAP R/3
- Sybase ASE

Agent Application Program Interfaces

Off-the-shelf Sun Cluster 3.0 agents are not available for every application. To enable you to create your own resource types, Sun supplies two APIs with Sun Cluster 3.0: the Resource Management API (RM-API) in the SUNWscsev package) and the higher-level Data Service Development Library (DSDL in the SUNWscsdk package). RM-API provides low-level C and callable shell script interfaces to basic data service operations. DSDL provides a library for accessing information about the cluster. This library enables you to avoid repetitive and error-prone coding.

The SunPlex agent builder, scdsbuilder(1HA), enables customers, professional service staff, and system integrators to build simple application agents very quickly. Accessed through a GUI, the agent builder directs the back-end code generator programs to output C or ksh routines for the resource type being constructed with the DSDL.

Data Service Constructs

Sun Cluster 3.0 takes an object-oriented approach to the creation of the components needed to build highly available and scalable data services. The three main constructs used are the *resource type*, the *resource*, and the *resource group*. The following sections describe the details of each of these constructs.

Resource Types

The basic building block for all data services is the resource type package, which Sun Cluster 3.0 also refers to as agents. Sun Cluster 3.0 ships with three standard resource types: SUNW.LogicalHostname, SUNW.SharedAddress, and SUNW.HAStorage.

- SUNW.LogicalHostname is the resource type that provides the logical IP address for failover services, such as Oracle or failover web services. This address resource is placed in a failover resource group that is instantiated on one cluster node at any one time. The logical IP address can, for example, be configured on hme0:2. Consequently, the logical IP address is only available to applications that are located on the same cluster node.

- SUNW.SharedAddress is the resource type that provides the logical IP address for scalable services, such as the iPlanet and Apache web servers. This address resource is placed in a failover resource group that is instantiated on one cluster node at a time. The logical IP address itself, for example, can be configured on hme0:2 but it is also configured on the loopback interfaces (lo0) of cluster nodes running scalable services that depend on this address.

- SUNW.HAStorage is a resource type that enables application resources that depend on global devices or CFS paths to synchronize their startup with the availability of the storage resources upon which they depend. A SUNW.HAStorage resource is placed in an application failover resource group and subsequent application resource definitions are made dependent on it. The relevant devices and path names are specified as extension properties of the SUNW.HAStorage resource.

Assuming you have a license to use additional agents, you can load the Sun resource types from the Sun Cluster agent media by using the scinstall(1M) command, and you can register them in the cluster framework by using scrgadm(1M). If you do not register the resource type, any attempt to create a resource of that type fails and returns an error.

The Solaris package that contains a resource type has all of the methods (programs or shell scripts) needed to start, stop, and monitor the application. In addition, a resource type registration (RTR) file provides the path to methods, the names of the methods, settings for any standard resource properties, and definitions of specific resource extension properties. Registering the resource type with the cluster framework with scrgadm(1M) enables the resource group manager daemon (see "Resource Group Manager Daemon" on page 105) to locate the methods necessary to control applications and start them with the right parameter settings. Thus, a general resource type can be written for use by multiple applications, rather than a specific instance of an application.

TABLE 3-3 lists the resource type properties that define all the possible callback methods that can be used to control and monitor a target application. At a minimum, you only need to define the start and stop properties unless you use the prenet or postnet method. The methods can be either compiled programs or shell scripts.

TABLE 3-3   Resource Type Properties

Property	Function
START	Starts the application
STOP	Stops the application
UPDATE	Updates all properties when the application properties have been changed
VALIDATE	Checks the property settings for a resource of this type
PRENET_START	Does start actions that must be done before network interfaces are "configured up." Called by RGM before calling the start method of any network-address resources on which a resource of this type depends.
POSTNET_STOP	Does stop actions that must be done after the network interfaces are "configured down." Called by RGM after calling the stop method of any network-address resources on which a resource of this type depends.
MONITOR_START	Starts a fault monitor for a resource of this type
MONITOR_STOP	Stops a fault monitor for a resource of this type
MONITOR_CHECK	Called on each resource in a resource group before doing a monitor-requested failover of the group. Called by RGM before doing a monitor-requested failover of a resource of this type.
INIT	Initializes resources of this type. Called by RGM when a resource of this type is put under resource group manager control.
FINI	Removes resources of this type. Called by RGM when a resource of this type is removed from resource group manager control.
BOOT	Initializes resources of this type similar to the init method. Called by RGM on a node that joins or rejoins the cluster when a resource of this type is already managed.

Resources

Resources are instantiations of specific resource types. They inherit all of the methods registered for the resource type with the cluster framework. The definition of a resource will provide specific settings for standard and required extension properties, as defined in the RTR file. These settings can include path names to application configuration files, any TCP/IP ports they listen on, timeout settings, and so on. Multiple resources of a particular resource type can exist within the cluster without modifying the original programs or shell scripts.

Initially, without the application running, the resource is offline. The rgmd calls the application start methods when the resource group that contains the resource goes online.

When one resource relies on another, for example, when an NFS share relies on a running network interface, Sun Cluster 3.0 provides two types of dependency—strong and weak. When other resources, rsB, rsC, and rsD, must be online before a resource, rsA, can start successfully, you can set the resource_dependencies property for rsA to ensure that the resource group manager daemon honors these relationships.

When the dependency is weaker, the resource_dependencies_weak property ensures that rgmd calls the start methods of these resources before that of the dependent resource; that is rsB, rsC, rsD, and then rsA. However, in this case, there is no requirement for the start method to complete before rgmd calls the start method of rsA. To use a mathematical term, the resource dependencies form a *directed acyclic graph*. The RGM does not permit any cycles (loops) in the overall set of resource dependencies. The start and stop methods for a resource must ensure that the application actually starts or stops before returning control to the calling program.

You can then take resources online and offline individually with the scswitch(1M) command. If any attempt is made to disable a resource on which others depend, the command fails. The scswitch(1M) command is more often used to put whole resource groups online and or to take them offline. See "Resource Groups" on page 104. You can also disable monitoring of a specific resource, using the -M flag on the scswitch(1M) command.

Sun Cluster 3.0 supports both failover and scalable resources. A failover resource is one in which a particular invocation of an application can only occur on one node at any one time. A standard HA-Oracle database is a good example of such an application. A scalable resource differs from a failover resource in that it enables a specific instance of an application to run on more than one node at once. Both iPlanet and Apache web servers can be run in a scalable fashion. Today, all the other Sun-supported applications run in failover mode.

Applications must be relatively stateless to run as a scalable resource. This means that instances must not be required to share any state or locking information between them. Because web servers simply serve web pages to a user population, they are ideal candidates for this approach. Currently, no generic mechanism exists to enable state-based applications to coordinate their data access and enable them to run as scalable services. Sun Cluster 3.0 provides the RSM-API, but this API is reserved for use by the Oracle 8*i* OPS and Oracle 9*i* RAC products.

For details, see [PL01] at:

```
http://www.sun.com/software/whitepapers.html#cluster.
```

For resource types that can be run as a scalable service, you should set the
FAILOVER property in the RTR file to false. This setting enables you to set values
for maximum_primaries and desired_primaries resource group properties
to values greater than one. By changing these values, you can dynamically vary
application capacity and resilience in response to user load and business needs.

Resource Groups

Resource groups form the logical container for one or more of the resources
described previously. The resources contained in an invocation of a single
resource group are all constrained to run on the same node. The rgmd must put a
resource group online or offline on one or more nodes. Then, the rgmd on the
appropriate cluster nodes calls the methods for the resources in the resource
group to start or stop them as appropriate. You can place a resource group in an
unmanaged state so the rgmd does not attempt to move it or bring it online when
a reconfiguration occurs.

FIGURE 3-15 is an example of a failover resource group configuration.

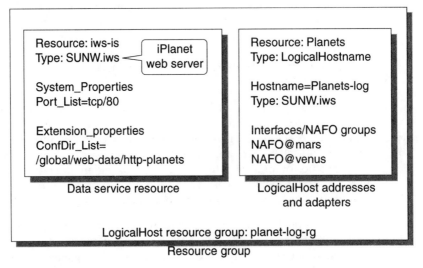

FIGURE 3-15 Failover Resource Group Configuration—Example

The rgmd can initiate a resource group migration in response to a scswitch(1M)
command request to move a service, or in response to the failure of a node that is
currently hosting one or more resource groups.

A failover resource group is only online on one node at a time, and that node hosts all of the resources in that group. In contrast, a scalable resource group can be online on more than one node at a time.

Resource groups also have a dependency property, RG_dependency. This property indicates a preferred order for putting other groups online or offline on the same node. It has no effect if the groups are put online on different nodes.

Resource groups have a number of standard and extension properties that enable fine-grained control of data services on a service-by-service basis. Your system administrator can change these properties while the cluster is running, to enable customers to manage the load on the cluster nodes.

When running multiple data services, you should configure each unrelated service into its own resource group. To maintain optimal performance, each data service should rely, when possible, on separate device groups for their cluster file systems and global device services. This enables you to colocate the primary I/O path with the data service at all times. Multiple instances of an Oracle database server are a good example. When data services depend on one another, they generally benefit from being in the same resource group.

Resource Group Manager Daemon

The rgmd is the user-level program that synchronizes the control of resource groups and resources within the cluster. It uses the cluster configuration repository to discover which user-level programs it must call to enact the relevant resource methods.

When the rgmd must put a resource group online or offline on a given node, it calls the methods for the resources in the resource group to start or stop them as appropriate.

Whenever the cluster membership changes, the kernel cluster membership monitor drives the resource group manager daemon. In turn, rgmd uses the "fork-exec" daemon, rpc.fed, to fork and execute data-service-method programs. These daemons communicate by using local SunRPC calls on each node. The rpc.fed daemon is a multithreaded program that blocks the RPC call until the execution of the program completes or times out, then returns exit status to the caller.

When moving a resource group between nodes, the rgmd must be absolutely certain that a resource has stopped on one node before it restarts the resource on another node. See "Multiple Instances" on page 29. If this rule is not strictly enforced, a nonscalable application could be run on more than one node simultaneously and, therefore, corrupt its data. If the rgmd cannot be certain that it stopped the application, it sets a STOP_FAILED flag on the appropriate resource.

You must clear this flag manually before the application can be restarted. You can then ensure that the application is actually down before you clear the flag to restart the resource.

The rgmd also enables considerable flexibility in the management of resource and resource group properties without requiring you to take down applications or the cluster. For example, you can add extra nodes to a two-node cluster running a scalable web service. Then, you can modify the scalable web resource group to allow it to run on the new node without stopping the existing web services. Similarly, if a web service is already running three HTTPD instances across a four-node cluster, you can decrease this to two or increase it to four without interrupting service.

Parallel Services

Parallel applications such as Oracle 8*i* OPS or Oracle 9*i* RAC are considered special and, as such, are outside the control of the resource group manager. These applications differ from standard Oracle, running in a failover mode, by having multiple instances of Oracle, running on multiple nodes and sharing a common set of data files. Although IBM DB2 is a parallel database, it does not perform concurrent I/O from multiple nodes to the same raw device, a shared disk architecture. Instead it uses a shared-nothing architecture, moving functions and data between nodes to satisfy queries.

Under normal circumstances, Oracle caches data from its data files or tablespaces in its system global area (SGA). Numerous in-memory latches or locks maintain the integrity of SGA by ensuring that multiple users on that server do not corrupt the data through uncontrolled simultaneous access. The latches effectively synchronize the access of users to the underlying data. When the parallel version of Oracle is running, a distributed lock manager (DLM) must keep the data in multiple SGAs coherent and synchronized. This action ensures that data cache integrity is maintained for multiuser access across multiple nodes. The DLM communicates between the nodes through the private interconnect, the implementation of which ensures resilient internode communication.

Unlike the global file service, the Oracle parallel implementations require concurrent local access to the underlying disks from each of the nodes on which it is running. This means that regular disk I/O is not being proxied across the interconnect, as is the case in which a service runs remotely from the primary I/O path. However, when the SGA on one node must share a data block that is currently cached on another, the data is passed between the nodes through the private interconnect. Oracle calls this technology *cache fusion*. Cache fusion is a new feature in Oracle 9*i* RAC.

Arbitration

This section describes how Sun Cluster 3.0 software architecture handles arbitration problems and other issues, including split brain, multiple instance, and amnesia. "Arbitration Schemes" on page 20 and "Failures in Clustered Systems" on page 29 discuss these issues.

Cluster Membership

Sun Cluster 3.0 defines the concept of membership as a group of nodes that can successfully communicate with every other node in the group through the private interconnect. This concept is critical to the success of a cluster product that is performing distributed computing operations. The cluster membership monitor (CMM) must ensure that only one cluster incarnation is in progress at a time.

To determine membership and, more importantly, to ensure data integrity, the CMM must achieve the following:

- Account for a change in cluster membership, such as a node joining or leaving the cluster
- Ensure that a faulty node leaves the cluster
- Ensure that the faulty node stays out of the cluster until it is repaired
- Prevent the cluster from partitioning itself into subsets of nodes

Given these requirements, the Sun Cluster 3.0 CMM protects a cluster against these failures:

- *Split brain*—All communication between nodes is lost and the cluster becomes partitioned into subclusters, each of which believes that it is the only partition. See "Split Brain" on page 29.
- *Amnesia*—The cluster restarts after a shutdown with cluster configuration data older than at the time of the shutdown. See "Amnesia" on page 30.

Sun Cluster 3.0 avoids split brain by using the majority vote principle (see "Majority Voting and Quorum Principles" on page 108), coupled with the use of quorum disks to circumvent undesirable situations that would otherwise compromise cluster availability.

Avoiding potential data corruption means that the cluster must ensure that it is using the latest configuration information held in the CCR. Take, for example, the case in which an administrator shuts down one node, A, of a clustered pair, and then changes the cluster configuration on the remaining node, B. If node B is then shut down and node A is brought up, node A will have out-of-date configuration information. This situation is known as amnesia.

As another example, consider the case where the last member of a cluster, A, places SCSI-3 PGRe keys on the quorum disks defined in the CCR. When another node, B, tries to start up a cluster before node A has restarted, the booting process on B stops because B cannot acquire the necessary quorum disk votes to achieve majority—B cannot do so because the reservation that A placed on the disks is persistent and specific to A.

Changes in cluster membership drive the cluster reconfiguration sequence that, in turn, can cause services to migrate from failed or faulty nodes to healthy ones through rgmd. The process of fencing off a node is vital for ensuring that user data is not corrupted. See "Fault Containment" on page 12. This is especially true when parallel services are running and making simultaneous changes to a common set of data files. If the CMM did not actively fence off or shut down errant nodes, these nodes would be able to continue to service user requests and write to the data files in the mistaken belief that they are the only nodes that remain in the cluster. This action would inevitably lead to corruption when both nodes update the same data page in an uncontrolled fashion.

CMM Implementation

Sun Cluster 3.0 implements its CMM as a kernel module. Therefore, resource starvation is less likely to affect the CMM than a user-level daemon would. Consequently, Sun Cluster 3.0 can support shorter timeouts to allow faster failure detection. Note that these times are typically small relative to the time taken to recover an application, which tends to dominate failover times. The CMM determines connectivity to other nodes through the cluster transport mechanism. Only when the last path to a node is declared down does the CMM fence off the potentially failed node.

Majority Voting and Quorum Principles

The cluster membership model is independent of the cluster storage topology and volume manager employed. The basic principle relies on the concept of a majority, that is, more than half of a particular quantity. Once the initial scinstall(1M) completes on all cluster nodes and scsetup(1M) is run to assign the first quorum disk, the cluster is taken out of "install mode." Thereafter, each node within the cluster is given one vote. The quantity, Vn, represents the total number of node votes. For a cluster with no quorum disks configured to continue, a majority of nodes must be able to communicate with each other over the private interconnect. A majority is calculated as $int[Vn*0.5]+1$, in which the *int* function computes the integer portion of its operand. If this condition is not met, nodes in the particular subcluster panic because they lose majority. A subcluster is any subset of nodes that constitute the entire cluster.

This algorithm has undesirable consequences for a two-node cluster because shutting down one node automatically brings down the other node. To overcome this, a quorum disk is used. A quorum disk is simply a nominated disk somewhere in the shared storage of the cluster. A quorum disk that is multihosted to M nodes is given $M - 1$ votes. For a dual-hosted quorum, this disk only receives one vote. Defining the total number of votes contributed by quorum disk as Vq, the total number of votes now available to the cluster (defined as Vt) is, therefore, $Vt = Vn + Vq$. A subcluster must still gain a majority of the available votes to continue. However, this is now calculated as $int[Vt \times 0.5] + 1$.

A quorum disk must be defined for a two-node cluster. This arrangement enables any single node that obtains the vote of the quorum disk to maintain majority and continue as a viable cluster. The CMM forces the losing node out of the cluster.

For clusters with N nodes, where N is greater than two, $N - 1$ quorum votes should be used. In certain topologies, $N - 1$ can serve to prevent several nodes from panicking from loss of majority after you have shut down $N/2$ of the cluster nodes.

CMM Reconfiguration Process

A kernel CMM reconfiguration consists of 11 steps following the `begin_state` and `qcheck_state` phases. All cluster nodes execute these steps in order and in lockstep. That is, cluster nodes do not start the next step until all cluster nodes complete the current step. If membership changes during any of these steps, all nodes return to the `begin_state` phase.

Once the quorum algorithm decides on a quorum of cluster members, the cluster nodes execute these steps. Thereafter, the ORB and the replica framework, and indirectly the CFS and device configuration service, perform the appropriate actions for a node that is leaving or joining the cluster. See "Disk Fencing" on page 112. When a node joins the cluster, the replica framework can add a secondary for a device group, and so forth.

The CMM has two user clients: `rgmd` and Oracle 8*i* OPS or Oracle 9*i* RAC. Both register their own set of steps. When a reconfiguration occurs, the user clients, `rgmd` and Oracle 8*i* OPS or Oracle 9*i* RAC, are driven through their steps.

SCSI-2 and SCSI-3 Command Set Support

To prevent errant cluster nodes from writing to a disk and potentially corrupting user data, Sun Cluster 3.0 uses SCSI reservation. The ability to reserve a disk is part of the SCSI command set used by all cluster storage that Sun supports. For details on how SCSI reservations are used, see "Disk Fencing" on page 112.

Most disks in use today support the SCSI-2 command set. SCSI-2 reservations are binary, allowing or disallowing access to a disk. Therefore, if a host in a cluster with more than two nodes reserves a disk that supports the SCSI-2 command set, all nodes but one are unable to access it once the reservation is in place. If the node or disk is reset, the reservation is lost because it is not persistent.

The SCSI-3 command set enables you to make group reservations for a disk. This, in turn, enables access by a set of nodes while disabling others. Group reservations are persistent, so they can survive node and drive resets. This feature is called SCSI-3 persistent group reservation (PGR). Sun Cluster 3.0 uses SCSI-3 PGR on disks that support and emulate the use of PGRe. On disks that do not, Sun Cluster 3.0 uses the SCSI-2 Tkown and Release commands.

SCSI-2 PGRe emulation includes:

1. Employing the alternate disk cylinders for storing the PGRe keys (different from the PGR keys that the drivers in question store) and the reservation key (there are 65 sectors, one each for the 64 possible nodes and an extra one for the reservation owner).

2. Emulating the SCSI-3 PGR ioctls. PreemptAndAbort uses Lamport's algorithm [Lamport74].

3. Using SCSI-2 Tkown and Release in conjunction with item 2 to ensure that the loser in the quorum race is removed from the cluster and hits reservation conflict, and is welcomed back into the cluster once it rejoins.

Sun Cluster 3.0 also implements a write-exclusive, registrants-only (WERO) form of SCSI-3 reservation. This type of reservation allows only registered initiators to update disk information. Fencing is done by ensuring that a WERO reservation is made, and by preempting the registration keys of the initiators of nodes to fence.

Cluster members place keys on the alternate disk cylinder at the beginning of the drive mentioned in item 1 when they join the cluster. The CMM removes the keys of removed members as part of the initial qcheck reconfiguration step, which precedes step one of the reconfiguration. This action is independent of whether the system uses PGR or PGRe.

Shared quorum disks have the keys of all the members in the last cluster reconfiguration, thus preventing amnesia. If the last cluster configuration had just one member, that key is the only key on the quorum disk. An amnesiac node would attempt to join the cluster and discover that it has been fenced away from the quorum disk.

As nodes join the cluster, they put their keys on the device. As some of the nodes leave the cluster, the current members remove the key of the departing node from the device. If a node panics while preempting a removed member that is removing its key, the CMM attempts another reconfiguration. If the remaining nodes can still form a cluster, they proceed to preempt the previously removed node as well as the node that just panicked.

If the remaining nodes do not form a majority, the cluster aborts. The quorum disk has the keys of these remaining nodes, the node that panicked, and the ousted node because the last successful reconfiguration had exactly those members.

Quorum Disk Vote

When cluster members lose contact with each other, they must attempt to acquire the votes of the quorum disks to maintain a majority. To achieve this, both nodes issue a SCSI-2 Tkown, or reservation, ioctl. The ioctl is atomic, so only one node is successful. If two nodes share multiple quorum disks, then, in a cluster with more than two nodes, both nodes attempt to acquire the votes for the quorum disks in the same order. The loser of the initial race drops out, thereby allowing the winner to obtain all of the necessary quorum disk votes and thus retain a majority. Writing the key of the owner to the alternate disk cylinder space makes the reservation persistent.

Uneven Cluster Partitions

Multinode clusters can be the subject of numerous failure scenarios, each of which should, ideally, result in the safe reconfiguration of the cluster to provide continued service on the remaining nodes. Some failures make it hard for the cluster to determine what the optimal outcome should be. For example, when a four-node, pair+M, cluster partitions 3 to 1, the three nodes should acquire the three nominated quorum disk votes and survive. However, a single node can win the race to the first disk and go on to attain majority, but this may not be the desired outcome. In an alternative scenario, in which the three nodes instantaneously lose communication with the single node (leading to a 1:1:1:1 split), either through a bizarre interconnect failure or by a simultaneous power failure, the single node should get the quorum disk votes and continue.

To resolve these two outcomes, the cluster membership algorithm introduces a staggered start in the race for the quorum disk reservation. Any majority partition is given a head start, on the basis that it should be the desired winner. If it fails to get the first quorum disk, either by being down or totally unresponsive, the node in the minority partition wins the race and goes on to attain majority.

The formula for this delay is $12 + N - R$, where N is the number of nodes not in this partition and R the number of known failed nodes. In the preceding scenario, the partition with three nodes would have a two-second start over the single node. This advantage accrues because the single-node subcluster will wait ($Delay = 12 + 3 - 0$) 15 seconds, whereas the three-node subcluster will only wait ($Delay = 12 + 1 - 0$) 13 seconds.

If the nodes in a minority partition cannot achieve majority, even with the addition of all of the quorum votes, they decline to participate in the race and panic out of the cluster.

Disk Fencing

Disk or failure fencing protects the data on disk against undesired access. See "Fault Containment" on page 12. The CMM must prevent unenclosed members from writing to any shared data disks to which they might be connected, in addition to protecting a cluster against using out-of-date configuration information.

The device configuration system (DCS) does the device group management. When the CMM is notified of a membership change, it notifies the DCS if a primary node for a device group has left the cluster. The CMM then chooses a new primary for the device group, using the properties stored in the CCR for that device group. The CMM then issues a DCS call to tell the node that it is now the primary node for the device group. During this call, the node fences off any nonquorum disks in the device group (note that quorum disks can still be used to store data). The node also takes the appropriate volume manager action of importing a VxVM disk group or taking ownership of an SVM disk set. The quorum algorithm reserves the quorum disks separately.

The DCS uses SCSI-3 PGR for multihosted devices and SCSI-2 for dual-hosted devices. In contrast, the quorum algorithm uses SCSI-3 PGR for multihosted devices and SCSI-3 PGRe for dual-hosted devices.

As part of the fencing process, MHIOCENFAILFAST is enabled on all disks. Any non-cluster member trying to access a disk with this set will failfast with a reservation-conflict panic message. See "Failfast Driver" on page 113.

For clusters that are running services such as Oracle 8i OPS or Oracle 9i RAC, the system uses the CVM feature of VxVM. This feature enables concurrent access to raw devices from more than one cluster node. If a cluster node fails, it is fenced off from all disks in shared CVM disk groups either through SCSI-3 PGRe for dual-hosted SCSI-2 disks, or through SCSI-3 PGR for multihosted devices. Thus, Oracle 8*i* OPS or Oracle 9*i* RAC clusters with more than two nodes require shared storage that implements SCSI-3 PGR.

Note – You should not attempt to alter any reservations placed on shared storage. The scdidadm(1M) command offers limited access to these reservations, but you should use it carefully.

Failfast Driver

The appropriate Solaris disk driver, either sd or ssd, handles failfast. If a device access returns a reservation conflict error when failfast is enabled, the driver panics the node. With failfast, you can also set up a polling thread that periodically accesses the device. The drive panics the node if the disk driver receives a reservation conflict error from the device.

Cluster Reconfiguration

The final job of the CMM is to drive the reconfiguration process. This task includes contacting the replica manager so that it can elect a new node to coordinate the replica managers. The primary I/O paths for the device groups of the cluster may also need to be changed. Changing the primary path requires the takeover of replica manager responsibilities.

If a cluster node fails, it is fenced off from all dual-hosted disks in shared CVM disk groups by simple SCSI-2 reservation. When multihosted storage is supported, the shared disk groups will use SCSI-3 PGR.

CHAPTER 4

Management Server

This chapter describes the role of the management server in the Sun Cluster 3.0 system. Unlike previous versions of the Sun Cluster software, the Sun Cluster 3.0 software does not require an administration workstation. However, to provide easy installation and management of Sun servers, the system needs a number of basic infrastructure services. This chapter describes the infrastructure services that a Sun management server provides to support the Sun Cluster 3.0 environment.

For a single cluster or a small group of servers, many of these services can be incorporated onto a single, small server such as the Netra™ T1 AC200. The SunTone™ Cluster Platforms portfolio includes such a server to provide rapid cluster installation and management. Larger sites or multiple clusters may require larger or multiple management systems. You can use the design of the management server for the SunTone Platforms portfolio as a guide to build your own management server, or you can use existing infrastructure services.

Note – The SunTone^{SM} program provides customers with a thorough evaluation of their business operations and information technology (IT) infrastructure, thereby helping to improve their quality of service and reliability. Currently, the SunTone Certification and Branding program has more than 1,400 applicants for certification—including service providers, independent software vendors (ISVs), and integrators—and provides more than 90 SunTone Certified Solutions. The SunTone Platforms portfolio is a new addition to the program, providing application-ready hardware and software stacks to help improve IT infrastructure deployment time and reliability. For more information, see http://www.sun.com/integratedplatforms.

This chapter contains the following sections:

- Design Goals
- Services
- Console Services

- Sun Ray Server
- Sun StorEdge SAN Surfer
- Sun Explorer Data Collector
- Sun Remote Services
- Software Stack
- Hardware Components
- Network Configuration
- Systems Management
- Backup, Restore, and Recovery
- Summary

These topics explain how the management server provides the infrastructure services you need to install and manage the cluster servers.

A number of ISVs provide software products that complement the Sun products described here. These products are not discussed here, but many provide valuable services for Sun customers.

Design Goals

The functions of a management server are to perform the following tasks:

1. Deploy software stacks and patches for system components:
   - Solaris operating environment
   - Sun StorEdge arrays
   - Network devices

2. Act as a point of control for management of systems components:
   - Sun Cluster 3.0 server nodes
   - Sun Fire cabinets using the FrameManager through Sun Fire system controllers
   - Sun StorEdge arrays
   - Sun StorEdge FC-AL switches
   - Sun terminal concentrator
   - Other components from third-party suppliers—network switches, uninterruptible power supplies (UPS), and so forth

3. Act as a central collection point for messages and alerts:
   - Sun Management Center server
   - UNIX system logger (`syslogd(1M)`, `logger(1)`)
   - Sun Remote Services or Sun™ Remote Services Net Connect server

- Third-party systems management and capacity planning software

4. Provide consistent access to system console devices, perhaps through a terminal concentrator:
   - Sun Fire system controllers
   - Sun Enterprise server serial port consoles
   - Sun StorEdge arrays
   - Other components that provide a serial port as the console device

5. Provide online documentation for all components. Most Sun documentation is available in AnswerBook™ format. Many documents are also available in Adobe® Portable Document Format (PDF).

Note – The management server must not become a critical component in the operation of a cluster. All cluster operations must be able to continue without impact if the management server fails. This is the default configuration for Sun Cluster 3.0 software that has no dependency on a management server. However, in case of a management server failure, you should implement an alternate operational procedure to access the system messages and console devices of servers to maintain serviceability of the cluster components. For example, a second client system with access to the console terminal server or a serial terminal device that can be connected to the serial port of a component to access the console can improve mean time to recover (MTTR) if a prolonged management server failure occurs.

Services

The primary purpose of the management server is to monitor and manage the cluster environment. The majority of the management server functions are beyond the normal management services associated with the Sun Cluster 3.0 environment. You can supply these services to other systems as the computing resources in the management server allow. The management server has enough CPU power and memory resources to consolidate logging messages from all cluster nodes and to implement the following servers:

- Sun Management Center
- SunPlex
- Network Time Protocol (NTP)
- AnswerBook

Console Services

The Sun Cluster cluster control panel (ccp) graphical user interface (GUI) is available from the SUNWccon package extracted from the Sun Cluster 3.0 client software. This GUI enables your system administrator to execute commands concurrently on all cluster nodes but does not provide a management interface. The ccp works with a terminal concentrator to provide a seamless connection to serial port consoles.

JumpStart

You can run JumpStart on the management server to automate the installation of all software modules and patches required by all cluster members of a Sun Cluster 3.0 environment. Using JumpStart and Web Start Flash technologies to load the required software and patches on the cluster nodes is a best practice, because it automates and expedites the software installation while reducing operator errors during a catastrophic failure recovery. In addition, the JumpStart technology provides a manageable environment in which you can collect the latest versions of the required software packages and associated patches in a single repository.

When you first turn on the management server, it customizes its JumpStart environment by requesting information specific to the customer locality (cluster name, cluster node names, Ethernet and IP addresses, time zone, name services, and so forth). After the management server customization and JumpStart software installation completes, all cluster members automatically boot as Sun Cluster 3.0 nodes.

After each cluster member reboots, the integrated hardware and software stack provides a *basic* Sun Cluster 3.0 environment. This basic Sun Cluster 3.0 environment still requires a service representative (or service-qualified customer) to perform the following tasks before you deploy the cluster into production:

- Configure the Sun Cluster 3.0 quorum disk. Quorum devices are resources the cluster infrastructure uses to establish a majority vote when determining cluster membership.

- Install a specific Sun Cluster 3.0 data service based on application needs. You can install any supported Sun Cluster 3.0 data services. A data service includes application and cluster routines (start, stop, monitoring, and so forth) required to integrate the application into the cluster environment.

- Configure the disk data. You can use the VERITAS Volume Manager or Solstice DiskSuite™ software to configure the data.

Consolidated Cluster Node Messages

The management server is a central repository for logs and informational, warning, and error messages for each cluster node (similar to Starfire™ domain logging by the System Service Processor). The /etc/syslog.conf files are modified on each cluster node to route system messages to the management server /var/adm/messages file.

The /var/adm/messages file aligns cluster node events over time to improve failure analysis. In addition, your system administrator can review cluster node events on the management server when a cluster node is down.

The Sun Management Center has a log file filter. This filter enables your system administrator to define patterns of messages that should be highlighted or ignored, and to quickly identify key messages in the midst of more routine informational messages.

AnswerBook2 Documentation Server

Sun distributes documentation for many products in AnswerBook format. The AnswerBook2 documentation server provides a facility to view Sun documentation with a web browser. This server renders documentation in HTML 3.2, sending it to a web browser for display, thus offering an integrated Webtop solution for Sun online documentation and providing navigation, search, and printing capabilities.

The server also supports the previous AnswerBook documentation format. The AnswerBook2 documentation server comes with the Solaris operating environment, and supports all Solaris locales. Thus, one server can handle multiple language requests from remote sites simultaneously.

This product is necessary for anyone who wants to access the Sun online documentation in a web environment.

AnswerBook2 organizes product documentation as collections of documents based on specific topics or products. Because of the size and number of the documents, including localized versions, the AnswerBook library may consume a significant amount of disk space.

Internet access to the AnswerBook documentation is available from http://docs.sun.com. Putting the documentation pertinent to a local site or system on the management server allows documentation access without requiring an Internet gateway.

Sun Management Center Server

The Sun Management Center application on the management server enables you to manage and monitor the hardware and Solaris operating environment on all cluster nodes. This software includes a restricted license that allows you to manage and monitor only the cluster nodes and management server.

The Sun Management Center environment uses a three-tier, agent-based, scalable architecture that provides a single point of management for system administrators. This software offers the following features:

- A Java GUI that you can access from the network, and a common look and feel for all Sun Management Center agents

- A web-based interface that makes management information available for access from web browsers anytime and anywhere

- Direct management of Sun Cluster 3.0 systems

- Object grouping, which provides an easy way to define and invoke complex tasks on a set of managed objects. For example, you can set up properties or change thresholds and alarm actions and then apply this complex assignment to a set of servers in the data center.

- Proactive event/alarm management and predictive failure analysis, which help increase system availability. This feature includes a new interactive knowledge base of events and alarm resolution that grows with customer experience.

- New filtering capabilities that help you pinpoint problems quickly, even in systems with a large number of objects or nodes

- Data view capability that enables you to create your own display configurations, using a convenient format

- Sun Management Center Developer Environment, a GUI tool that enables you to develop new Sun Management Center agents

The Sun Management Center application has several optional add-on features. A System Reliability Manager enables you to perform:

- Patch management
- File watch
- Operating system crash dump analysis
- Script launching

A Hardware Diagnostic Suite (HWDS) enables:

- Online testing to detect hardware faults
- Test scheduling to enable latent fault detection
- Integration with Sun Management Center for unified system management

The Sun Management Center integration modules include partnerships with ISV applications such as:

- Computer Associates Unicenter TNG
- Enlighten DSM
- Halcyon
- Hewlett–Packard OpenView VantagePoint Operations
- Tivoli Enterprise Software

Solaris Management Console

Using the Solaris Management Console™ 2.0 application, your system administrator can manage the Solaris operating environment remotely, no matter what the scale of the environment. Solaris Management Console 2.0 is a Java technology-based, client/server application from which your system administrator can manage one or more Solaris domains. All GUI-based administrative tools are integrated into the Solaris Management Console 2.0 software, providing a single, consistent interface to each tool.

The Solaris Management Console 2.0 application enables users and administrators to register servers running its software on the network. This software dynamically configures tree views of registered hosts and services, making it easier to manage each Solaris server. Solaris Management Console 2.0 software benefits IT departments, system administrators, and network administrators by reducing labor and support costs, increasing productivity, and improving the administration experience.

The Solaris Management Console 2.0 software enables your system administrator to launch applications on a remote server while monitoring the application through a light front-end GUI on the client. This capability eliminates the need for downloading large applications over the network and installing and running them on the client. The remote capability also enables your administrator to manage administrative and network services from home or any other location when a trouble call comes in.

One of the challenges facing system administrators is to keep their systems secure. Accordingly, the use of "root" types of user IDs must be restricted. This can have a negative impact on users or IT staff members who must perform tasks in a timely manner but lack root authorization. Role-based access control (RBAC) support enables a system administrator to delegate specific rights to users, distributing system administration responsibilities to where they are most efficiently performed while still maintaining control over the system. This ability to grant specific rights eliminates the "all or nothing" problem inherent with superuser or root user IDs. RBAC roles and rights can be assigned through the user manager.

Key features of the Solaris Management Console 2.0 application are:

- Role-based access control
- Easier Solaris administration by simplifying the task of administering both local and remote Solaris software servers
- Intuitive console
- Centralized systems administration
- Administration of multiple Solaris systems by a single console login
- Open and extensible environment that integrates Java applications, X.11 legacy applications, wizards, and HTML through the Solaris Management Console 2.0
- Software development kit (SDK)
- Access to all GUI-based tools—user manager, process manager, log viewer, job scheduler, mounts and shares manager, disk and partition manager, and serial port manager
- Complete integration with the Solaris 8 1/01 operating environment
- Context-sensitive help
- Single interface to administer the entire Solaris operating environment
- Decreased administrative time
- Web-based enterprise management (WBEM) initiative support

The primary difference between the Solaris Management Console and the Sun Management Center is that the latter is designed to manage Sun systems and the former is designed to simplify common system administration tasks.

NTP Server

Every aspect of managing, securing, planning, and debugging a network involves determining when events happen. Time is the critical element that allows an event on one network node to be mapped to a corresponding event on another. In many cases, these challenges can be overcome by the enterprise deployment of the Network Time Protocol (NTP) service.

The management server includes the xntpd(1M) daemon, which is bundled with the Solaris operating environment software to provide time synchronization services to all cluster nodes. Sun modifies the /etc/inet/ntp.conf and /etc/inet/ntp.client files on each cluster node to acknowledge the management server as the NTP server and also modifies the /etc/inet/ntp.conf and /etc/inet/ntp.server files on the management server to activate the NTP services.

For Sun Cluster nodes that have system service processors (SSPs) or system controllers (SCs) to provide NTP services, you can configure the management server as a higher level server than the SSP or SC. The domains act as clients. Thus, the SSPs and SCs operate as clients to the management server and servers to the domains. You can configure the management server, in turn, as a client to an external NTP server. Alternatively, you can connect the management server directly to a reference clock.

You can configure the relationship between NTP servers and clients to operate in the following modes—*NTP server*, *NTP client*, and *NTP peer*.

An NTP server provides time data to clients. Clients send a request to the server and the server sends back a timestamped response, along with information such as its accuracy and stratum (defined as the position of a member within the client, server, and peer hierarchy). An NTP server can broadcast multicast packets to improve efficiency when serving a large number of clients

An NTP client receives time responses from an NTP server or servers and uses the information to calibrate its clock. The client determines how far its clock is off and adjusts its time to match that of the server. The round-trip time for packet receipt determines the maximum error. To improve efficiency when a large number of clients is served, an NTP client can accept multicast packets from a server.

An NTP peer is a member of a group of NTP servers that are tightly coupled. In a group of two peers, equal at any given time, the most accurate peer acts as a server and the other peers act as clients. As a result, peer groups have closely synchronized times without specifying a single server.

Sun Ray Server

The Sun Ray™ 1.3 server software provides system management and administration services, including authentication of users, server group management, redirection of input and output to the Sun Ray appliances, and the screen display for Sun Ray appliances in a *hot desk* environment. This server-based software supports administrative functions such as managing authentication policies. With Sun Ray server software, you can attach local parallel and serial devices, print to both network and local PostScript printers, harness the compute power of the Solaris 8 operating environment, and drive multiple displays with a single mouse or trackball.

Sun Ray appliances are compact, network-based devices that provide remote keyboard, mouse, and display capabilities for a server. A hot desk environment can be set up so that you can leave a session on one appliance and regain the session on another appliance and use smart cards for user identification and integration with the hot desk feature. Sun Ray appliances are particularly useful to your operators or systems administrators because their sessions can follow them to different Sun Ray appliances located throughout a data center or an operations control center.

Sun StorEdge SAN Surfer

The Sun StorEdge SAN surfer software enables you to manage Sun StorEdge network Fibre Channel switches. This software runs on a management server and manages the switches through direct attach FC-AL or out-of-band through TCP/IP over Ethernet. These features are provided:

- Dynamic remote management of one or more storage area network (SAN) fabrics, switch, port, and device-level viewpoints
- Intelligent diagnostics to help identify faulty devices before they fail
- Hardware, broadcast, and name server zoning
- Customized event logging printable reports
- Password security with individual read/write access levels
- Simplified large fabric installation and repair with a mass-deployment tool set
- In-band (Fibre Channel) and out-of-band (Ethernet) access
- Capability to implement any standard GUI by using Telnet, SNMP, HTML, or SES with OSI-based architecture

Sun Explorer Data Collector

The Sun Explorer™ data collector software is a collection of scripts that gather system information and bundle it into a compressed file. You can send this data to Sun for use in tracking system configurations or analyzing problems.

Sun Remote Services

The Sun Remote Services Net Connect software enables you to detect and record events on systems remotely. This remote monitoring enables timely resolution of problems before productivity is impacted. This package requires installation of the Sun Management Center software as a prerequisite.

Through a Sun Remote Services (SRS) agent, the management server becomes the gateway to access the cluster nodes for service or upgrades. Since the management server is a central repository of the system logs, error messages that impact any of the cluster members trigger an action from the SRS site (FIGURE 4-1).

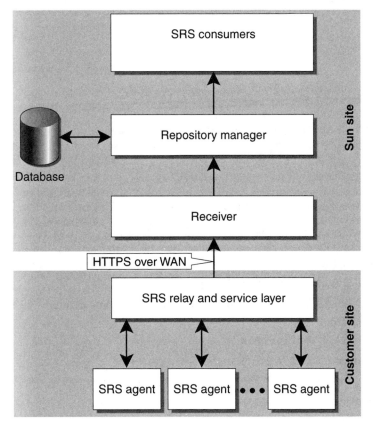

FIGURE 4-1   SRS High-Level Architectural Block Diagram

The SRS agent is configured at the customer site to provide specific contracted services. The SRS agent provides three basic functions—general service provision, event and alert service, and security services. The SRS relay and service layer aggregates and associates all agents at the customer site.

Software Stack

Sun loads the software required to implement all of the management server functions onto a single management server. The JumpStart environment of the management server contains all software components required to install all nodes in a Sun Cluster 3.0 environment, including the Solaris operating environment, the Sun Cluster 3.0 software, and any required patches.

Hardware Components

The hardware components required by the management server to support its activities are not very extensive. The bulk of the services provide read-only access to files, software packages when cluster nodes are installed, and online documentation. Other services include logging and monitoring. The only service that consumes significant resources is the Sun Management Center server, which requires a large amount of RAM for reasonable performance.

The SunTone Cluster Platforms portfolio includes a Netra T1 AC200 server as the management server. This server is a low-cost, carrier-grade, low-profile server with the following parts:

- One 500 MHz UltraSPARC processor
- 1-Gbyte RAM (sufficient for running as a Sun Management Center server for a cluster)
- One empty PCI card slot
- Slim profile, 1U rackmountable package
- Two internal 36.4-Gbyte UltraSCSI disk drives, mirrored
- Two serial ports
- Two USB ports
- Two FastEthernet ports
- Internal CD/DVD drive

This server is very flexible and works well as a management server for clusters.

Sun preinstalls the SunTone Cluster Platform management server at the factory with the software environment described previously in this section. A set of recovery CDs/DVDs enables you to recover to the factory-installed state in the event of a catastrophic failure.

The DVD drive on the management server enables you to load the recovery CDs/DVDs. CD0 contains a bootable copy of the Solaris operating environment configured to execute the recovery software. CD1 contains the Solaris operating environment (root), and CD2 contains the JumpStart server and Web Start Flash support files.

For increased availability, the management server includes a second internal SCSI disk to mirror the boot drive. Sun mirrors the boot disks at the factory using the Solstice DiskSuite software.

To eliminate the need for a keyboard, mouse, and monitor, an 8-port terminal concentrator (TC) connects the cluster nodes (FIGURE 4-2) to the console port of the management server, thus providing console access to all cluster nodes.

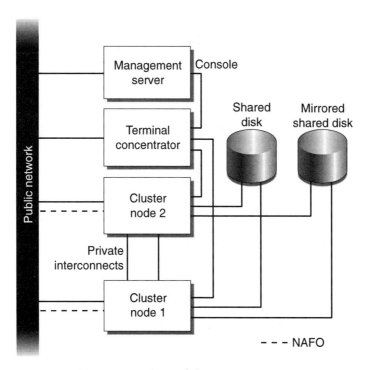

FIGURE 4-2   Environment Logical Connectivity

Network Configuration

The management server can be used as a gateway between a public network and a cluster administration network. This configuration enables you to separate the management of cluster nodes and storage from public networks in which access may not be strictly controlled. FIGURE 4-3 shows this configuration. The management server can act as a proxy to forward alerts and log messages to other systems on the public network. Meanwhile, users attempting to access the devices on the cluster management network directly must first log in to the management server. At a minimum, you can configure the management server to prevent routing between the networks. For more secure environments, you can use the management server as a firewall. For very secure environments, a separate firewall can provide stronger enforcement of security policies.

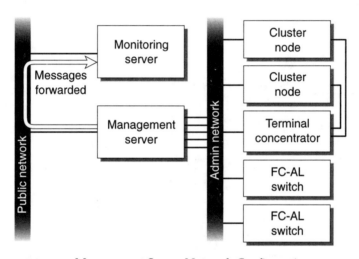

FIGURE 4-3   Management Server Network Configuration

Systems Management

The management server provides some beneficial capabilities to a Sun Cluster 3.0 system. Installation and recovery are particularly beneficial. Other system management capabilities can be equally important but may not require special considerations for clusters.

All JumpStart software components on the management server must include the latest patches and the latest versions supported by the Sun Cluster 3.0 software. The primary software components are:

- Solaris operating environment software
- Solstice DiskSuite software
- Sun Cluster 3.0 software and data services

Note – To learn more about the architectural details of a JumpStart environment, review the Sun BluePrints Online article "Building a JumpStart Infrastructure" [ANOL01]. The Sun BluePrints Online Article "Cluster Platform 220/1000 Architecture—A Product from the SunTone Platforms Portfolio" [Vargas01], describes the details of using a management server to install Sun Cluster nodes. These articles are located at: http://www.sun.com/blueprints. Select Sun BluePrints OnLine.

Backup, Restore, and Recovery

Successful data center operations require good backup, restore, and recovery processes. Good processes are even more important when a data center is providing highly available services. This section examines the backup, restore, and recovery options for use in a Sun Cluster 3.0 environment using the management server.

Note – The Sun BluePrints OnLine article "Building a JumpStart Infrastructure" [ANOL01] recommends a specific JumpStart directory structure as a best practice. This article was published after the Cluster Platform 220/1000 was developed. Future SunTone Cluster Platform products will adopt this JumpStart directory structure best practice.

Management Server

The management server is the focal point of Sun Cluster 3.0 system recovery. Recovery procedures for the management server itself are required. Since the management server acts as the JumpStart server for the cluster nodes, the management server plays an important part in the recovery of a cluster node.

The management server contains a large number of files—JumpStart profiles for the cluster nodes, copies of the Solaris operating environment used when installing clients, AnswerBook documentation, Sun Management Center support files, and so forth. Most of these files are static. You can restore these files from the distribution media. However, log files change regularly and tend to be relatively small, but they do require continuous backup.

The SunTone Cluster Platform 220/1000 includes a management server on which Sun preinstalls the cluster software environment at the factory. Sun does not preinstall the Solaris operating environment on the cluster nodes. You must install the Solaris operating environment and Sun Cluster 3.0 software by using the management server—the factory does not have the cluster name, host names, node names, IP addresses, and other site-specific information. The system administrator collects this information on site when the system is delivered and installed.

Tape Backup

If a tape backup system is available, you can do a full backup of the management server when major changes of the file systems occur, for example, updating the JumpStart directory structure with a new release of the Solaris operating environment. Incremental backups to save log or configuration file changes should be done on a regular schedule.

CDs and DVDs

A set of CDs or DVDs that contain the software image installed on the management server in the factory enables you to rebuild the management server to the factory-installed state. If a catastrophic failure causes the loss of the management server operating environment and you cannot recover the operating environment from backup tape, you can use this recovery process. Recovering to factory-installed state by using the CDs is significantly faster than reloading the dozens of packages installed on the management server from their distribution CDs.

Directly Attached Tape Drives

Cluster nodes may have directly attached tape drives. If not, you can use a network-based tape backup service such as remote ufsdump or a full-featured backup solution. For Sun Cluster 3.0 systems, you can also use the global file system (GFS) to share a tape device between cluster nodes. In any case, backup to tape is preferred because the recovery time for reloading a cluster node and reinstalling the data services can be long. Keeping at hand a ufsdump of the cluster node environment for rapid recovery purposes is a best practice.

Web Start Flash Technology

For rapid recovery, you can use the Sun Web Start Flash technology to store the existing cluster node operating environment. This technology is significantly faster for loading the Solaris operating environment than JumpStart installation or ufsrestore, especially when you use it in conjunction with the management server to provide rapid recovery of the installed nodes.

The Sun Web Start Flash process is:

1. Create a Web Start Flash archive (flar format) with flarcreate.

2. Copy the Web Start Flash archive onto the management server.

3. Configure the management server to install the cluster node from the Web Start Flash archive.

During node recovery, the node uses the JumpStart technology to install the Web Start Flash archive. Using Web Start Flash in this manner enables you to recover a cluster node with almost all of its configuration information intact. This is an improvement over a clean Solaris operating environment and Sun Cluster 3.0 software installation, which will not have all of the configuration information of the node.

JumpStart Software

In the case of catastrophic loss of the cluster nodes operating environment when a tape backup does not exist, you can reinstall the nodes from the management server using the JumpStart software. This recovery method reloads the operating environment, but you will have to make the agent configuration and any other system changes manually.

Summary

In this chapter we described a collection of infrastructure services that a management server such as those used in the SunTone Cluster Platforms can provide. A management server provides a single point of management for the cluster or a group of clusters for:

- Installation and recovery
- Logging, alerts, and configuration records
- Systems management, such as the Sun Management Center server
- Convenient online documentation

A management server example was described, including the recovery process of the management server itself. You are encouraged to implement a systems management architecture such as this in your Sun Cluster system designs.

CHAPTER 5

Case Study 1—File Server Cluster

This chapter contains a case study of a hypothetical company, referred to as the Firm, that needs a file server cluster. This case study defines the Firm and its computing requirements—an HA-NFS service running on a SunTone Cluster Platform 220/1000 server.

This chapter contains the following sections:

- Firm Description
- Design Goals
- Cluster Software
- Recommended Hardware Configuration
- Summary

Firm Description

The Firm is a decentralized software development company. Independently managed groups develop the Firm's products. Each group supports its own computing needs and infrastructure. The Firm provides only a few universal information technology (IT) services. Each group is responsible for providing and supporting their other IT needs. The groups use Internet access and domain name service the most. Each group contains 25 to 250 people who work on a specific product at their site. Smaller groups work as collectives of individuals, while larger groups tend to have one or two levels of management with associated isolation of resources.

One group is working on a new product code named Prospect-J. The Prospect-J development has a critical time-to-market requirement, known internally as "the impossible deadline." Deadline pressure is causing the developers to work on the product interactively and nearly continuously.

The Firm does not have raised floors, hardened data centers, or a central operations control center for monitoring critical IT services.

Design Goals

To support the Prospect-J development team, the Firm is implementing a highly available, yet low-cost, file service. The design goals are based on the business case, server requirements, cluster services, and expected service levels.

Business Case

The completed financial analysis shows that every day the Firm delays bringing Prospect-J to market could cost $100,000 in revenue. The expected primary cause for missing the schedule is interruptions in the development and test process.

To avoid interruptions in the development and test processes caused by the inaccessibility of source code, resulting from a file-system-related failure, the Firm decided to implement a highly available network file service. The Firm's founder believes that mistakes caused by tired employees can be more costly than those caused by hardware failure. The founder uses the phrase "you can get almost as much work finished in 11 hours as you can in 10" to illustrate his point of view. To help guard against the effects of human error, daily archival of the source code is required.

Server Requirements

To support the Prospect-J development, the development group needs a highly available network file server that must meet the following requirements:

1. Support developers whenever they want to work. Essentially, this requirement demands continuous availability.

2. Support nightly builds of software for testing the following day

3. Tape backup of all files to enable easy retrieval of a specific file on a specific date by a user without system administrator privileges

4. Acquire a system quickly to meet the impossible deadline

5. All administration tasks must be done from a remote location because the system does not have operators on duty continuously. Error reporting and status must be deliverable through two-way email for use by cell phones or pagers.

6. Spare parts must be available in a reasonable time frame but are not required on site.

7. Reserve file-locking semantics during a failover

8. Provide NFS file services

9. Support up to 100 users during peak periods. The user workload is sporadic and unpredictable.

Note – The Firm expects the system to supply file services only. Other systems will compile, edit, and handle other file manipulation.

Cluster Services

The Firm requires the following cluster services:

- Network file system (NFS)
- Common Interface File System (CIFS)
- Daily file backup

Expected Service Level

The Firm is concerned about the time to market for Prospect-J. The developers tend to work nonstandard hours. The Firm expects the developers to work longer hours as the deadlines approach. The group starts the daily builds in early morning and expects them to be completed by 0800, when the test team begins work. For this reason, the system must be available continuously with minimal downtime.

The deadline for completing Prospect-J development is within nine months. Therefore, the Firm is not planning any downtime for upgrades, routine maintenance, or capacity expansion.

Because no scheduled downtime is available, the group leader first must approve emergency patches and then decide when the system administrator can apply these emergency patches. Also, because no planned downtime is available for upgrades, the plan of record for rolling back emergency patches is to revert to the previous daily backup.

Design Priorities

The senior management of the Firm gave the group a prioritized list (TABLE 5-1) of major features. If a design decision involved a trade-off between two major features, the group used this prioritization to make a decision.

TABLE 5-1   Major Feature Priorities

Feature	Priority
Availability	1
Cost	2
Reliability	3
Recovery	4
Security	5
Performance	6
Serviceability	7

Availability

Availability is the highest priority for the Prospect-J development file server cluster. Any downtime before the development deadline will cause a slippage and subsequent loss of revenue opportunity.

Cost

The Firm wants to keep the cost of the system as low as possible without compromising the desired time-to-market deadline.

Reliability

Component reliability is more important than typical highly available installations because the Firm does not have a hardened data center. Also, the Firm will not stock spare parts on site.

Software reliability is expected to be high. The Firm does not intend to change the software components. The file services, clustering, and backup software will be used as is, with little or no customization. The firm will not develop any new software to install on the cluster.

Recovery

Recovery takes two forms—recovery of the cluster when down and recovery of archived files. Cluster recovery from a failure is expected to be as automated as possible because no operator is available continuously. Recovery of archived files must be done without operator assistance by a backup-and-restore software product.

Security

The system contains some of the Firm's proprietary and intellectual property. The system does not contain confidential personnel information, credit card numbers, or any other data that would make the Firm legally vulnerable if it were stolen.

The Firm is concerned about security problems causing an outage. Therefore, they will restrict login access to the system to a few responsible administrators. Physical security is a minor concern, but the lack of a hardened data center with controlled physical access puts the Firm at risk. The building that contains the system and developers has a part-time receptionist and a card access system that controls building access.

Some of the Firm's developers work in remote locations and connect to the Firm's internal network through a virtual private network (VPN). A separate group maintains the VPN and all Internet access points. As an added precaution, the Firm uses network address translation (NAT) to help prevent direct access to internal systems from the Internet. File service will be restricted to a set of hosts that will be maintained.

Performance, Sizing, and Capacity Planning

Predicting performance requirements and anticipating write workloads is difficult because the write workloads will be intermittent. The file service clients support local file caching, which reduces the read workload. The Firm does not expect that a sustained workload will exist for any significant period of time other than for backup.

Serviceability

The Firm does not have a centralized IT support organization. The Firm will rely on component supplier service contracts for installation, parts replacement, and any system troubleshooting.

Cluster Software

The Sun Cluster 3.0 software includes the highly available Network File System (NFS) data service package, SUNWscnfs, without additional licensing charges. The HA-NFS data service is currently a failover service—the Sun Cluster 3.x software road map includes a scalable NFS agent in the future.

A failover service executes on a single cluster node until the fault monitor agent detects a service anomaly. Once a fault is detected on a data service, the system restarts the data service on the same node or an alternate node. The Firm has decided to use the Sun Cluster 3.0 HA-NFS service to serve two separate file systems:

- The workspace file system includes the developers' home directories and workspaces used to store any work in progress.
- The build file system contains the configuration controlled sources, build environment, test suites, and test results.

This requirement allows the Firm to distribute the NFS service between two cluster nodes by creating two separate HA-NFS data services: workspace and build. During normal operations, the system shares the NFS load across the nodes, based on the file systems. The only caveat with this configuration is that a failure on a cluster node reduces the performance of the surviving node because it must host two HA-NFS data services at the same time. The Firm considered this and believes that their configuration will be adequate, even in the degraded mode.

Software Configuration

The primary service provided by this cluster is NFS, which has been a standard part of the Sun operating environment since 1985. The Sun Cluster 3.0 HA-NFS agent includes the fault monitors and recovery mechanisms required to provide failover NFS service. This service is easily installed on Sun Cluster 3.0.

NFS Overview

The NFS environment provides transparent file access to remote files over a network. File systems of remote devices appear to be local. Clients access remote file systems by using either the mount command or the automounter.

The terms client and server describe the roles that a computer plays when sharing file systems. If a file system resides on a computer disk and that computer makes the file system available to other computers on the network, that computer acts as a server. The computers that are accessing the file system are called clients. The NFS service enables any computer to access file systems of any other computer and, at the same time, provides access to its own file systems. Thus, a computer can play the role of client, server, or both at any given time on a network.

Note – Cluster nodes should not be NFS clients of file systems that are served by the cluster.

The objects that can be shared with the NFS service include any whole or partial directory tree, or a file hierarchy, including a single file. Unlike the Sun Cluster 3.0 GFS, peripheral devices such as modems and printers cannot be shared through NFS.

In most UNIX system environments, a shared file hierarchy corresponds to a file system or to a portion of a file system. However, NFS support works across operating systems, and the concept of a file system might be meaningless in other, non-UNIX environments. Therefore, the term file system used throughout this book refers to a file or file hierarchy that can be shared and mounted over the NFS environment.

NFS Characteristics

The NFS protocol enables multiple client retries and easy crash recovery. The client provides all of the information for the server to perform the requested operation. The client retries the request until the server acknowledges the request or until the request times out. The server acknowledges writes when the data is flushed to nonvolatile storage.

The multithreaded kernel does not require the maintenance of multiple nfsd or asynchronous-block I/O daemon (biod) processes; they are both operating system kernel threads. There are no biods on the client and only one nfsd process on the server.

Random patterns are characteristic of NFS traffic. NFS generates requests of many types, in bursts. The capacity of an NFS server must address the sporadic nature of NFS demands. Demand varies widely but is relatively predictable during normal activity.

Most requests from applications follow this pattern:

1. The user reads in the sections of the application binary, then executes the code pages leading to a user dialog, which specifies a data set on which to operate.

2. The application reads the data set from the remote disk.

3. The user can then interact with the application, manipulating the in-memory representation of the data. This phase continues for most of the runtime of the application.

4. The modified data set is saved to disk.

More sections of the application binary can be paged in as the application continues to run.

The NFS client negotiates with the server about using NFS version 2 or NFS version 3. If the server supports NFS version 3, version 3 becomes the default.

NFS version 3 contains several features to improve performance, reduce server load, and reduce network traffic. Since NFS version 3 is faster for I/O writes and uses fewer operations over the network, the network is used more efficiently. Note that higher throughput may make the network busier. NFS version 3 maintains the stateless server design and simple crash recovery of version 2, along with its approach to building a distributed file system from cooperating protocols. TABLE 5-2 lists the high-level features of NFS versions 2 and 3.

TABLE 5-2   High-Level Features of NFS Versions 2 and 3

Feature	NFS v2	NFS v3
Stateless protocol	Yes	Yes
Default transport protocol	UDP/IP	TCP/IP
Maximum transfer size	64 Kbytes	4 Gbytes
Maximum file size	4 Gbytes	1 Tbyte
Asynchronous writes	No	Optional

The Firm's workload is mostly small, attribute-intensive text files. This workload justifies the use of a slower, more cost-effective network infrastructure for connecting the clients and the server. In this case, the Firm uses FastEthernet for its client or public networks.

Arbitration

NFS is a stateless protocol. This makes detection of a failed server slightly difficult. The system must monitor four processes on an NFS server to determine if it is providing all NFS services properly:

1. The network file system daemon, nfsd, handles file requests, reads, writes, attribute lookups, and so forth.

2. The mountd processes file system mount requests. mountd allows or disallows a client from accessing a file system. The system only accesses mountd when a client wants to mount or unmount a file system. The network file system daemon, nfsd, handles file I/O requests.

3. The network lockd handles file and record locking requests. The paragraphs that follow describe the network lockd and the network status monitor daemon, statd(1M), in detail.

4. The statd recovers file and record locking requests in the case of a server or client failure. The paragraphs that follow describe the network statd in detail.

The starting order of these processes is important. When the system enters multiuser mode at run level 2, it starts statd before lockd. When the system extends multiuser mode by offering network services at run level 3, it starts nfsd before mountd.

The Sun Cluster 3.0 HA-NFS agent monitors all four of these daemons. If a daemon stops running, the agent attempts to restart the daemon. The operation of these daemons is independent of the file systems served. Any NFS file server has all four daemons running. Only one instance of each daemon is running, no matter how many file systems are being served.

The system must export each file system being served by using the share(1M) command. For convenience, you can enter share commands in the /etc/dfs/ dfstab file so that the system starts the NFS service and exports specified file systems automatically at reboot. The Firm's configuration specifies two different resource groups. Each group serves different file systems— the workspace file system and the build file system. The agent start and stop scripts share or unshare the appropriate file system by having a separate dfstab for each resource group—/etc/dfs/dfstab.workspace and /etc/dfs/ dfstab.build.

Each client connects to the server through a logical IP address that follows the resource groups. For example, the *workspace-server* logical IP address belongs to the resource group that serves the workspace files and is associated with the dfstab.workspace share commands. Similarly, the *build-server* logical IP address is associated with the dfstab.build share commands. From the client perspective, the workspace and build file systems are served by two different servers regardless of the state of the cluster. This greatly simplifies client file system management.

Synchronization

NFS is a stateless protocol, although some clients may want to use file or record locking on files served by NFS. The NFS protocol has a built-in method of file and record lock synchronization that is independent of the cluster framework. The network lockd and the network statd manage the locks.

The lockd is part of the NFS lock manager, which supports NFS file record locking operations. The lock manager does the following tasks:

- Forwards fcntl(2) locking requests for NFS-mounted file systems to the lock manager on the NFS server.
- Generates local file-locking operations in response to requests forwarded from lock managers running on NFS client machines.

State information kept by the lock manager about these locking requests can be lost if you kill lockd and reboot the operating system, or if the system fails over the HA-NFS service to another node in a cluster. The system can recover some of this information as follows.

When the server lock manager restarts, it waits for a grace period for all client-site lock managers to submit reclaim requests. Also, statd notifies client-site lock managers of the restart and promptly resubmits previously granted lock requests. If the lock daemon fails to secure a previously granted lock at the server site, it sends SIGLOST to a process.

Network Status Monitor

The statd is an intermediate version of the status monitor. It interacts with lockd to provide the crash and recovery functions for the locking services on NFS. The statd keeps track of the clients with processes that hold locks on a server. When the server reboots after a crash, statd sends a message to the statd on each client notifying it that the server has rebooted. The client statd processes then notify the client lockd that the server has rebooted. The client lockd then attempts to reclaim the lock(s) from the server.

The statd on the client also informs the statd on the server(s) holding locks for the client when the client has rebooted. In this case, the server statd notifies the server lockd to release all locks held by the rebooting client, allowing other processes to lock those files.

Note – The NFS protocol is stateless—a client only detects a server crash when the service recovers.

Recommended Hardware Configuration

The Firm decided to deploy a Sun Cluster 3.0 environment on a pair of Sun Enterprise™ 220R servers using a Sun StorEdge™ D1000 array. These low-cost, workgroup components provide ample capacity for the planned NFS service. A Netra T1 AC200 server provides the management infrastructure services. A terminal concentrator (TC) allows easy, remote access to server consoles. For customer convenience, Sun mounts all of the components in a single rack. The paragraphs that follow describe the hardware features that the Firm considered in making this decision. FIGURE 5-1 shows the logical configuration.

Management Server

Chapter 4 describes the management server in the SunTone Cluster Platform 220/1000 server. In this configuration, a low-cost, single-processor Netra T1 AC200 server is ideal.

The management server connects to a TC that provides access to the console for the management server and the server consoles of the cluster nodes.

The management server also acts as backup-and-restore server. A differential UltraSCSI card in the single PCI slot drives a Sun StorEdge™ L9 tape autoloader library. "Backup, Restore, and Recovery" on page 152 describes this library in more detail. TABLE 5-3 lists the parts for the management server and other support components.

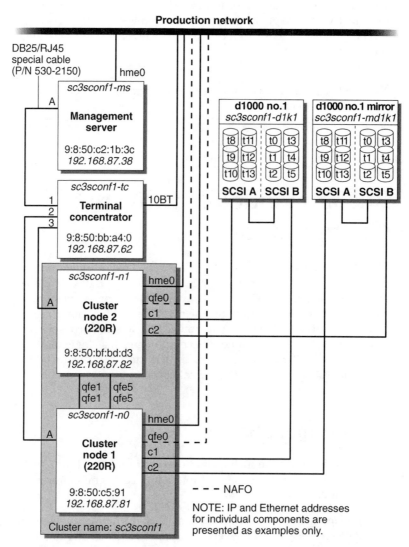

FIGURE 5-1 NFS Cluster Logical Configuration

TABLE 5-3   Management Server and Support Components Parts List

Quantity	Description
1	72-inch StorEdge expansion rack. Includes power sequencers with independent power cables and individual peripheral power cables (distributed among the two power sequencers)
1	Netra T1 AC, one 500 MHz UltraSPARC processor, 1 Gbyte of memory, and internal 18-Gbyte UltraSCSI drive for the management server
1	Optional internal 18.2-Gbyte UltraSCSI drive for the management server
1	RJ45/DB25 Netra serial port adapter for the management server
1	Terminal concentrator kit
1	Terminal concentrator mounting bracket
3	5-meter terminal concentrator RJ45/DB25 cable to access management server and cluster node consoles
2	436 Gbytes (12 × 36.4-Gbyte 10K RPM disks) Sun StorEdge D1000 with two power supplies, two fan trays, four UltraSCSI differential host ports and rackmount rails
4	4-meter SCSI 68 TO VHDC differential UltraSCSI cable

Options

The Netra T1 AC200 management server offers little room for expansion or options. The only hardware option is to add more memory, up to two gigabytes.

Nodes

The cluster nodes are two CPU workgroup servers. These servers provide a cost-effective cluster solution with limited expansion capability. The number of PCI slots limits the amount of I/O devices. Also, only two CPUs can be added without upgrading to a larger server.

The Sun Enterprise 220R is a workgroup server optimized for rackmounting. The key features are:

- One or two UltraSPARC II processors running at 450 MHz with 4 Mbytes of E-cache
- Up to 2 Gbytes of ECC protected main memory
- One 5.25-inch peripheral bay that can house a CD/DVD, 4mm, or 8mm tape drive

- Two serial ports. One port is used as a console device.
- One parallel port
- One Quad FastEthernet port with unshielded twisted pair (UTP) and media independent interface (MII)
- Four full-length PCI slots. One PCI bus has a dedicated slot, another PCI bus is shared among three slots.
- Rack-optimized 4U design
- One or two load-sharing, hot-swappable power supplies

The cluster nodes are built to provide sufficient redundancy for the cluster. All four PCI slots have Sun Quad FastEthernet™ cards and dual UltraSCSI cards for the interconnects, public networks, and shared storage. TABLE 5-4 lists the parts for each node.

TABLE 5-4 NFS Cluster Node Parts List

Quantity	Description
1	Sun Enterprise 220R server, two 450 MHz UltraSPARC II processors, 4-Mbyte E-cache, 2-Gbyte memory, two 36-Gbyte 10K RPM, 1-inch high internal UltraSCSI disks, internal DVD, Solaris server license, two power supplies
2	Quad FastEthernet PCI card
2	Dual, differential UltraSCSI PCI card
2	5-meter null RJ45 Ethernet cable for the cluster private interconnects

Options

The nodes have no hardware expansion options or unused PCI, CPU, or memory slots.

Options Considered But Discounted

The Sun Enterprise 220R can support a keyboard and graphics card. However, the Firm sees little need to add such devices to a rackmounted server.

An alternate node choice is the Sun Enterprise™ 420R server. This server has room for more processors, up to four, and memory, up to 4 Gbytes. While the extra computing power and memory might be useful for some applications, they do little to enhance the performance of the target environment, workgroup-sized NFS service. This server also has four PCI slots. However, one of the PCI slots is a short slot because of mechanical restrictions. The short slot changes the I/O configuration so that instead of two Sun Quad FastEthernet cards, only one will fit physically. Two of the long slots contain the shared storage HBAs. The remaining slots, one long and one short, are available for cluster interconnects and public networks. The redundant interconnect would have to use a single FastEthernet card in the short slot. The loss of three FastEthernet interfaces reduces the capability of providing multiple, redundant public network interfaces. Given the network limitations and the fact that additional computing power is not needed, the Firm does not believe the Sun Enterprise 420R is a viable alternative.

Boot Environment

The boot environment consists of two, hot-pluggable, 36.4-Gbyte UltraSCSI disks. These disks share a common UltraSCSI bus that is built into the motherboard. The factory mirrors the boot disks with Solstice DiskSuite™. Although the common UltraSCSI bus is a single point of failure (SPOF), it is not critical to the overall cluster services because they failover to the other node in case of a SCSI bus failure.

Shared Storage

The shared storage is low-cost, UltraSCSI disks in a Sun StorEdge D1000 array. Sun can rackmount these with the cluster nodes. The storage uses Solstice DiskSuite software instead of a hardware RAID controller.

This array does not have an embedded hardware RAID controller. Combining this array with the VERITAS Volume Manager software or with the RAID capabilities that Sun embeds with the Solaris operating environment achieves software RAID solutions. This array has two UltraSCSI channels (four UltraSCSI connections). The the Sun StorEdge D1000 backplane is split into two 4- or 6-drive segments. Two of the UltraSCSI connections can be jumpered to create a single 8- or 12-drive segment. This array is a software RAID solution that offers many capabilities and features:

- Slots for 12 single-ended, hot-pluggable, UltraSCSI drives. Configurations are available with 72 to 436 Gbytes of storage, using 1-inch high, 18- or 36-Gbyte, 10K RPM disk drives.

- Two independent UltraSCSI buses with differential interface to a host. The buses can be daisy-chained to form one physical bus. The differential UltraSCSI interface allows total cable length up to 25 meters.

- Redundant, hot-swappable, load-sharing power supplies. Power supply fault sensing and failover.

- Redundant, hot-swappable cooling fan trays with two fans each. Fan tray fault sensing and failover.

- Environmental sensing
- Software RAID using Solstice DiskSuite software
- Higher RAS than a Sun StorEdge™ MultiPack disk drive
- Compact, 4U height, mountable in standard 19-inch racks

Options

The cluster nodes have two dual differential UltraSCSI adapters. Each Sun StorEdge D1000 array uses only one of the UltraSCSI buses per node. A minimum of two Sun StorEdge D1000 arrays is required to eliminate all SPOFs in the cluster. The cluster can support up to two additional Sun StorEdge D1000 arrays before reaching capacity. This support would provide approximately 436 Gbytes of file system space, which is more than the Firm anticipates requiring for this project.

Options Considered But Discounted

Sun can upgrade the Sun StorEdge D1000 array to include a hardware RAID controller, the Sun StorEdge™ A1000 array. However, Sun Cluster 3.0 currently does not support the Sun StorEdge A1000 array.

The Sun StorEdge MultiPack disk drive is another low-cost storage option for clusters. However, the StorEdge MultiPack cannot be rackmounted. This limitation exposes the system to mechanical packaging risks.

The Sun StorEdge T3 Array provides FC-AL hardware RAID capabilities. However, this option adds significant costs. FC-AL host bus adapters (HBAs) are more expensive than UltraSCSI HBAs, and the Sun StorEdge T3 Array is significantly more expensive than the Sun StorEdge D1000 Array on both a unit and cost-per-gigabyte basis. Also, the potential storage capacity for the StorEdge T3 array (nine disks) is less than that of the Sun StorEdge D1000 (twelve disks).

The VERITAS Volume Manager was not used because the extra cost of a license would increase the cost of the cluster, which is against the design priorities.

Network and Interconnects

FastEthernet is the chosen technology for the cluster interconnect, cluster administration network, and public network.

Options

The Firm can connect the cluster administration network directly to the public network. This would facilitate access to the console serial ports if the management server is down. Alternatively, the Firm can connect the cluster administration network to other devices, such as the system administrator's desktop workstation. TABLE 5-5 lists the network port assignments for the FastEthernet interfaces on each cluster node.

TABLE 5-5   NFS Cluster Node Network Port Assignments

Port	Description
Onboard FastEthernet	Cluster administration network, NAFO group 1
QFE No.1, port 0	Cluster interconnect
QFE No.1, port 1	Public network, NAFO group 2
QFE No.1, port 2	Unused
QFE No.1, port 3	Unused
QFE No.2, port 0	Cluster interconnect
QFE No.2, port 1	Public network, NAFO group 2
QFE No.2, port 2	Unused
QFE No.2, port 3	Unused

Options Considered But Discounted

Gigabit Ethernet is an option for the cluster interconnects. However, adding Gigabit Ethernet requires the removal of the Sun Quad FastEthernet cards. In such a configuration, the public network has to use the FastEthernet interface on the motherboard. This reduces the potential availability for the public network because there is no redundant public network interface. The public network would be a NAFO group with one interface. The internode traffic the Sun Cluster 3.0 HA-NFS generates is minimal and does not warrant the performance gains achieved by using Gigabit Ethernet and the subsequent loss of NAFO on the public network.

FIGURE 5-2 shows the NFS cluster network configuration options selected.

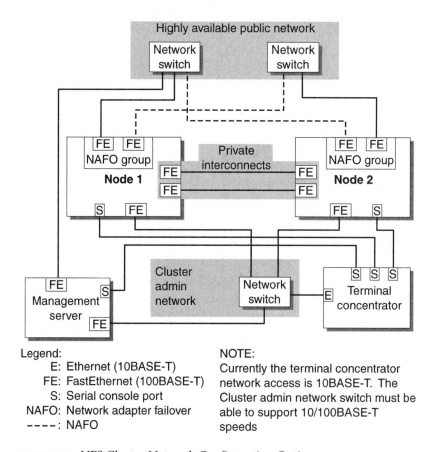

Legend:
E: Ethernet (10BASE-T)
FE: FastEthernet (100BASE-T)
S: Serial console port
NAFO: Network adapter failover
----: NAFO

NOTE:
Currently the terminal concentrator
network access is 10BASE-T. The
Cluster admin network switch must be
able to support 10/100BASE-T
speeds

FIGURE 5-2 NFS Cluster Network Configuration Options

Environmental

The cluster uses components designed for office environments. The Firm can supply
110 or 220 VAC and 50 or 60 Hz power. The audible noise generated by the fans is
quiet enough to be comfortable in an office setting. These considerations are
important to the Firm, because they lack a raised floor data center environment.
However, the Firm decided to place the components in a single rack, such as the Sun
StorEdge expansion cabinet, to use floor space efficiently, and to reduce the risk of
accidental physical disruption. Also, the Firm decided to install a rackmountable
uninterruptible power supply (UPS) to provide power in the case of a blackout.
FIGURE 5-3 shows the NFS cluster rack configuration.

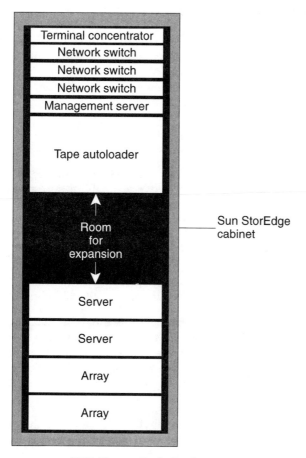

FIGURE 5-3 NFS Cluster Rack Configuration

Options

The cabinet has some room for expansion. This area could be used in the future for additional disk capacity or other components.

Options Considered But Discounted

A four-rail, Telco-style rack is another possibility. However, these racks do not provide protection from accidental mechanical disruption. Also, the Firm must bolt these racks to the floor, making deployment in their office environment difficult.

Backup, Restore, and Recovery

File server users expect their production data to be guaranteed by a backup-and-restore solution. At a minimum, the system administrator should back up the user files daily, using the incremental backup option, which backs up only files that have changed since the last backup to the tape media. The proposed backup-and-restore solution for the HA-NFS server is the Solstice Backup™ software, which executes on the management server and provides automatic backup and ad hoc restore services to file server users of the HA-NFS logical host. The logical host abstraction makes current ownership of the HA-NFS service disk data irrelevant.

The Solstice Backup 6.0 software is Sun's branded version of Legato NetWorker® 6.0 software, which provides backup and recovery capabilities for midsize to large heterogeneous UNIX, Microsoft Windows, Novell, and Linux environments. The Solstice Backup 6.0 software provides a system administrator's interface to implement backup and recovery policies and to establish an unattended, incremental backup schedule for the user files on the HA-NFS server. The Firm can group file server users according to different file access needs, and create separate backup schedules to implement a continuous backup strategy. File server users can do ad hoc backups and recover their own files using a graphical online index tool.

The management server has a dual-channel differential ultrawide SCSI PCI card that provides connectivity to a Sun StorEdge L9 Tape Autoloader. The tape autoloader consists of a robotic system that manipulates data cartridges from nine separate slots into a single DLT™ 8000 tape drive. Each tape cartridge has a native (no software or hardware compression) capacity of 40 Gbytes, which provides an accumulated capacity of 360 Gbytes of storage.

The native tape drive transfer rate is 6 Mbytes/sec and the transfer rate for the Ethernet network connection between the management server and the Sun Cluster 3.0 nodes is 100 Mbytes/sec (approximately 8 Mbytes/sec). It is safe then to assume that the transfer rate between the Sun Cluster 3.0 nodes and the tape media is between 4 to 6 Mbytes/sec. (The 4 Mbytes/sec figure assumes that the production network is busy). FIGURE 5-4 shows the expected backup times.

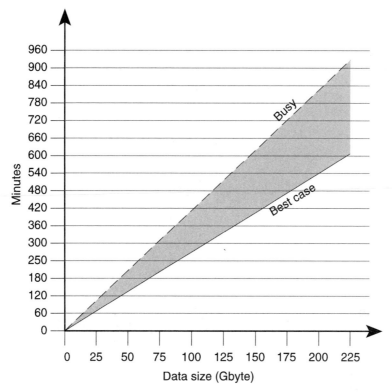

FIGURE 5-4 Expected Backup Times

Assuming a native transfer rate of 4 to 6 Mbytes/sec for the tape connection, and assuming that the entire file user community generates 5 Gbytes of new and modified files every day, the daily incremental backup will take 14 to 20 minutes.

$$IBT(6MB) = \frac{5GB \times 1,000\frac{MB}{GB}}{6\frac{MB}{s} \times 60\frac{s}{minute}} = 13.89 \text{ minutes}$$

$$IBT(4MB) = \frac{5GB \times 1,000\frac{MB}{GB}}{4\frac{MB}{s} \times 60\frac{s}{minute}} = 20.83 \text{ minutes}$$

where:

IBT = incremental backup time

Assuming a native transfer rate of 4 to 6 Mbytes/sec for the tape connection, a full backup of the entire shared disk (218 Gbytes) will take 10 to 15 hours.

$$FBT(6MB) = \frac{5GB \times 1,000 \frac{MB}{GB}}{6 \frac{MB}{s} \times 60 \frac{s}{minute} \times 60 \frac{minutes}{hour}} = 10.09 \text{ hours}$$

$$FBT(4MB) = \frac{5GB \times 1,000 \frac{MB}{GB}}{4 \frac{MB}{s} \times 60 \frac{s}{minute} \times 60 \frac{minutes}{hour}} = 15.14 \text{ hours}$$

where:

FBT = full backup time

Note – Chapter 4 of the *Sun BluePrint Backup and Restore Practices for Sun Enterprise Servers* [SKB00] describes a model for sizing distributed tape backup systems.

Justification

A basic service level agreement (SLA) for file server users involves daily backups. To guarantee the validity of the data, the system administrator makes the daily backups when file server users are idle, to be certain the data is not changing while the tape backup is occurring.

Options

A backup solution alternative is the VERITAS NetBackup software.

Summary

In this chapter we described a case study to provide a solution for a highly available file service. The business case drove the requirements of high availability and low cost. The solution selected included an NFS service provided by a Sun Enterprise 220R server and Sun Enterprise D1000 array, similar to the SunTone Cluster Platform 220/1000.

The software environment of the HA-NFS data service was described in detail. The manner of recovering NFS file locks that provide client level synchronization was described in detail.

You can use this case study as a reference for designing clusters using Sun workgroup servers.

CHAPTER 6

Case Study 2—Database Cluster

This chapter contains a case study of a hypothetical company, referred to as the Company, that needs a database cluster. This case study defines the Company and its computing requirements—an Oracle 9*i* Real Application Cluster (Oracle 9*i* RAC) running on Sun Fire™ 4800 mid-range servers using Sun StorEdge T3 arrays as the shared storage.

This chapter contains the following sections:

- Company Description
- Information Technology Organization
- Design Goals
- Business Case
- Requirements
- Design Priorities
- Cluster Software
- Recommended Hardware Configuration
- Summary

Company Description

The Company is a global Fortune 1000 company with a centrally managed information technology organization (ITO). The company manufactures products in several factories, some of which are operational 24 hours a day, and distributes its products globally. The sales force is based in offices located in major metropolitan areas around the world. The Company outsources customer service call centers to a number of independent firms located in the major countries proportional to the installed base.

A top-level analysis of the critical computing services shows that some systems must be available continuously. These systems may have different service availability guarantees based on the expected mean time to repair and recover (MTTR). Systems that require high availability have short MTTR, whereas other systems may only require a MTTR measured in days.

The following systems require continuous availability:

- Manufacturing support, for factories that operate continuously
- Electronic commerce (e-commerce)
- Sales support
- Order entry
- Customer management

A number of business-critical services do not require continuous availability. The impact of an outage of short duration in these systems is deemed to be acceptable. As a result, the service levels may not require highly available systems. The Company does not believe that these systems currently justify the costs of clustering. These systems are:

- Financial and accounting
- Human resources
- Payroll
- Product development support
- Data warehouse and business intelligence
- Desktops, palmtops, or other user interfaces

Information Technology Organization

A primary data center is located at corporate headquarters. This site hosts the bulk of the business-critical systems. The primary data center is hardened, so it has reliable power sources, air conditioning, and communications infrastructure.

The Company staffs the primary site continuously with operators who maintain a diligent watch over the business-critical systems. A senior operator is assigned as a duty officer for each shift. The duty officer has the responsibility and authority to make decisions regarding the operation of systems providing business-critical services. All operators understand the well-defined problem reporting, communication, and escalation processes. The ITO director has the ultimate responsibility and authority over all IT systems.

A secondary data center is located in a different city. The secondary site acts as the disaster recovery site and hosts some non-business-critical systems. Multiple transportation options exist between the primary and secondary data center, so that personnel and freight can travel reliably between the two sites in under four hours. This allows the secondary site to operate as a "lights out" data center. The secondary site is not a hardened data center but does have reliable power sources.

A high-speed, private network is in place between the primary and secondary data centers. Private networks exist between the primary site and manufacturing plants. All sites have access to the Internet through local service providers and a virtual private network (VPN). The VPN can be used as an alternate network path in the case of private network outages. The network infrastructure is fully redundant for the primary and secondary sites to provide reliable communications between all of the systems in the data centers.

Physical security of the primary and secondary sites is implemented so that access is restricted to authorized personnel only. Internet security is implemented by a classic firewall design. The Company uses a variety of mechanisms designed to prevent and detect unauthorized gateways or equipment to implement intranet security, and believes that the security infrastructure is sufficient for the needs of the Company.

Design Goals

The Company wants to implement a top-level architecture that will provide a platform for their business-critical applications on the Oracle 9*i* RAC database system. FIGURE 6-1 shows the top-level architecture of this database.

The Oracle 9*i* RAC database system is located in the primary data center. The secondary data center contains a single system that the Company uses as a standby system and for the following tasks:

- Standby database service for disaster recovery, using Oracle Data Guard
- Backup of the database to tape, using Oracle Recovery Manager. Periodically, the company makes and stores duplicate copies of the full environment in a secure vault.
- Reporting jobs for the marketing organization
- Data migration to a data warehouse for further analysis
- Point-in-time copying of the database for testing the development of new software on separate test systems located at the secondary data center

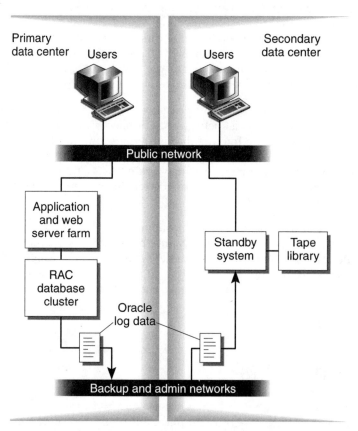

FIGURE 6-1 Top-Level Architecture for Oracle 9i RAC Database System

Using the secondary system for these non-business-critical operations relieves the primary database system of several resource-intensive operations. At the same time, the disaster recovery plan for activating the secondary site is always ready to be initiated. The secondary system utilization is high enough to justify sizing the system appropriately to meet the I/O and computation tasks of the secondary site users but not impact the sizing of the primary system.

If a disaster occurs, the Company will relegate the development and reporting users to work off-peak hours or relocate them to separate systems, as necessary. Decoupling the requirements of the primary and secondary sites allows the IT architects to design systems that provide appropriate user service levels for the business.

The remainder of this chapter describes the design of the Oracle 9i RAC cluster located at the primary data center.

Business Case

The Company has a number of business-critical services that must operate continuously. Two services, e-commerce and customer management, continuously support a number of users. Collected data (FIGURE 6-2) shows the average number of users accessing these systems on a per-hour basis over several months. At any given time, more than 190 users are active on the two systems. A trend analysis shows that the number of users is increasing at approximately a 20 percent compound annual rate.

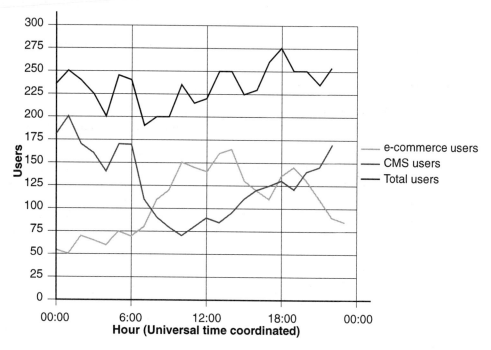

FIGURE 6-2   Active Users

These services generate approximately $200 million a year, with an estimated 22 percent compound annual growth rate. The current, unclustered systems have a measured, average annual outage rate of 37 hours a year.

Capacity planning analysis shows that the current systems are likely to reach saturation during peak usage within the next year. The developers are also increasing the complexity of the applications on the e-commerce site. The effect of the new applications on system performance is not yet known, so a system that can easily expand its performance capacity is recommended.

The financial analysis assumes a five-year life cycle. The Company uses a three-year capital depreciation schedule. The recurring and nonrecurring costs were estimates.

The results of the analysis show that a profit can be made if the availability for the e-commerce and customer management system is improved from the current measured 37 hours per year to less than 2 hours. The budget permits a mid-range, clustered system to replace the current single-server system.

Requirements

The requirements analysis was completed by a cross-functional team representing the key stakeholders. The critical requirements are:

1. Service availability so that measured unplanned downtime is less than two hours a year.

2. Applications are written to support an Oracle 9*i* RAC database.

3. Components must be easily expandable to increase capacity without requiring a redesign of the application environment or data center infrastructure.

4. In case of a disaster, the applications must be running on the secondary site within 6 hours. Planned transfer to the alternate site should occur in less than 30 minutes. Note that the unplanned disaster case has a greater time allowance than the planned disaster case. This is specified so that the disaster plan can be exercised while the service level is maintained, but an actual disaster may require additional time to accommodate safe transfer to the secondary site.

The marketing department wants to perform data analysis on the information collected by the system. This analysis does not have to be done on live operational data so it is not a critical requirement, but marketing wants the data to be accumulated daily.

Services Required

The required system services are:

- Customer management system (CMS™), which is accessed by a variety of external and contract vendors. This service provides a single point of management for all of the Company's customers.

- E-commerce database services. These services include storage and management of outbound marketing information, as well as any applications that interface to the other back-office applications.

Several Oracle 9*i* RAC database instances located at the primary data center will provide these services.

A number of systems, such as web, authentication, and directory servers, provide the supporting infrastructure for these services. These systems are not described here.

Service Level Expected

The Company realizes that the systems are expected to grow over time. However, even the best planners cannot accurately predict potential changes, especially for the new development being done on e-commerce applications. To balance the Company's application availability requirements with the rate of expected change, the ITO developed a schedule for planned system changes. This schedule helps to restrict changes to planned times that the users can rely on for planning purposes. Every effort is made to enable rollback of any scheduled changes within a short period of time. Thus, if a regression occurs, the Company can return the system to operation by rolling back the changes. TABLE 6-1 lists the schedule for planned service changes. At all other times, the Company expects the services to be operational.

TABLE 6-1 Planned Service Schedule

Planned Service Changes	CMS	E-commerce
Major software updates	Annually	Biannually
Minor software updates	Biannually	Quarterly
Scheduled patch maintenance	Monthly	Monthly
Emergency patch maintenance	As needed	As needed
Hardware platform replacement	Annually	Annually
Hardware upgrades	Quarterly	Quarterly

Performance problems are another source of service outages. The ITO operations staff continuously monitors the performance of the systems for the following conditions:

- Hung processes
- Processes consuming more CPU time than expected
- Available CPU resources
- Low memory conditions
- Unbalanced I/O workloads

In addition, the development of new software requires the delivery of a probe that can be used to test the operation of the software. The Company distributes this probe throughout the Company, and the operations staff will monitor the performance results looking for anomalies.

Design Priorities

To provide guidance for the ITO when making design decisions, the Company prioritized the major features of the system. These priorities give the ITO the freedom to implement the best possible system while carefully considering the business requirements of the Company. TABLE 6-2 lists the priorities. The ITO uses these priorities to resolve the decision when the design involves a trade-off between two major features.

TABLE 6-2   Major Feature Priorities

Feature	Priority
Availability	1
Reliability	2
Serviceability	3
Security	4
Recovery	5
Cost	6
Performance	7

Availability

Availability is the highest priority. The Company realizes that many external users have direct system access. The availability of the service provided to these customers directly impacts the highest-rated critical-to-quality issue of the external users. The system architecture must be optimized to provide available services. This availability includes scheduled and unscheduled outages. The Company expects to offer services in the event of a number of failures, including component failures and a disaster at either the primary or secondary data centers. In addition, all software and hardware upgrades should have minimum impact on service availability.

Reliability

Reliability is given a high priority too. Component reliability affects service availability. If components are unreliable and require frequent servicing, the probability of being able to deliver the required services decreases. Component reliability drives the requirements for component features such as these:

- RAID-protected persistent storage—ECC protection on system main memory
- Onsite and offsite backup media storage
- Onsite spare parts
- Hot-pluggable hardware field replaceable units (FRUs)
- Software upgrade procedures that minimize required downtime and allow rollback to the previous state

Serviceability

The Company ITO has enough operators to provide continuous support for the systems at the primary data center. However, not all operators are experts in all systems. As a result, the Company relies on its organizational ability to call in resources as needed. Internal personnel work toward providing a continuous human presence in the event of an abnormal event that requires systems to be serviced. The component supplier service contracts are written to provide phone and rapid onsite support for critical components.

At the component level, the Company wants to purchase only components that can be easily serviced. For hardware, this includes:

- Uniquely identifiable parts
- Hot-pluggable parts
- Clear and unambiguous labels and indicators

Security

The Company believes that the physical and network security are sufficient. However, both the e-commerce and CMS databases can contain customer confidential information that must be protected. The obvious places for protecting this information is in the applications themselves. The Company places special emphasis on testing the e-commerce applications for unauthorized access to sensitive data. The CMS system is largely off-the-shelf, so that the data security requirements are met by the supplier. In addition, any copies of the database used for reporting or development are restricted. To prevent eavesdropping, the Company encrypts the logs shipped to the secondary site.

In addition to online security, all copies of the database are kept at secure sites. These copies include backup data located in the data centers. Periodic offsite copies of the backups are kept in a physically secure vault with controlled access.

Recovery

The recovery of the system in the event of data corruption or disaster is important. To ensure that the database can be successfully recovered, the Company tests the offsite backups before shipment to the offsite vault. The Company also tests the other backups periodically to ensure that the daily, incremental backups are good.

Cost

The Company performed a cost analysis and determined that the costs of a mid-range, clustered system are in line with the desired system profit over its lifetime.

Performance

The services the system provides are interactive in nature. The large number of external online users makes prediction of the system performance over time somewhat difficult. The ITO will measure capacity over time and will size the systems in accordance with projected performance requirements. In addition, the ITO philosophy is to purchase systems that have internal expansion capability so the Company can expand CPU, memory, and I/O within reason over the lifetime of the system.

Cluster Software

TABLE 6-3 lists the selected base software stack. The applications that run on top of the base are not described here, since they are not publicly available.

TABLE 6-3   Oracle 9i RAC Cluster Software Stack

Software	Version	Description
Oracle RAC	9i	Database system
VxVM	3.1.1	VERITAS Volume Manager
Sun Cluster software	3.0 update 1	Cluster platform
Solaris operating environment	8 7/01	Operating environment
Sun Management Center agents	3.0	Agents for managing the cluster with the Sun Management Center software

The Oracle 9i RAC database system allows two or more cluster nodes to simultaneously perform transactions against a single database. These nodes can operate in two modes:

- *Active-active* is a type of architecture in which multiple nodes synchronize their accesses to database objects.

- *Active-passive* or *primary-secondary* is a type of architecture in which one node performs work against the database while a second node stands by, ready to take over processing if the first node fails.

The Oracle 9i RAC uses a shared disk architecture (FIGURE 6-3) so each node in the cluster has direct access to the shared disks. All database instances access the data files and control files. The Oracle 9i RAC requires replication of many pieces of the Oracle database architecture across each participating cluster node. For example, each node starts an Oracle database instance comprising the necessary background processes—the system monitor (SMON), process monitor (PMON), log writer (LGWR), and database writer (DBWR) simultaneously.

A distributed lock manager (DLM) process runs on each instance and coordinates data block synchronization by creating an in-memory database of lock objects that are equally distributed among all instances.

Background processes that support the DLM include the Global Enqueue Service monitor (LMON) and the Global Enqueue Service daemon (LMD). Moreover, each node maintains its own system global area (SGA) in memory, including the database buffer cache, the redo log buffer, and the shared pool.

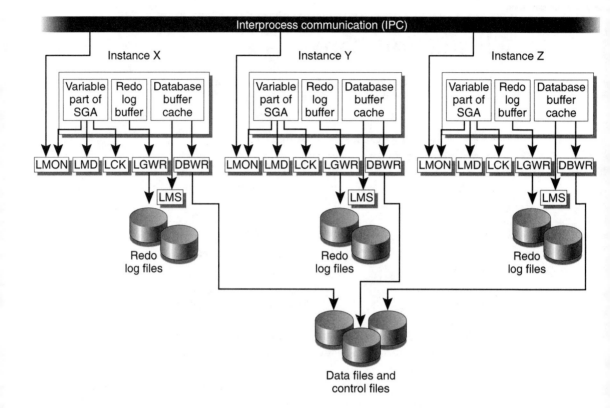

FIGURE 6-3 Oracle 9*i* RAC Architecture

On disk, the system assigns each node its own redo log files and rollback segments. The system uses these redo log files to return the database to a consistent state following a system crash. These log files record changes made to the blocks of any object, including tables, indices, and rollback segments. The log files guarantee preservation of all committed transactions in the event of a crash, even if the resultant data block changes are not yet written to the data files. Rollback segments store the "undo information," for example, the information needed to cancel or roll back a transaction, should the application choose to do so.

Rollback segments also provide a form of SQL statement isolation. A long-running query against a set of tables must only see their contents as they looked at the time the query began. This is known as *read consistency*. If another transaction modifies the data blocks of the same tables later, the rollback segments will store the "before images" so that the earlier, long-running query can return a result set, isolated to the time at which it began.

The Oracle 9*i* RAC package fits into a market segment in which availability takes precedence over scalability. Hence, Oracle 9*i* RAC is also offered as an active-passive solution. In active-passive mode, all client connections remain on the primary node and only fail over to the secondary node if the primary fails. This active-passive configuration fails to address completely the concept of client connection (application) failover.

During a failover, graceful reconnection of the client to the surviving node without the client having to authenticate again is preferable. Moreover, if the client was processing a query, it would be beneficial to restart the query after failover, without user intervention. Oracle RAC Guard provides an application failover mechanism. RAC Guard meets the requirement of managed failover for an Oracle 9*i* RAC active-passive configuration. Oracle RAC Guard is an additional layer of software packages that, for architectural reasons, reside on top of the Oracle 9*i* RAC.

With this active-passive configuration, Oracle 9*i* RAC is well adopted by the industry. Applications need not be designed for parallel operations to gain the benefits of a quick failover; this approach lowers the MTTR, thereby improving overall availability. The downside to this approach is that the secondary node, which is basically standing by for a failover with a warm instance, is underused. The solution to gaining full use of the secondary node depends on synchronization technology improvements.

Arbitration

The Oracle 9*i* RAC has many performance and availability improvement optimizations. Many of these optimizations center around the architecture, in which internode communication is expensive in terms of latency. For arbitration, Oracle distributes the ownership locks across nodes in the cluster. Oracle calls this *lock mastering*. From an arbitration perspective, lock mastering is the metadata about locks. Each node knows which node is mastering each lock and where to send synchronization requests.

The Oracle 9*i* RAC can move the lock mastery dynamically between nodes. When the cluster is built, the nodes must arbitrate to decide where to master the locks. If a node fails, the surviving nodes must arbitrate to assign new masters for the locks previously held by the failed node.

Performance optimization is possible when a node that dominates access to a set of locks can become the master for those locks. This control reduces the amount of lock traffic by changing global accesses into local accesses.

Lock Mastering

To synchronize requests for resources from multiple instances, the DLM maintains an in-memory database of locks distributed randomly among all active cluster nodes. When the system requests an object for global role access, its object ID is applied to a hashing function, which identifies the instance responsible for coordinating its access. This instance acquires a global cache service (GCS) lock for the object from a reusable pool of locks. All other instances within the cluster can apply the same hashing function to the object and, therefore, know exactly which instance to contact for permission to access the object in a shared or exclusive mode. Such an instance is "mastering the lock" for that object. Randomly assigning lock mastering among all active instances distributes the DLM workload equitably.

Node Joining the Cluster

When a new node joins the cluster, it starts an instance and mounts the same database as the other instances. Sun Cluster Group Services makes GCS aware that new instance has joined the Oracle 9*i* RAC and is ready to be assigned its share of the workload of mastering the GCS locks.

The Oracle 9*i* RAC relies on an integer M, which is a multiple of the maximum number of possible instances, as defined by the PARALLEL_SERVER_INSTANCES parameter. Rather than interrupting all access to the database while performing a full remastering, the DLM gradually, over time, migrates some of its resource mastering workload over to the joining instance, thereby maximizing availability.

Node Leaving the Cluster

When a node leaves the cluster, only the resources it was mastering need to be remastered. Locks already mastered to the surviving instances are unaffected.

Once Sun Cluster Group Services notifies the Oracle 9*i* RAC of the departing node, software package, such as that found in the Oracle RAC Guard, attempts to restart the instance on the failing node. If a restart is not possible, SMON, on the first surviving node to observe the instance failure, does the instance recovery at the same time the remastering of the locks occurs. All transactions that had been performed on the failed instance are recorded in the redo log files of that instance, but only those transactions committed before the newest checkpoint are guaranteed to have been written out to the data files. Since the redo log files for all instances reside on raw devices, the instance that is performing recovery can access the redo log of the failed instance. It either commits to the data files those transactions that had committed after the final checkpoint (also known as "rolling forward") or rolls back those that had not by reading "before images" found in the rollback segments of the failed instance. SMON also frees up any resources that those pending transactions may have acquired. During the roll-forward period, the database is only partially available. Other instances can only access data blocks they currently have buffered. They cannot perform any database I/O, nor can they ask GCS for any additional resource locks.

Similar processing occurs when more than one, but not all, of the instances fail simultaneously. The system must remaster the GCS locks on the failed instances to the surviving instances, and the SMON of a surviving instance must perform roll-forward and rollback operations against the redo log files and rollback segments left behind. However, in this case, the Oracle 9*i* RAC takes advantage of the system change number (SCN), the timestamp known on all instances of the database. SMON reads the redo log files once to identify the "recovery set," that is, the data blocks that have a sequence of modifications recorded but are missing a subsequent block written record.

During the second and final pass, SMON issues a sorted merge of the failed redo log files, based on SCN. When SMON identifies a block belonging to the recovery set built in pass one, it constructs the last known version of the block (which may involve applying the redo information from more than one failed instance), writes the version to disk, and frees the lock associated with it. This process avoids repeated writes of the same data block. Note that, if the latest known version of the data block resides on one of the failed instances, the system can obtain a more recent past image version of the block over the cluster interconnect from a surviving node, rather than rereading the block from disk.

Crash Recovery

In the unlikely event that all instances fail, the first instance restarted after the failure performs instance recovery on the redo log files of all failed instances, including its own, if necessary. This is known as "database crash recovery." It is also possible to initiate the recovery from an entirely separate instance that was not participating in the cluster before failure. As in a single-instance database recovery, database access begins once the roll-forward phase is complete. Rolling back uncommitted transactions can occur in parallel with the creation of new work. Naturally, no lock remastering occurs during crash recovery, since the DLM is starting over.

Automatic Lock Remastering

To reduce traffic on the cluster interconnect, it is preferable to have the instance that performs the majority of accesses to a given resource also act as the mastering node for that resource. This method reduces the handling of DLM requests across instances. The data structures of the Oracle 9*i* RAC allow it to pinpoint a given table space that is being used exclusively by one instance. In this case, Oracle 9*i* RAC gradually migrates all lock mastering for that tablespace to the instance that is accessing it. Since the migration happens over a period of time, there is no noticeable slowdown or lack of availability.

The Oracle 9i RAC also performs some heuristics on the DLM traffic. For example, if the DLM notices that one instance repeatedly requests the same lock from a remote mastering instance, and if it is the only instance that is making these requests, the DLM eventually migrates the mastering of that lock to the requesting node. In this case, the notion of each instance mastering an equal share of the GCS locks is lost, but the benefit is reduced traffic over the cluster interconnect.

Synchronization

The Oracle 9i RAC synchronization mechanism is similar to that used by directory-based cache-coherency protocols in microprocessor designs. One significant difference is the fault recovery. Microprocessors encountering faults cannot guarantee that the software is unaffected, so they send an interrupt which, in the case of the Solaris operating environment, panics the operating system. The Oracle 9i RAC must not stop the database when it detects a fault. The Oracle database has features, such as the transaction logs, that enable it to recover the data in case of a failure. When a fault that causes the loss of a node occurs, the Oracle 9i RAC keeps the database up while it arbitrates the new cluster configuration, recovers the data from the failed node, and synchronizes any locks.

Local GCS Lock Mode Versus Global

Versions of the Oracle RAC prior to 9i allowed only one instance at any time to hold a version of a data block considered "dirty," that is, the image in the buffer cache does not match that on disk. If one instance held an exclusive lock on the data block, all other instances were only allowed to hold null locks on the same block, essentially giving up their locks. Oracle RAC 9i allows the data block to be dirty in more than one instance and hence introduces the concept of a global management role. The exclusive lock in a local role operates somewhat independently of the DLM. This permits writing its buffer to the on-disk version without prior consent. However, the same lock in a global role requires coordination from the DLM for this I/O and yet allows other instances to obtain a shared lock on the same block. Accompanying this update functionality is the concept of a PI block, which adds complexity to both the DLM algorithm and recovery. The role of a data block is updated from local to global when it is dirty and another instance requests the block for additional write access. This situation results in two distinct versions of the data block in memory, each different from the copy on disk.

Cache Fusion Read-Read Example

As the bandwidth for interconnects increased and the transport mechanism for "content and control" improved, Oracle introduced cache fusion for transferring data across nodes through the interconnect. *Cache fusion* is aptly named, since it describes an architecture that treats all of the physically distinct RAM of each cluster node logically as one large database SGA, with the interconnect providing the physical transport among them (FIGURE 6-4).

Before Oracle 9*i* RAC, transferring a data block from one node to another involved writing the block from the database buffer cache of the holding node to the shared disk storage. The requesting node read the data block from disk into its own cache. However, passing data through persistent disk writes adds significant latency and a corresponding performance penalty. In some cases, application performance is several orders of magnitude slower than cache fusion.

Cache fusion implements cache synchronization, using a write-back model. The DLM processes on each node manage the synchronization by using the clustered interconnect for both inter-DLM traffic and data block movement between nodes.

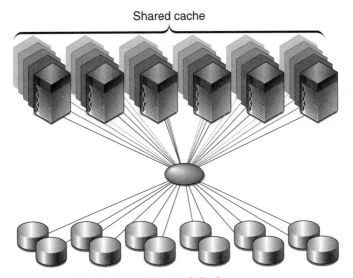

FIGURE 6-4 Oracle 9*i* RAC Logical Cache

FIGURE 6-5 shows a two-node cluster in which cache fusion performs as follows:

1. Node B requests data block 1008 from the database.

2. Node C already has the data block in its buffer (SGA). Node D is also the manager of the DLM lock on this resource.

3. Lock information is exchanged over the cluster interconnect through an integrated DLM.

4. The system transfers the data block from the buffer on node C across the cluster interconnect to node B.

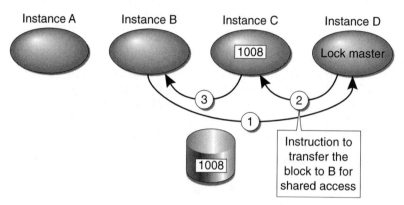

FIGURE 6-5 Two-Node Cache Fusion

Good scalability is possible because the time required to transfer the data block over the cluster interconnect is significantly less than the time required for node A to write the data block to shared disk and for node B to read the data block. This model also frees the application from having to resolve all lock management issues in a very fine-grained manner.

Cache fusion is a good fit for applications that require parallel operations on resources. However, using standard IP-based network technology for the cluster interconnect still causes a small amount of latency. Message-passing on the interconnect usually occurs on the UDP/IP stack, and the system copies data to local buffers in the UDP/IP drivers before transferring it to the remote node. Therefore, one cache fusion operation (a data-block buffer transfer) results in two copying operations, one local and one remote.

Remote Shared Memory (RSM) eliminates the local copying requirement inherent in previous transport implementations. RSM comprises local and remote adapters that provide mapped memory segments to copy message data directly into a remote address space. Effectively, some global memory space is known to all nodes involved.

Once RSM is implemented, Oracle 9i RAC will do cache fusion by copying buffers directly into the remote memory space of the interconnect adapter card. In effect, the interconnect adapter card is a mapped extension of the memory of the remote node. The result is a lower latency for data block transfers and improved performance scalability.

Recommended Hardware Configuration

The company decided to implement a two-node Sun Cluster solution using the Sun Fire midframe server and Sun StorEdge arrays (FIGURE 6-6). The following sections describe the hardware features the Company considered in making this decision.

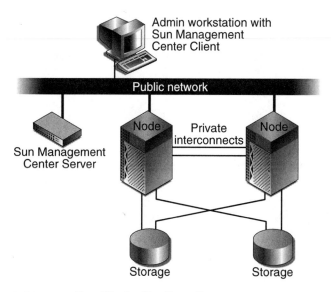

FIGURE 6-6   Sun Cluster Configuration

Management Server

The management server described in Chapter 4 provides a single management point for the cluster. Many of the functions of the management server are available in other infrastructures. The ITO identified the functions that are critical to direct management or recovery of the cluster. The management server is ready to support the cluster when needed. The management server is not used to support the critical services of other systems. The functions served by the management server and those served by other infrastructure servers are these:

- Sun Management Center server
- JumpStart service for the cluster nodes
- Network Time Protocol (NTP)
- Consolidated system log messages archive (not to be confused with Oracle logs)

Optionally, the Company can put the management server in a separate cabinet. However, the ITO currently believes that keeping the management server located with the cluster hardware helps avoid confusion.

Nodes

The Company has chosen to implement a medium-sized cluster, using Sun Fire™ 4800 mid-range servers for the nodes. However, a larger mid-range server, the Sun Fire™ 6800 server, is available from Sun. This server shares many of its components with the Sun Fire 4800 server. The Sun Fire 6800 server provides an upgrade option in case the Company requires more computing or I/O capabilities in the future and the current servers are full.

Options

The Sun Fire 4800 server is based on UltraSPARC III technology. This server, which was based on the UltraSPARC II technology, replaces the popular Sun Enterprise™ 4500 server in the Sun product portfolio. The key configuration options are:

- One to three system boards containing two or four processors, each with up to Gbytes of main memory
- Two to twelve CPUs in two CPU increments
- CPUs run at 750 MHz or 900 MHz
- 2 to 96 Gbytes of main memory
- One or two system controllers that control the configuration of the platform and act as console devices
- One or two hot-pluggable I/O assemblies that can contain either eight PCI or six cPCI slots
- PCI assemblies containing eight slots assigned to four PCI buses. Two buses have one dedicated slot each. The other two buses each have three slots. Most slots accept full-length cards. However, there is a hardware component that limits two slots for short cards only.
- cPCI assemblies contain six individually hot-pluggable slots assigned to four cPCI buses. Two buses have one dedicated slot each. The other two buses each have two slots.
- Redundant Sun Fireplane™ interconnect switches
- N+1 redundant, hot-pluggable power supplies; internal power is configured to share the load across all components in the chassis
- Two redundant transfer units (RTUs), which provide automatic switching between dual power feeds. The RTUs supply AC power to the power supplies.

- Redundant, hot-pluggable fan trays

The Sun Fireplane interconnect switches run at 150 MHz. Each port on this interconnect can transfer data at a rate of up to 9.6 Gbytes/sec. The CPU/memory boards transfer at 9.6 Gbytes/sec. I/O assemblies can only transfer data at 2.4 Gbytes/sec. A marketing claim of 33.6 Gbytes/sec (three at 9.6 plus two at 2.4 Gbytes/sec) is described as an "aggregate bandwidth." Benchmarks have shown sustained rates of nearly 9.6 Gbytes/sec, which is far greater than the possible I/O bandwidth.

The UltraSPARC III processor ranges in speed from 600 to 900 MHz in 150 MHz increments to match the Sun Fireplane interconnect speed. Further speed enhancements are planned. The UltraSPARC III has sophisticated cache-coherency (synchronization) circuitry built into the processor. The UltraSPARC III design was intended to reduce the latency between the processor and main memory, including the cache-coherency steps, for hundreds of processors running a single Solaris operating environment instance. The cache coherency uses both a *snooping protocol* and a *distributed directory-based protocol*.

In the snooping protocol, all processors look at, or snoop, on the address bus to see what cache transactions are occurring. The problem with snooping protocols is that the benefits for all processors seeing all address bus transactions is difficult to scale to large numbers of processors without compromising latency.

In the distributed directory-based protocol, each processor contains a list of the processors that have cached data. This list avoids the requirement of all processors seeing all transactions by adding a directory lookup to each processor's local directory. This potentially adds latency, depending on whether the cached data is local or remote, but this additional latency scales better for larger systems. Sun Fire servers use both techniques—snooping protocols on processor boards containing up to four processors, and distributed directory-based protocols between boards. As previously described, the Oracle 9i RAC implemented a similar directory-based method for caching between cluster nodes.

Full hardware redundancy is designed into the Sun Fire 4800 server. Components such as system clocks, system controllers, power, and cooling are fully redundant. The Sun Fireplane interconnect can be configured redundantly, too. All data paths use end-to-end ECC error protection. In addition, fault isolation is improved over the previous generation of servers so that faults can be isolated to the FRU that has faulted. A variety of advanced mainframe-class features, such automatic system recovery (ASR), hot CPU upgrades, and dynamic reconfiguration deliver exceptional serviceability.

ASR occurs when the system is powered on. Optionally, ASR can occur when the system reboots after a hardware error is found. The additional end-to-end ECC and other enhanced fault isolation features combine with ASR. These features are a significant improvement over the previous generation of Sun Enterprise servers. Faulty components are blacklisted, similar to the blacklist feature in the Sun

Enterprise 10000 server. Hot CPU upgrades allow upgrades to faster CPUs while the Solaris operating environment and applications continue to be available. Dynamic reconfiguration enables you to add or remove system hardware resources (CPUs, memory modules, and I/O controllers) without shutting down the Solaris operating environment or powering down the system.

For proper operation, the dynamic system domain features in a Sun Cluster environment require special design and processes. For more information, contact a Sun Service provider.

With Solaris processor sets, Solaris Resource Manager software, and dynamic system domain features, the system has the flexibility to accommodate changing resource requirements across multiple applications.

The Sun Fire 4800 server can be used as a deskside system, placed in a Sun Fire cabinet, or mounted in an industry-standard 19-inch rack.

A stated previously, the Company decided to purchase a pair of Sun Fire 4800 servers for use as nodes in the Oracle 9*i* RAC database cluster. TABLE 6-4 lists the node parts.

TABLE 6-4   Sun Fire 4800 Server Node Parts List

Description	Quantity
Sun Fire cabinet	1
Sun Fire 4800 Server base package—factory-racked	1
PCI I/O assembly for Sun Fire 4800 Server	2
CPU/memory board with four 900 MHz CPU, 32-MB ECache, 4 x 2 Gbyte memory	2
Sun Enterprise power cord, U.S. version	4
Optional RTS AC Module for Sun Fire Server	1
Redundancy Kit for Sun Fire 4800 Server (includes one power supply, one fan tray, and one system controller)	1
Media tray with two 36-Gbyte disks and one DVD	1
Media tray with two 36-Gbyte disks and one DDS4 tape drive	1
SunSwift™ UltraSCSI and SunFastEthernet adapter	4
Sun StorEdge PCI single FC network adapter	4
Gigabit Ethernet PCI adapter 2.0	5

TABLE 6-5 lists the node I/O configuration.

TABLE 6-5 Sun Fire 4800 Node I/O Configuration

I/O Bay	PCI Slot	PCI Controller/ Bus	Card	Connector	Target
IB 8	0 (short)	0, B	1032A: PCI UltraSCSI and SunFastEthernet adapter	HD68, SCSI	D240 No.1, left bus
				RJ-45, SunFastEthernet	Cluster administration network switch
	1 (short)	0, B	6799A: PCI FC-AL network adapter	SC, FC-AL	FC-AL switch No.1
	2	0, B	Unused		
	3	0, A	1141A: PCI Gigabit Ethernet NIC (MMF)	SC, Gigabit Ethernet	Cluster interconnect No.1
	4	1, B	Unused		
	5	1, B	1032A: PCI UltraSCSI and SunFastEthernet adapter	HD68, SCSI	D240 No.2, left bus
				RJ-45, SunFastEthernet	No connection
	6	1, B	6799A: PCI FC-AL network adapter	SC, FC-AL	FC-AL switch No.3
	7	1, A	1141A: PCI Gigabit Ethernet NIC (MMF)	SC, Gigabit Ethernet	Public network switch No.1

TABLE 6-5   Sun Fire 4800 Node I/O Configuration *(Continued)*

I/O Bay	PCI Slot	PCI Controller/ Bus	Card	Connector	Target
IB 6	0 (short)	0, B	1032A: PCI UltraSCSI and SunFastEthernet adapter	HD68, SCSI	D240 No.1, right bus
				RJ-45, SunFastEthernet	No connection
	1 (short)	0, B	6799A: PCI FC-AL network adapter	SC, FC-AL	FC-AL switch No.2
	2	0, B	Unused		
	3	0, A	1141A: PCI Gigabit Ethernet NIC (MMF)	SC, Gigabit Ethernet	Cluster interconnect No.2
	4	1, B	1032A: PCI UltraSCSI and SunFastEthernet adapter	HD68, SCSI	D240 No.2, right bus
				RJ-45, SunFastEthernet	No connection
	5	1, B	1141A: PCI Gigabit Ethernet NIC (MMF)	SC, Gigabit Ethernet	Backup network switch

Options Considered But Discounted

The Sun Fire 4800 server is available in a deskside configuration. However, deskside configurations are not suitable for data center environments, where rackmounted servers are preferred. Exposed cables are a problem with deskside or desktop systems. It is very difficult to secure the cables and ensure that they are properly maintained. For example, the minimum cable bend radius can be violated if the cable cannot be secured to ensure that the bends are within tolerance. Exposed cabling increases the probability that cables can be accidentally damaged. Also, it is difficult to secure a collection of deskside components in seismically active areas. It is better to place servers designed for highly available services in racks so the Company can control their mechanical configurations.

Boot Environment

The boot environment uses Sun StorEdge™ D240 media trays. The Sun StorEdge D240 media tray is a compact, scalable, and highly flexible storage solution, specifically designed to support the Sun Fire servers for the boot disk and removable media solution. The slim, two-rack unit (2U), rackmounted configuration can accommodate a range of storage devices including removable hard disks, DVD-ROM, and tape backup.

The Sun StorEdge D240 media tray features a single or dual SCSI bus configuration that supports up to two independent server boot domains per system. Dual, hot-swappable, load-sharing power supplies power the media tray. FIGURE 6-7 shows the front view of the media tray.

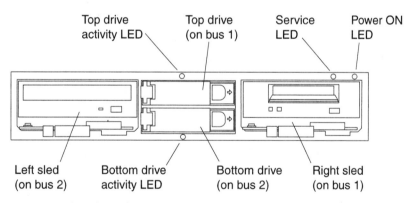

FIGURE 6-7 Sun StorEdge D240 Media Tray—Front View

Electrically, the SCSI bus can be split into two, with one 3.5-inch disk and one 5.25-inch bay per bus (FIGURE 6-8). This provides containment for faults on the SCSI buses. The dual power supplies are load sharing and fully redundant. The FRUs are independently replaceable, so the Company can replace any active component without disrupting other active components. The Sun StorEdge D240 media tray can support two independent SCSI buses without introducing opportunities for common mode faults.

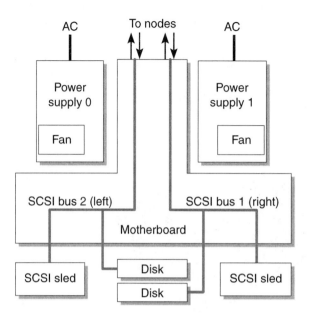

FIGURE 6-8   Sun StorEdge D240 Media Tray—SCSI Bus Configurations

The ITO has a policy that all boot devices on production servers must be mirrored to improve availability. In addition, an upgrade procedure with rollback capability must be designed into the boot environment. This allows the Company to install patches or add new versions of the software stored on the boot disks without risking the existing operational environment. When feasible, the Company can use a separate disk for the upgrade procedure, to help ensure fault containment if a problem occurs during patch installation or upgrades. Solaris Live!™ Upgrade software is used to manage the boot environments. FIGURE 6-9 shows the boot disk layout selected for each node in the cluster.

Fault tree analysis (FTA) and Event Tree Analysis (ETA) (see Appendix D) of this design show that there is a potential risk in the case of multiple failures. If the primary boot drive or the SCSI bus serving the primary boot disk fails, the system activates the hot spare. This puts the new primary boot disk and boot mirror on the same SCSI bus. During the time required to service the first failure, the configuration is vulnerable to a second failure on the second SCSI bus. This vulnerability exists only for the time required to repair the first failure, which reinforces the importance of repairing failures quickly and maintaining low MTTR rates. FIGURE 6-10 shows this failure scenario.

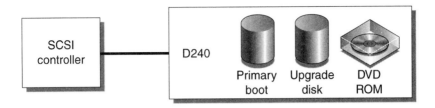

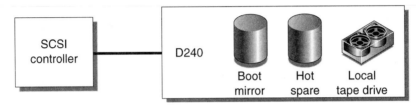

FIGURE 6-9 Production Server Boot Disk Environment

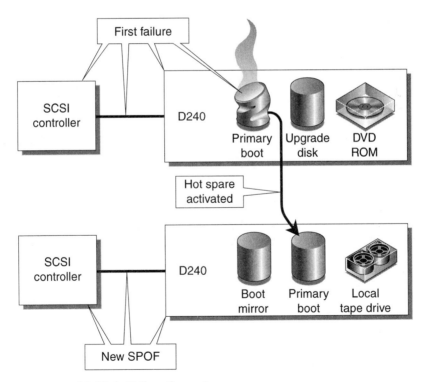

FIGURE 6-10 Multiple Failure Scenario

An alternate design using the split bus capability of the Sun StorEdge D240 couple with two SCSI controllers was considered. FIGURE 6-11 shows this alternate design.

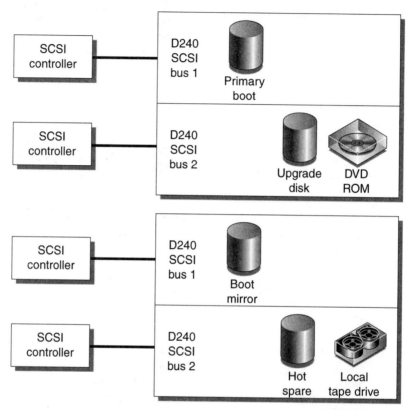

FIGURE 6-11 Alternate Design for Production Server Boot Disk Environment

The alternate design consumes more server I/O slots than the original design. A preferred solution would be to use a dual SCSI controller card. Sun currently sells both a single-ended (6540A) and differential (6541A) UltraSCSI card; however, these cards do not have firmware that would enable them to be used as boot disk controllers. Currently, a dual SCSI PCI controller with boot firmware is not available from Sun.

It is rare that you can consider such multiple failure scenarios owing to complexity. However, when the number of components is small and options exist to help build additional redundancy, the analysis can prove beneficial.

Shared Storage

The Company decided to use the Sun StorEdge T3 array as the shared storage for the cluster. TABLE 6-6 lists the required shared storage parts.

TABLE 6-6   Oracle 9*i* RAC Shared Storage Parts List

Description	Quantity
2620-Gbyte Sun StorEdge T3ES; includes eight T3 arrays configured in four partner groups in one 72-inch StorEdge Expansion cabinet, two eight-port FC switches with five GBICs each.	1
Power cords	4

The key specifications of the Sun StorEdge T3 array are:

- Advanced architecture that uses full Fibre Channel connectivity, switched-loop design, and failover security
- Path failover with mirrored cache with hot-swap and redundant RAID controllers, power supplies, cooling fans, backup batteries, interconnect cards, and drives
- Modular flexibility combined with full, front-to-back fiber architecture allows configuration for high-transaction, high-bandwidth, or high-performance computing
- Compatible with Jiro™ technology for storage network interoperability and manageability
- Linear scalability to a massive 169 Tbytes on a single server
- Multiple platform failover support on a variety of host servers and operating systems
- Sun Remote Services (SRS) program support for continuous remote systems monitoring

The Sun StorEdge T3 array presents one or two logical unit numbers (LUNs) to a host. In the Solaris operating environment, LUNs are synonymous with single disks. Each LUN presents one disk in /dev/rdsk/c*t*d*s[0-7]. Each LUN can have a different RAID configuration. The Company can configure a disk in the array as a hot spare to improve MTTR in case of a disk failure in a data-protected LUN. LUN configurations can be created as follows:

- RAID 1—Minimum of two disks regardless of whether a hot spare is used. Up to eight disks with a hot spare. Up to nine disks without hot spare.

- RAID 5—Minimum of three disks (two data plus one parity). Up to eight disks (seven data plus one parity) with hot spare or nine disks (eight data plus one parity) without hot spare. Sun StorEdge T3 array hardware and firmware have been optimized for RAID 5. In most cases, RAID 5 outperforms RAID 1 or RAID 1+0.

- RAID 0—Single LUN with up to nine disks. No hot spare is possible because RAID 0 does not offer data protection. Use of RAID 0 is advised only in conjunction with an external form of data protection, such as host-based mirroring across two Sun StorEdge T3 arrays, or in the rare case when host-based RAID 5 stripes across multiple trays is used. This configuration is *not recommended* for highly available systems, since the mean time between failure (MTBF) of a single LUN configuration is 1/9th that of a single disk. Also, since the mean time to recover (MTTR) includes synchronization of up to 657 Gbytes, using 73-Gbyte disks, and can be excessive. This combination of low MTBF and high MTTR is the direct opposite of the desired state in a highly available system.

For shared disks in Sun Cluster environments, the LUN is the unit of control by the logical volume managers. For data services in which a shared nothing data model is used (every service except Oracle 8*i* OPS or Oracle 9*i* RAC), only one node can access the LUN at a time. You should consider this limitation in the design of systems in which the number of available LUNs in the Sun StorEdge T3 array limits the number of resource groups that can be implemented.

The modular architecture used in the Sun StorEdge T3 array allows either single or dual controller configurations. The single controller configuration has several SPOFs and only clusters with host-based mirroring support it. The dual controller configuration, also called partner pair, provides full redundancy. TABLE 6-7 summarizes several other implications of using the Sun StorEdge T3 array in clusters.

TABLE 6-7   Sun StorEdge T3 Array With Sun Cluster Configurations

Configuration		Analysis
Single controller	Pro:	Best performance because the controllers do not have to synchronize their caches.
	Con:	Many SPOFs. Requires host-based mirroring. May have high MTTR because of host-based mirror synchronization.
Dual controller (partner pair)	Pro:	Fully redundant configuration. Cache is mirrored between controllers. Redundant paths to disks are used.
	Con:	Mirrored cache synchronization has small impact on write performance.
	Con:	Controller boot time is nearly doubled because the master controller boots before the alternate controller.

Note – In the case of a failure, host-based mirroring across single Sun StorEdge T3 array controllers can take a long time to synchronize, thus increasing the MTTR of such configurations. Configuring the LUNs as RAID 1 or RAID 5 with a hot spare can significantly reduce the MTTR when a single disk fails.

Options

The Sun StorEdge T3 array system designed by the Company can be easily expanded over time. Disks can be upgraded as newer, denser, or faster disks become available. More Sun StorEdge T3 arrays can be added modularly to expand storage capacity or performance as required.

Options Considered But Discounted

Systems designers who need higher performance, minimized planned downtime, and higher availability should use Sun StorEdge T3 array single bricks that use host-based mirroring. Designers who need controller failover capabilities and better space utilization with hardware RAID 5 should use Sun StorEdge T3 array partner pair configurations.

Currently, the Sun StorEdge T3 array in the partner pair configuration can take as long as six minutes (worst case) to boot.

The Sun Cluster 3.0 software includes a cluster file system (CFS) that can be used instead of VxVM for Oracle 9*i* RAC clusters. However, Oracle 9*i* RAC does not currently support the CFS.

The Sun StorEdge T3 array is available in a desktop configuration. As discussed previously, it is better to place highly available systems in racks so you can control the mechanical configuration.

Network Interconnects

Network interconnects, also called private networks, are connections between cluster nodes used for internode cluster-related traffic. Public networks are network connections to other systems. This terminology can be confusing, especially when multiple public networks are being used. For example, backup networks, system administration networks, demilitarized zone (DMZ) networks, and user networks are all considered public networks from the Sun Cluster software perspective. Sun Cluster systems are not supported as gateways between networks.

Oracle 9i RAC is a service that depends on the performance of the cluster interconnect for scalability. DLM traffic (small packet) and data (large packet) traffic are sent over the interconnects. Sun Cluster 3.0 software supports a minimum of two and a maximum of six private cluster interconnects. All interconnects must be accessible by all nodes. Network switches are used for clusters with more than two nodes. The Sun Cluster software will multiplex its internode traffic across the cluster interconnects. This increases the bandwidth between the cluster nodes though it does not necessarily decrease latency between them.

Scalability in Oracle 9i RAC depends on the latency and bandwidth for the internode traffic. The Sun Cluster 3.0 software allows improvements mentioned previously to increase bandwidth. But the latency imposed by bandwidth, called the payload latency, is only one of the contributors to overall interconnect latency. The other contributors include length of cables, signalling technology, and overhead required for packets. Generally, the only way to reduce this latency is to change the interconnect technology. Currently, Sun Cluster 3.0 supports Sun Quad FastEthernet (100BASE-T) and Gigabit Ethernet FC-AL/P Combination Adapter (1000BASE-SX or 1000BASE-T) interconnects.

The Company uses separate backup, system administration, and user networks. The new system integrates seamlessly into the existing network structure. FIGURE 6-12 shows the cluster network design.

Cache fusion is a good fit for applications requiring parallel operations on resources. However, a small amount of latency still exists when standard IP-based network technology is used for the cluster interconnect. Message passing on the interconnect usually occurs on the UDP/IP network protocol stack. This is more efficient than using the TCP/IP protocol stack, since the UDP/IP protocol stack is optimized for reliable networks. The TCP/IP protocol stack contains protocol overhead to help ensure delivery on unreliable networks. In this context, the reliability of the network is based on the routes and packet sizes permitted or fragmentation required to pass through remote gateways. Also, in this context, the cluster interconnect is considered reliable; thus the lower latency UDP/IP protocol stack is a good choice.

The Company decided to use two Gigabit Ethernet cards as the node interconnects. This choice provides the highest bandwidth of the currently available technologies. It also is identical to the other network infrastructure in use, thus simplifying management and leveraging existing staff competencies.

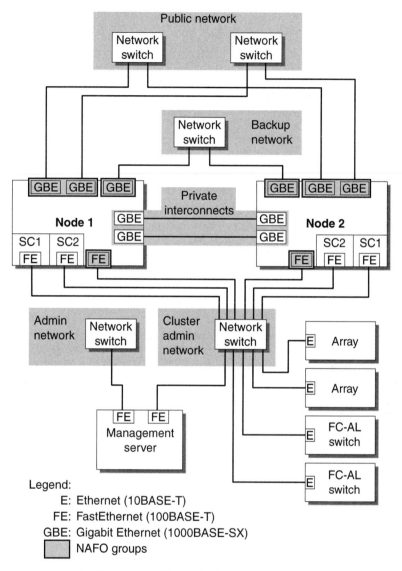

FIGURE 6-12 The Company's Network Design

Options

A few spare PCI slots are available. In the future, the Company can use these slots to add cluster interconnects if the capacity plan requires additional interconnect bandwidth.

Options Considered But Discounted

The Company considered using FastEthernet as additional node interconnects. This is possible because the connection to the administration network is FastEthernet. If these interconnects are implemented with a Quad FastEthernet card, three spare FastEthernet connections exist. However, such a configuration complicates the sizing and capacity planning for the interconnect traffic. Thus, the Company will implement any additional interconnects with Gigabit Ethernet, which is consistent with the original configuration.

Environmental Requirements

The data center environment must be properly maintained to support highly available systems. This section describes the power, temperature, and humidity issues that must be considered. The Company has taken these considerations into account in the design of their hardened, primary data center.

Power Sources

The Sun Fire 4800 server is installed in a Sun Fire cabinet. This cabinet uses a sophisticated redundant transfer unit (RTU) that can choose between power sources to provide power to the entire cabinet. Four independent 30-amp single-phase redundant transfer switch (RTS) modules (two per RTU) supply AC power to the systems. Each RTU supplies power to three bulk AC to 48 VDC power converters configured in an N+1 redundant mode; two of the three converters must be functioning to power each system. FIGURE 6-13 shows the Sun Fire cabinet power distribution.

Separate circuit breakers, located on isolated power grids, supply the dual AC connections to the RTU. The building that houses the primary data center does not have feeds from separate power sources—only one transformer and power grid supplies the entire building. Since separate power sources are not available, an uninterruptible power supply (UPS) unit with a diesel-fueled generator is connected to one RTS module to provide power in the event of a grid power failure.

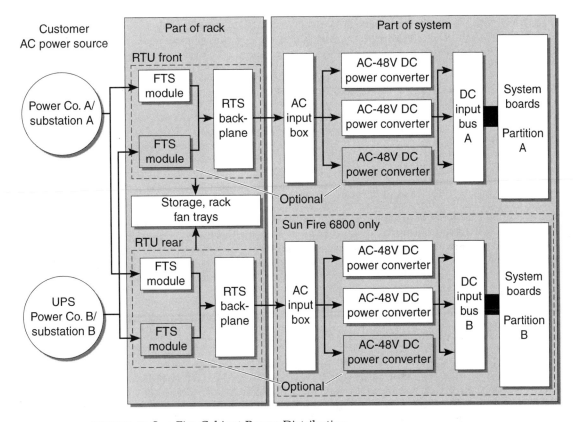

FIGURE 6-13 Sun Fire Cabinet Power Distribution

RTUs have no single point of failure. All the failover logic is in the redundant RTS modules. Each RTS module is hot-swappable and has service LEDs for serviceability.

The RTU is a very fast switch with microprocessor control and decision-making programming to take an incoming feed from either one power source or the other. It monitors the health of incoming power and can switch between a failing feed and a good feed before the system would experience a *brownout*. This feature provides a reliable, single, AC source that can also be used by peripherals with single AC input cables. Exceptional redundancy and real-time checking are built into the RTU to meet stringent safety requirements.

The RTU communicates with the system controller through a FrameManager to provide information on the status of AC power. The system controller also controls the RTU to facilitate service procedures. Monitoring the AC power status is a normal part of the operations of the data center. Alarms alert the operators to important changes.

To prevent catastrophic failures, the design of the power system ensures that all systems in the data center receive adequate power. Dedicated AC breaker panels are in place for all power circuits that supply power to each system. These installations comply with applicable local, state, regional, or national electrical codes.

By default, the Sun Fire 4800 server has three power cords. This does not supply fully redundant power to both RTUs. To help ensure adequate power, the Company added a fourth RTS and power cord.

Ambient Temperature

An ambient temperature range of 70°F to 74°F (21°C to 23°C) is optimal for system reliability and operator comfort levels. Most computer equipment can operate within a wide temperature range, but a level near 72°F (22°C) is desirable because it is easier to maintain safe associated relative humidity levels at this temperature. The Company implements multiple HVAC systems to provide $N+1$ redundancy. An electronic system that can generate alerts when the equipment is not performing properly monitors the HVAC systems.

Ambient Relative Humidity

Ambient relative humidity levels between 45 percent and 50 percent are the most suitable for safe data processing operations. Under certain circumstances, most data processing equipment can operate within a fairly wide environmental range (20 percent to 80 percent), but the optimal goal should be between 45 percent to 50 percent for several reasons:

- This range helps protect computer systems from corrosion problems associated with high humidity levels.

- This range provides the greatest operating time buffer in the event of environmental control system failure.

- This range helps avoid failures or temporary malfunctions caused by intermittent interference from static discharges that occur when relative humidity is too low.

Electrostatic discharge (ESD) is easily generated and less easily dissipated in areas in which the relative humidity is below 35 percent and becomes critical when levels drop below 30 percent. The 5 percent relative humidity range may seem unreasonably tight when compared to the guidelines used in typical office environments or other loosely controlled areas, but it is not difficult to maintain in a data center because of the high-efficiency vapor barrier and low rate of air changes normally present.

Backup, Restore, and Recovery

The Company uses multiple backup-and-restore packages for the systems in the data center. At one time, the Company attempted to standardize on a single backup and restore software package for all systems. The problem was that a single software package that supports many heterogeneous systems can never be tightly integrated with any of the systems. The advantage of this loose integration is that migration of data between systems is relatively easy and the Company preserves its investment in training. The disadvantage of the loose integration is that the MTTR for recovering the boot environment of a system is longer; an operating system must first be loaded, followed by the backup software package to restore the boot environment. The Company solves this by using both the native backup for the boot environment and a heterogeneous backup system, Sun StorEdge™ Enterprise NetBackup. The boot environments are backed up by using both. Other data is primarily backed up by using Sun StorEdge Enterprise NetBackup.

The company backs up the Solaris operating environment and boot environment two ways—a ufsdump is written to the local tape, and a Sun StorEdge Enterprise NetBackup copy is scheduled daily. The system operator generates a ufsdump in conjunction with the Solaris operating environment fssnap utility. A separate ufsdump to local tape is written before and after any scheduled maintenance. The use of fssnap allows a consistent copy of the boot environment to be backed up, even when the system is fully operational and the boot environment files are changing. The Sun StorEdge Enterprise NetBackup copies are made to facilitate recovery of individual files from a given date. This type of backup is difficult to accomplish with ufsdump. However, in an emergency, the recovery of a ufsdump of the boot environment is much faster than the same recovery using Sun StorEdge Enterprise NetBackup. Thus the ufsdump has a lower MTTR for the boot environment than Sun StorEdge Enterprise NetBackup.

Note – The Solaris boot environment for Sun Cluster 3.0 systems includes both the root file system, /, and the /global file system.

The company uses Sun StorEdge Enterprise NetBackup to back up the Oracle 9i RAC environment and database. For normal backup operations, the Company only does the backups on the disaster recovery system located at the secondary data center. The secondary system has directly attached tape drives to facilitate rapid backup and restore. Thus the primary cluster is not required to back up the Oracle environment or database every day. For ad hoc recoveries, the secondary site provides the recovery data.

In case of a disaster exercise or actual disaster, the secondary site contains the primary service point. There is no change in the backup procedures at the secondary site. When the primary site is to be brought back online, the latest tapes are physically shipped from the secondary site to the primary site. The Oracle environment and database are restored to the primary site cluster with a network-attached backup server. This operation can take several hours or days. When the primary site is ready to go online, the changes made at the secondary site are applied, bringing the primary site up to date. When the primary site cluster is synchronized and ready for service, users are redirected to the primary site cluster.

Options

Many options are available to the Company for backup, restore, and recovery. Fortunately, you can decouple these from the system design. Decoupling these options enables you to phase in improvements in storage technology as they become economically feasible.

Options Considered But Discounted

Backups can be made of the Oracle environment and database at the primary site with directly attached tape drives. However, this approach complicates the cluster design, since tape drives are not random access devices, making them difficult to cluster reliably. This solution also places a performance penalty on the database while the backup is being done. This penalty is not so much on CPU or memory, but on disk contention. A properly designed backup system exposes the slowest link in the hardware chain. This link is usually the disk drives, tape drives, or network (in the case of backups across a network.) Many system and database tuning procedures concentrate on the performance of the disks. Any additional disk contention causes a measurable performance penalty.

Using a network connected to a backup server is possible. However, as the size of the data grows, network backups do not scale well. Directly attached tape drives can back up at near media speed. Currently, a single Gigabit Ethernet network can only supply a small number of tape drives operating at media speeds. Thus, the network is the backup bottleneck. This option also suffers from the performance impact similar to that of the direct attached tape drive scenario described previously.

Summary

In this chapter we described a case study to provide a solution for a highly available Oracle 9i RAC database service. The business case drove the requirements of high availability and expansion options. The selected solution included Sun Fire 4800 servers and StorEdge T3 arrays.

The software environment of the Oracle 9i RAC database was described in detail. Oracle cache fusion was examined along with its arbitration, migration, and database lock recovery methods. The synchronization methods used by cache fusion are very similar to the directory-based coherency protocols used in other computer systems components. These cache fusion synchronization methods were described in some detail, though you are encouraged to refer to the Oracle documentation on the subject.

You can use this case study as a reference for designing clusters that use Sun mid-range servers.

Sun Cluster 3.0 Design Checklists

The design checklists in this appendix can help you keep the business requirements in focus while proceeding with your Sun Cluster 3.0 design. You can use these checklists as general, high-level design guidelines for Sun Cluster 3.0 systems.

Remember that the details of component versions, patches, interoperability, and support change regularly. The latest configuration matrices and version information are available from the Sun Service providers.

This appendix contains the following checklists:

- Business Case Considerations
- Personnel Considerations
- Top-Level Design Documentation
- Environmental Design
- Server Design
- Shared Storage Design
- Network Design
- Software Environment Design
- Security Considerations
- Systems Management Requirements
- Testing Requirements

Business Case Considerations

The business case describes the reason for building the system, the expected costs, and the expected return on investment. In many cases, this list also includes the service level agreement (SLA). As the service level approaches continuous availability or 100 percent service availability, the costs increase dramatically. With today's technology, it is virtually impossible to expect 100 percent service availability, so you must weigh a reasonable expectation of service availability against the cost of availability. Here are the business-related tasks you must perform:

- ❑ Define the project.
- ❑ Identify the stakeholders.
- ❑ Identify the customers.
- ❑ Develop high-level data flow and work flow diagrams that describe the customer processes and how they are enhanced by the system under design.
- ❑ Identify critical applications.
- ❑ Determine the business risks.
- ❑ Define the metrics for success.
- ❑ Determine availability requirements for each critical application. These may vary widely depending on when the users require access to the service.
- ❑ Determine recovery requirements. You can describe these requirements as the mean time to recover (MTTR) for each critical application.
- ❑ Determine planned maintenance requirements, maintenance windows, time zone considerations, and regular and emergency maintenance processes.
- ❑ Determine the performance requirements.
- ❑ Negotiate SLAs with the customers.
- ❑ Identify the suppliers.
- ❑ Verify that the suppliers can deliver appropriate service and support to match the SLA.
- ❑ Determine an implementation timeline and expected project life cycle.

Personnel Considerations

Do not overlook the personnel who are more important for delivering highly available services than hardware or software. To achieve highly available service, you must design, implement, and maintain the system properly. Personnel can represent single points of failure (SPOFs), too. For example, if a system architect or designer leaves the company, the remaining staff may not be able to maintain the system in a manner that delivers highly available services. You must put in place personnel processes that eliminate the "personnel SPOFs":

- Implement a safety program. Train all personnel on safety features and processes.
- Build a *team* to design, implement, and maintain the system.
- Document the system design and share the design information with all team members.
- Train all operators and maintenance personnel on the system implementation and function of all major components.
- *Arbitration* problems can occur with personnel. It is important that the personnel responsible for delivering the highly available services are identified and understand their responsibilities. Also, the authority to make decisions that affect the design or operation of the highly available services must reside with the responsible people—"Every ship needs a captain and every airplane needs a pilot."
- Clearly identify the chain of command. All team members should know the key decision makers.
- Implement a delegation-of-authority process to provide continuous coverage.
- *Synchronization* problems occur with personnel much like they do in computer systems. Establish clear, consistent, and regular communication among the various team members. This communication is essential for success. Also, include a process in the user SLA for alerting the users when an event that can directly affect them occurs.
- Implement redundant communication methods for team members—meetings, conference calls, email aliases, cell phones, pagers, chat rooms, instant messaging, bulletin boards, and so forth.
- Implement authoritative communication channels to end users—message of the day, newsletter, system status web site, bulletin board, email aliases, and so forth.

Top-Level Design Documentation

Clearly show the major components and the services provided by the system in the top-level design. Here are the top-level design documentation tasks you must perform:

- Describe the major components and their relationships.
- Describe the user interfaces and interfaces to other computer systems, factories, stakeholders, and so forth.
- Describe the business process flows through the system.
- Determine the dependencies on external systems.
- Develop a disaster recovery plan.
- Identify the required "soft" infrastructure services—synchronized time Network Time Protocol (NTP), network management (Simple Network Management Protocol (SNMP)), systems management (Solaris web-based enterprise management (WBEM)), backup, restore, archive, directory, and so forth.
- Identify the required "hard" infrastructure services—venue, physical access, and so forth.

Environmental Design

You should design the venue that contains the components of a highly available system to reduce or eliminate outages that are the result of environmental effects. Loss of power, excessive heat, floods, and fire can cause system outages. Place the system in a location where people can work safely. Consider the following environmental design tasks and features:

- Define the procedures to be used when an environmental failure occurs. Test these procedures regularly.
- Implement redundant power sources. Uninterruptible power supplies (UPSs), generators, and multiple power grid connections help provide power supply redundancy. If possible, use separate power feeds with different paths to multiple substations to help eliminate the failure mode in which a substation power failure occurs.
- Implement an automatic switchover to alternate power sources. Automatic transfer switches (ATSs) are preferred over manual switches for switching between multiple power sources.

- Implement automatic monitoring and alarms, and multiple air cooling units, if possible. Proper cooling requires both temperature and relative humidity control.
- Monitor and control airborne contamination. Particulate matter and dust can clog air filters, causing excessive heat buildup. Conductive materials such as metal filings can cause short circuits. Corrosive materials such as salt spray and quicklime dust can cause failures in electrical components, wiring, and connectors.
- Use fire suppression equipment that does not cause permanent damage to electronic equipment—FM-200, halon (if permitted), carbon dioxide fire extinguishers, and so forth. In earthquake-prone areas, local codes may require equipment to be secured to the floor.
- Use flood and fire detectors and test them regularly. Natural disasters such as floods, fires, and earthquakes can cause system outages.
- Label all components clearly. Clear labeling is especially important for redundant systems because there are multiple, identical components. Good labeling helps prevent failure modes, such as the field service person turning off the power to service an active component.
- Implement a cable management system that clearly labels and routes cables. Secure the cables routed inside cabinets according to the manufacturer's specifications.
- Install all equipment according to manufacturers' specifications.
- Restrict physical access to the site and the system to help prevent accidents caused by unauthorized personnel.
- Perform high-level fault analysis of the data center infrastructure.

Server Design

Server design requires the analysis of many features and options. Generally, low-end servers have fewer availability features and options than high-end servers. Here are the server design features and options you must consider:

- Multiple power supplies in dual, $N+1$, or $2N+2$ redundant mode. Hot-swappable power supplies can reduce the MTTR.
- Multiple power inputs to the expansion racks and multiple power sequencers in the racks. Dual-grid options are available for some products.
- Automatic system recovery (ASR).
- Environmental monitoring and alarm capability.
- Hot-pluggable field-replaceable units (FRUs).

- Console access. For most Sun servers, this access is through the serial port. Some servers also offer Ethernet connections for console services. You can use a terminal concentrator to provide access to serial ports through the network. A single terminal concentrator can support many servers.

- Server key switches. These switches must be in "locked" position for production use.

- System server capacity. CPU, RAM, and I/O must be sufficient to handle the load in case a node fails. Also, consider the capacity required during the recovery of data services.

Shared Storage Design

Shared storage devices are devices connected to more than one host. Using the Sun Cluster 3.0 software, you can make these devices highly available. Shared storage devices differ from local storage devices that are directly connected to only one host. You can make local and shared storage devices globally available by using the Sun Cluster software; however, only shared storage can be made highly available to the cluster and be accessible when a node has failed. You can use any storage devices the node platform supports for local storage. Shared storage devices have additional restrictions. Some features of storage devices that contribute to increased availability are these:

- Dual redundant, $N + 1$, or $2N + 2$ power supplies.

- Internal battery backup or integrated UPS.

- Multiple power sources.

- Redundant or $N + 1$ cooling.

- Hot-pluggable FRUs.

- Hardware RAID controller with data-protected, nonvolatile cache.

- Multiple host support. This requires SCSI-2 reservation support or the equivalent for devices that support two hosts. Devices that support more than two hosts require SCSI-3 persistent group reservation (PGR).

- Spare disk drives that can be enabled when an active drive fails.

Before you complete your system design, verify support of shared storage, host bus adapter (HBA), and server configurations. Also, use reliability block diagram (RBD) analysis (see "Reliability Block Diagram Analysis" on page 240) to verify that the storage subsystem design provides reliable access to at least half of the storage devices.

Network Design

Highly available systems are often interconnected with other systems or networks. End-to-end system availability requires that all of the components provide reliable service. Here are the network design tasks you must perform:

- ❑ Document the network design. Sun Cluster systems tend to have many networks. Label cables to match the network design to help avoid cabling mistakes.

- ❑ Use network hubs or switches as interconnect junctions. Design these junctions to avoid potential common mode faults. For example, use separate power sources.

- ❑ Use highly available network design techniques. Use redundant and automatically recoverable network routers, and monitor the network equipment.

Software Environment Design

The software environment is critical to supporting highly available services. The software stack used in modern computer systems is complex and increasing in complexity faster than the hardware environment. Designing and maintaining a stable software environment is critical to providing highly available services. Here are the software environment design tasks you must perform:

- ❑ Maintain appropriate maintenance updates and patch levels on all software and firmware.

- ❑ Implement a patch or update validation and installation process. Ideally, the installation process should have rollback capabilities. For Sun systems, the PatchPro service, Sun Alert patch reports, and security bulletins are available on the http://sunsolve.sun.com web site.

- ❑ Implement a software upgrade process. You can use the Solaris LiveUpgrade software to manage upgrades and rollbacks with minimum disruption of service.

- ❑ Automate the software installation process. Use Solaris JumpStart and WebStart Flash technology to create and rapidly install customized software stacks.

- ❑ Simplify the boot disk layout. A simple, consistent boot disk layout can improve serviceability and ease software upgrades.

- ❑ Use appropriate resource management techniques to provide sufficient capacity to services that require rapid response times.

- ❑ Configure syslog to forward log notices to one or more log hosts.

- ❑ Enable system accounting.

- Use distributed naming services to simplify system administration and avoid unintended dependencies or SPOFs in the naming service design.
- Avoid dependencies on external systems that may not be reliable—network file system (NFS) mounts, name services, or Dynamic Host Configuration Protocol (DHCP.)
- Select a node name that describes the system. Cryptic node names can cause confusion and communication errors among personnel.

Security Considerations

Security is an important part of a highly available system. An insecure system is difficult to make highly available; unauthorized access can cause an outage, and recovering from a security breach can be very time consuming. Software environment security affects every part of the software stack. Any weak link can compromise the rest of the system. Here are the security features and options you must consider:

- Develop a comprehensive security strategy. This strategy should include physical as well as electronic security.
- Use passwords that are difficult to guess.
- Assign an account or login only to personnel who require access to the system.
- Do not share accounts; instead, share roles. Use appropriate grouping techniques such as UNIX groups or Solaris role-based access control (RBAC), for defining roles.
- Use encryption, when appropriate, to protect confidential or sensitive data.
- Implement written policies and procedures for handling security matters.
- Implement security hardening as appropriate.

Systems Management Requirements

Systems management includes processes and tools for effectively operating computer systems. A rule of thumb is that process problems cause 40 percent of outages. Good systems management processes can greatly reduce the occurrence and duration of outages. Here are the systems management tasks you must perform:

- Train all personnel who are responsible for implementing or operating the systems. Complex systems, such as clusters, require personnel trained to handle crisis situations.

- Produce and maintain runbooks. Store documentation in a library that has continuous access. Online access is convenient, but keep physical copies of important troubleshooting and recovery documentation.
- Archive system logs and accounting records for reference.
- Use the Sun Management Center software to monitor and manage Sun systems.
- Use web-based enterprise management (WBEM) and complex information manager (CIM) tools to manage Sun systems using web-based interfaces.
- Perform regular audits of system configurations.
- Use capacity planning tools to record trends in capacity usage, and use the Sun HighGround™ Storage Resource Manager to manage heterogeneous storage.
- Implement change control procedures for all systems management processes.

Testing Requirements

You must test systems and processes to ensure proper operation before rolling them into production environments. Consider the following test requirements:

- Implement a staging area for testing the environment of highly available services.
- Use test or staging systems for training operators and systems administrators for production systems. Test systems management processes before implementing them on production systems.
- Maintain a comprehensive set of tests and automated test suites. Extend this test suite to cover problems that have been encountered in previous outages to help prevent them from recurring.
- Implement an interoperability testing system to detect problems with integrating equipment or software.

Sun Cluster Technology History and Perspective

The first half of this appendix describes the evolution of the new Sun Cluster 3.0 product. It briefly describes the features and main release dates of the Sun clustering software that preceded the Sun Cluster 3.0 release—SPARCcluster™ PDB™ 1.*x*, Solstice HA 1.x, and Sun Cluster 2.x. The second half of this appendix contains brief descriptions of the features and capabilities of Sun Cluster 2.2 and contrasts them with the features and capabilities of Sun Cluster 3.0.

This appendix discusses the following topics:

- SPARCcluster PDB 1.x and SPARCcluster HA 1.x History
- Sun Cluster 2.x
- Sun Cluster 2.2 and 3.0 Feature Comparison

SPARCcluster PDB 1.*x* and SPARCcluster HA 1.*x* History

Before the release of Sun Cluster 2.0 in October 1997, Sun had two products that addressed different aspects of clustering— Sun SPARCcluster HA 1.*x* and Sun SPARCcluster PDB 1.*x*. The following sections outline the features, functions, and release histories of these two products.

SPARCcluster PDB 1.*x*

The Sun SPARCcluster PDB 1.0 system was announced in November 1994. This announcement marked Sun's initial entry into the clustering arena. However, first customer shipment was not until March 1995. Supported hardware configurations were very restrictive. This server supported only two-node configurations consisting of either SPARCserver™ 1000E or SPARCcenter™ 2000E systems running the Solaris 2.4 operating environment and using SPARCstorage™ model 100 or 200 arrays. Similarly, application support was limited to the Oracle 7.1.6 Parallel Server (OPS).

The only common feature between Sun SPARCcluster PDB and an Oracle 8*i* OPS or Oracle 9*i* RAC solution in Sun Cluster 3.0 is the continued use of the VERITAS Cluster Volume Manager (CVM) product to control concurrent access to the underlying storage. Originally, the CVM was a separate product, but it is now incorporated in the core VERITAS Volume Manager (VxVM) product as a licensable feature.

The Sun SPARCcluster PDB 1.1 system was announced in January 1996. New features included a multithreaded DLM to improve performance and CVM Dirty Region Logging (DRLs) to speed up recovery. The latest release of Oracle Parallel Server, v7.3.2, was also supported then.

Following the release of the new UltraSPARC-based Enterprise servers, the product was rebranded as Ultra Enterprise™ Cluster PDB and version 1.2 was announced in October 1996. It supported the Ultra Enterprise 2, 3000, 4000, 5000, and 6000 servers, as well as the older generation SPARCserver 1000E and SPARCcenter 2000E systems, and required the use of the Solaris 2.5.1 operating environment. Support for Informix OnLine XPS 8.10 and Sybase MPP 11.0 parallel databases was added, along with low-end SCSI-based MultiPack storage configurations, rather than the more expensive, fiber channel SPARCstorage array. A new Scalable Coherent Interface (SCI) interconnect was also introduced as an alternative to FastEthernet. A system monitoring capability was delivered by integrating Sun SyMON™ into the system. Version 1.2 was the final release of the product before its functionality was merged into Sun Cluster 2.0.

SPARCcluster HA 1.*x*

The Sun SPARCcluster HA 1.0 server was announced in July 1995. The first customer shipments were in October that year. Unlike the Sun SPARCcluster PDB server, this software focused on making standard applications highly available rather than on running parallel applications. The fault management software used by the Sun SPARCcluster HA server was known as Solstice HA. Because this software effectively defined the product, it was often referred to by this name rather than as SPARCcluster HA.

The initial release supported HA-NFS version 2 (with lock recovery) and HA-Oracle 7 with IP failover. This support was achieved through a series of fault monitors that are conceptually identical to those used in Sun Cluster 3.0. Unlike SPARCcluster PDB, SPARCcluster HA used Solstice DiskSuite 4.0 to provide volume management functions.

Hardware and software requirements for Sun SPARCcluster HA 1.0 were very similar to Sun SPARCcluster PDB 1.0. Clusters were limited to two-node configurations, using only SPARCserver 1000E or SPARCcenter 2000E systems (mixed node clusters were not supported) running under the Solaris 2.4 operating environment. Storage was provided by SPARCstorage model 100, and later, 200 arrays using 10BASE-T, 100BASE-T, or FDDI for the cluster interconnects. Unlike Sun Cluster 3.0, SPARCcluster HA 1.0 had no HA-API toolkit to extend the product.

The 1.1 release, scheduled for May 1996, was never publicly released. Instead, new features were deferred until release 1.2 in October 1996. These features included:

- Support for the new Sun Enterprise™ 2, 3000, 4000, 5000, and 6000 servers. These servers were also supported in mixed configurations.

- A new HA-API toolkit, to allow additional services to be developed

- Support for Informix Online XPS 7.0 and Sybase MPP 11.0 database software

- Solaris 2.5.1 operating environment as the minimum operating system release for the product

The final release of Ultra Enterprise HA 1.3 server in April 1997 saw the product rebranded along lines similar to the Ultra Enterprise PDB product. Features included:

- Support for SPARCstorage™ RSM™ 214 arrays, as well as multipacks for low-end Enterprise 2 clusters

- Support for Solstice DiskSuite 4.1. This support introduced the concept of mediators for dual-disk string configurations. Previous generations required a minimum of three arrays.

- Added support for Netscape Internet Services

- Support for FDDI as a cluster interconnect, allowing nodes to be 2 kilometers apart when Fibre Channel arrays were used.

No new hardware or software was qualified on the product except the Solaris 2.6 operating environment.

Sun Cluster 2.x

The Sun Cluster 2.0 product was released in October 1997. This release began to merge the features offered by SPARCcluster PDB 1.2 and Solstice HA 1.3 software. This effort took 18 months, culminating in the Sun Cluster 2.2 release.

The initial Sun Cluster 2.0 release supported the following features:

- VERITAS Volume Manager (VxVM) only

- VERITAS File System (VxFS) was required to provide file system logging because Solstice DiskSuite was not supported
- Solaris 2.5.1 support, with Solaris 2.6 support following in December of that year
- Support for Ultra Enterprise 1, 2, 3000, 4000, 5000, 6000, and 10000 and SPARCcenter 1000E and 2000E
- Up to four nodes in an $N+1$ storage topology
- Agent support for Oracle 8i OPS parallel RDBM, Informix XPS, Sybase MPP, Netscape (news, web, and mail), DNS, and NFS
- Support for Sun RSM Array™ 2000 and Sun Enterprise Network Array™ A5000 (as it was then known, before the StorEdge rebranding)
- An HA-API for writing custom agents

Sun Cluster 2.1 was released in April 1998 and added support for the following:

- Solaris 2.6 operating environment
- Two-way initiated Sun StorEdge A3000 array
- A scalable storage topology supporting up to four nodes, using the Sun StorEdge A5000
- Clustered pair and ring storage topologies
- Four-node Oracle OPS implementations
- Sun Enterprise 450 and Sun Enterprise 3000 support with disk multipack
- Year 2000 compliance
- Sun Quad FastEthernet for both public and private networks
- Public Network Monitor and NAFO
- An HA-SAP agent
- A third-party IBM DB2 agent

The first release of Sun Cluster 2.2, in April 1999, completed the planned merger and added support for:

- Solaris 7 operating environment
- The Netra t1120 and Netra t1125 servers
- Sun Gigabit Ethernet as a public network
- New HA agents for Tivoli, Lotus Notes, BEA Tuxedo, and Netscape Lightweight Directory Access Protocol (LDAP)
- Volume management using either Sun StorEdge Volume Manager (VxVM) or Solstice DiskSuite
- Campus clusters separated up to 10 kilometers using Sun StorEdge A5000 arrays

Two subsequent product updates, known as Solaris 8 4/00 and Solaris 8 7/00, respectively, occurred in April and July 2000. These updates added support for newly released hardware and software.

Sun Cluster 2.2 and 3.0 Feature Comparison

Sun Cluster 2.2 and Sun Cluster 3.0 are fundamentally different products, despite having very similar goals—provision of highly available and scalable application services. The differences stem from the fact that Sun Cluster 2.2 is predominantly a layered product, using a combination of programs, shell scripts, and daemons to achieve its goals. In contrast, Sun Cluster 3.0 is highly integrated with the Solaris 8 operating environment and delivers much of its functionality through kernel modules and agents. The common feature between the two products is the implementation of application fault monitors in the future.

Starting with the low-level components, such as the cluster interconnects and kernel drivers, this section describes the features that Sun Cluster 2.2 delivered and contrasts them with the features offered by Sun Cluster 3.0.

Cluster Interconnects

Both the Sun Cluster 2.2 and Sun Cluster 3.0 products require dedicated networks between the constituent cluster nodes for the exclusive use of the cluster framework. These networks provide the infrastructure for the transmission of heartbeat messages to determine connectivity between nodes, application-level messages, and data transfer for the new Sun Cluster 3.0 global features (for example, transmission of application and data transfer messages for the Oracle 8i OPS DLM and the Oracle 9i RAC cache fusion data).

Sun Cluster 2.2 requires two private connections to provide a backup level of resilience. Sun Cluster 3.0, however, supports a minimum of two and a maximum of six private interconnects because of the higher demands that the new global features place on the system. This means that, potentially, a Sun Cluster 3.0 system can tolerate more interconnect failures before it has to fence off a node that can no longer communicate with its peers.

FIGURE 3-5, FIGURE 3-6, and FIGURE 3-7 show the types of cluster topologies Sun Cluster 3.0 supports—Clustered Pair, N+1, and Pair+M. Sun Cluster 2.2 supports a ring topology that is not supported by Sun Cluster 3.0. Sun Cluster 2.2 does not support the scalable Pair+M topology.

Switch Management Agent

The Sun Cluster 2.2 switch management agent daemon, smad, is a user-level daemon responsible for managing communication sessions on the private interconnects. It is also dependent on a kernel module, called smak, that can be loaded. The smad communicates with its peers by sending and receiving UDP packets at regular intervals. This process is often described as the cluster heartbeat. This process differs from the lower level DLPI mechanism used by Sun Cluster 3.0. When SCI is used, smad also performs the heartbeat checks on these links.

In Sun Cluster 2.2, the physical network interfaces on the private interconnects are assigned IP addresses in the range of 204.152.65.1 to 204.152.65.20. These are Sun-registered, private, nonroutable network numbers. The smad process then configures an additional logical IP address in the range of 204.152.65.33 to 204.152.65.36 on one of the physical network interfaces. If a physical link fails, smad migrates the logical link to the alternate physical interface, allowing processes that depend on the IP link to continue uninterrupted. If both links fail, smad signals the cluster membership monitor to initiate a cluster reconfiguration.

Membership Monitor

Membership is an important concept for any platform that tries to execute state-based applications in a distributed computing environment. Without careful coordination, applications can be started more than once without each other's knowledge. The resulting uncontrolled access to the underlying data structures causes data corruption.

The cluster membership monitors (CMMs) of the two product releases are substantially different. Both CMMs use the concept of membership to prevent split-brain syndrome. However, the Sun Cluster 2.2 version does not protect against amnesia, as the Sun Cluster 3.0 CMM does. Instead, this function is left to the cluster configuration database (CCD) daemon, described in subsequent paragraphs. Similarly, Sun Cluster 2.2 implements the CMM as a user-level daemon known as clustd, whereas Sun Cluster 3.0 implements the CMM as a highly available kernel agent. When the CMM is engaged (the return step of the cluster state machine), all pending I/O to the shared cluster storage is complete and the system blocks new I/O, pending the outcome of the membership changes.

The Sun Cluster 2.2 CMM rules for deciding the outcome of membership changes are fairly complex. See the rules and scenarios in the *Sun Cluster Environment Sun Cluster 2.2* book [SunSCE01], page 60 onward. This is due, in part, to the fact that Sun Cluster 2.2 design uses SCSI-2 disk reservation rather than SCSI-3 persistent group reservations (PGR), thus restricting its ability to fence off multihosted disks in a scalable cluster storage topology.

To guarantee data integrity, failure fencing is critical. Because SCSI-2 reservations are binary, a valid cluster node with rightful access to the data can be fenced off in a scalable storage topology. To guarantee that failed nodes in a scalable storage topology are fenced off, the Sun Cluster 2.2 CMM uses a "shoot down" mechanism that connects the nodes to their console ports, through the terminal concentrator, and forcibly halts the nodes. This shoot-down mechanism is the only mechanism that ensures that failure fencing works. When nodes are already down, because of a power outage, the CMM pauses cluster operation pending authority from the system administrator to continue a partition. The Sun Cluster 3.0 system does not require system administrator intervention for this condition.

The Sun Cluster 2.2 CMM algorithm is driven primarily by cluster membership transitions, rather than an overall vote count, as is Sun Cluster 3.0. Similarly, the disk fencing and quorum disk algorithms depend on the volume management product (Solaris Volume Manager (SVM) or VxVM) and storage topology used. "Quorum Voting" on page 214 and "Failure Fencing" on page 215 describe the potential outcomes in more detail.

To simplify the description of the results of the CMM algorithm, the concept of a *partition* is introduced here. A partition is a subcluster consisting of any number of nodes from the previous working cluster. The CMM bases its decisions on the concept of *majority partition* and *minority partition*. A majority partition has at least $N/2+1$ of the N nodes participating in the previous working cluster, whereas a minority partition has less than $N/2$ nodes.

With storage topologies that are not scalable, any partition that has less than a majority aborts and any partitions with a majority continue automatically. When a partition contains exactly half the nodes and it was initially a two-node cluster, an arbitration process is required to break the impasse. Then a quorum disk is used to break the tie.

For Sun Cluster 2.x clusters that use a scalable storage topology, if a partition contains fewer nodes than needed for majority, the CMM waits for a total of `Exclude Timeout` + `Scalable Timeout1` seconds before trying to reserve the nominated quorum disks and terminal concentrator port. This delay allows other potentially larger partitions to form a new cluster first and shoot down this partition. If this partition is not shot down, and the minority partition successfully obtains the port and quorum disk, this partition continues as a cluster. Otherwise this cluster aborts.

When a majority partition exists, the partition attempts to acquire a lock on the terminal concentrator port, and then resets any nodes in the minor partition. If the partition fails to get a port lock, all the nodes of the partition abort. Finally, if both partitions consist of half the nodes, each partition attempts to obtain the port lock and subsequently shoots down the nodes in the other partition. Otherwise, the partition stalls pending operator assistance or uses a deterministic policy to decide which partition should continue.

Once the CMM has determined the new cluster members, it fences off any shared storage to prevent potential data corruption. The `clustd` process then continues to execute the remaining 12 reconfiguration steps, by calls to the `reconf_ener` program, during which the system reenables the I/O to the shared storage. The *Sun Cluster Environment Sun Cluster 2.2* book describes the 12 reconfiguration steps on page 44.

Quorum Voting

For Sun Cluster 2.2 clusters using VxVM as the volume management product, a nominated quorum disk provides the additional vote to break the deadlock. For nonscalable architectures, one quorum disk is defined between each pair of nodes. The two nodes connected to the quorum disk issue a SCSI-2 reservation `ioctl` on the shared device. Because the `ioctl` is atomic, only one call succeeds and gains the reservation. The other call fails and drops the node out of the cluster.

Cluster nodes use a similar mechanism at startup. When two nodes share a quorum disk, the first node to enter the cluster attempts to reserve the device to ensure that no other cluster is in progress. If this reservation fails, the node aborts out of the cluster. When the reservation succeeds, the node releases the reservation only when it can communicate successfully over the interconnect networks with the peer node that is sharing the quorum disk.

For scalable topologies, the preceding approach does not work. According to the preceding argument, the introduction of the second node would release the reservation, thereby creating the opportunity for an entirely separate cluster to form, by the same route, from the remaining nodes. As a workaround, a telnet process directed to a port on the terminal concentrator locks the port. While the session remains active, a cluster is in progress.

Clusters based on SVM use a different approach that combines failure fencing with split-brain resolution. Disk sets under the control of SVM have a continual SCSI-2 reservation on them. Any attempt to take control of a disk set currently owned by another node results in a reservation conflict and, subsequently, a node panic.

When a split-brain scenario occurs, each node releases the disk sets under its control and attempts to reserve the disk sets of the other node. This action causes at least one node to panic out of the cluster. The remaining node then re-establishes reservations on all disk sets it owns. The outcome of such a race is somewhat nondeterministic, but no more so than the race for the quorum disk under VxVM.

Failure Fencing

For nonscalable cluster topologies and topologies that use VxVM for volume management, failure fencing is achieved through SCSI-2 reservations. For the SVM approach, see "Quorum Voting" on page 214. The successful partition places a SCSI-2 reservation on all shared storage, protecting it from corruption by failed cluster nodes.

Successful partitions in a scalable topology use the shoot-down method described previously to fence off failed nodes. Once shut down, the fenced nodes are unable to join the cluster until they can communicate with an existing cluster over the private interconnects. Because no SCSI-2 reservations are used, the data is more vulnerable than it might be in a Sun Cluster 3.0 system.

By employing SCSI-2 reservations, the Sun Cluster 2.2 framework precludes the use of technologies such as alternate pathing (AP) and dynamic multipathing (DMP). In contrast, Sun Cluster 3.0 uses SCSI-3 PGR calls and can benefit from, and use, the new Solaris 8 Sun StorEdge Traffic Manager storage multipathing framework. This framework is also called multipathing I/O (MPxIO).

Cluster Configuration Database

Sun Cluster 2.2 stores its configuration information in a cluster configuration database (CCD). Like Sun Cluster 3.0, Sun Cluster 2.2 implements CDD as a set of flat text files stored on the root file systems of the respective cluster nodes and updated by using a two-phase commit protocol. The CCD files rarely take up more than a few kilobytes.

Because Sun Cluster 2.2 was not designed to use persistent keys on its quorum disks, the CCD is not completely protected against amnesia, that is, the uncertainty that the cluster configuration information being used might not be the latest version. The Sun Cluster 3.0 CCR, however, is completely protected. An explanation of the files and daemons used to implement the CCD helps to provide an insight into these limitations.

Nodes participating in a Sun Cluster 2.2 cluster do not boot directly into a cluster. Instead, they have to wait until they are explicitly directed to start, or join, a cluster by the system administrator issuing the scadmin(1M) command. This manual procedure creates a nondeterministic recovery time when the entire cluster must be rebooted.

The CMM of the node that starts a new cluster must first determine a number of facts, including the cluster name, the potential nodes and their IPs addresses, and what the nominated quorum disk is. To find this information, CMM consults the *cluster_name*. cdb file in the /etc/opt/SUNWcluster/conf directory. This file is not automatically replicated, so any changes to it must be propagated to other nodes—failure to do so can prevent a node from joining the cluster. The failure to manually propagate changes to the *cluster_name*.cdb file introduces the opportunity for latent faults.

The CCD is stored in two separate files located in the /etc/opt/SUNWcluster/ conf directory—a ccd.database.init file containing static information that allows the CCD to initialize and a ccd.database file for the dynamic data that changes when the cluster is running. A checksum protects the integrity of these files. A node is unable to join the cluster if the ccd.database.init files differ.

The ccd.database.init file effectively provides the Sun Cluster 3.0 CCR read-only mechanism (see "Cluster Configuration Control" on page 89); however, the ccd.database.init files are never updated.

The dynamic portion of the CCD, ccd.database, is updated by the user-level CCD daemon (ccdd). This update uses the two-phase commit protocol, implemented as RPCs over the cluster interconnects, to ensure that ccdd makes consistent updates to the cluster node CCD databases.

For any updates to occur, a majority of CCDs must be available. Effectively, that is a majority of cluster nodes running. If one node of a two-node cluster is not running, this restriction is inconvenient. To overcome this, you can configure a shared CCD database on two mirrored disks, dedicated to this purpose alone. Of course, this is a huge waste of space for such a small database. This copy of the data is stored in /etc/opt/SUNWcluster/conf/ccdssa/ccd.database.ssa; it is only active when one node is not participating in the cluster. Creating an extra copy of the CCD ensures that the majority requirements are always met because one node CCD copy plus the shared CCD copy holds two of the three existing copies of the data. This facility is only available to clusters that use VxVM for volume management.

Using a shared CCD in a two-node cluster prevents amnesia by ensuring that the latest information always is held in the ccd.database.ssa file. However, clusters with more than two nodes do not support the use of a disk-based, shared CCD. Instead, they must rely solely on the node's copies to attain majority. This still has the potential for a cluster to restart with the wrong, amnesiac, information in the CCD. A particular scenario in which this occurs is a four-node cluster with nodes A, B, C, and D. If changes are made to the CCD while D is shut down and then nodes A, B, and C are stopped and D is started, there is nothing to prevent D from using its erroneous CCD data, even though it cannot be updated.

Consequently, the Sun Cluster 3.0 implementation offers a far stronger guarantee that accurate configuration data is always being used. This assurance also comes without any additional management overhead—all the files it relies on are updated automatically. This method eliminates the manual intervention steps and greatly reduces the opportunities for latent configuration errors.

Data Services

Both cluster products can provide basic failover capabilities for crash-tolerant applications and support for parallel applications. However, Sun Cluster 2.2 lacks the new scalable services enabled by the global features introduced by the Sun Cluster 3.0 framework.

The terminology used between the two releases varies because of the inherently different capabilities and design philosophies of the two products. TABLE B-1 contrasts the terms the two releases use.

TABLE B-1   Sun Cluster 2.2 and 3.0 Terminology Differences

Sun Cluster 2.2	Sun Cluster 3.0
Data service, for example: Oracle or NFS	Resource type
Data service instance	Resource
Logical host	Resource group, but does not contain any disk sets
Disk sets (SVM) or disk group (VxVM), managed as part of the logical host	Device group, managed as a separate resource
Sun Cluster 2.2 logical hosts	N/A

Logical hosts are the basis for all Sun Cluster 2.2 highly available services except Oracle 8*i* OPS. A logical host contains one or more disk groups or disk sets, a logical IP address per subnet, and one or more applications, for example, Oracle, NFS, or a web server. A logical host is the smallest unit of service migration between nodes.

The obvious and immediately discernible difference between a logical host and a Sun Cluster 3.0 resource group is the necessary inclusion of the disk sets and disk groups within its definition. This requirement stems from the absence of global file service functionality in Sun Cluster 2.2. Instead, the 11th step of the cluster reconfiguration, driven by the CMM, imports the disk group/disk sets defined in the logical host, checks the file systems of the relevant volumes, and then remounts the volumes on the new host. All this work is handled by user-level processes such as vxdg(1M), metaset(1M), fsck(1M), and mount(1M).

When several applications share a single logical host, the failure of any of its applications, necessitating a logical host migration, results in all the applications being moved, regardless of their condition. When fine-grained control is required, separate logical hosts, each with its own disk groups and disk set, must be created to facilitate independent migration. Sun Cluster 3.0 does not require such an implementation, although without additional device groups, some of the resource groups incur some remote I/O. FIGURE B-1 shows the Sun Cluster 2.2 logical host.

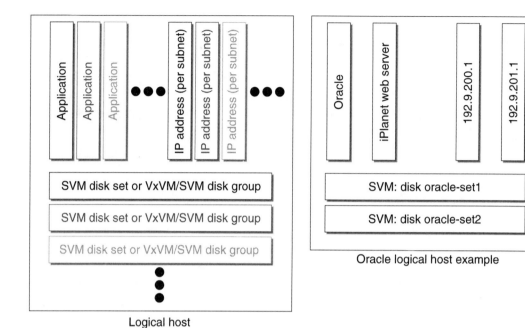

Logical host

Oracle logical host example

FIGURE B-1 Sun Cluster 2.2 Logical Host

Availability

By the time Sun Cluster 2.2 7/00 was released, a large collection of data services existed. The Sun and third-party agents included these services:

- Oracle Enterprise Server and Applications
- IBM DB2 Enterprise Edition
- Sybase ASE
- IBM Informix Dynamic Server
- Network File System (NFS)
- Domain name service (DNS)
- Solstice Internet Mail Server
- Apache web server
- iPlanet Enterprise, Messaging, News, and LDAP Servers
- SunPC™ NetLink
- SAP R/3
- Lotus Notes/Domino
- Tivoli Framework

- NetBackup
- BEA Tuxedo
- Open Market Transact
- Adabas

Custom agents could be created with the 1.0 HA-API; however, no equivalent of the SunPlex Agent Builder Wizard was available to speed development. Agents that required subtly different setting usually required the creation of multiple versions of the same scripts because the data service infrastructure lacked the Sun Cluster 3.0 resource type registration (RTR) file concept that allows so much of the parameterization of resource types. This shortfall causes considerable management and development overhead when you trying to maintain a single code base for an agent.

Control

A collection of programs and shell scripts that are registered with the cluster framework by the hareg(1M) command starts, stops, and monitors the data services defined in the logical host. Whenever the cluster is reconfigured, a callback mechanism executes these programs and scripts, during steps 11 and 12 of the cluster state machine.

Compared with the two options offered by the Sun Cluster 3.0 release, Sun Cluster 2.2 has no way to enforce strict data service dependency. The illusion of logical host dependency can be created, but only by the registration of the services in a specific order. Any subsequent change in any of these data services can break the artificial ordering.

Cluster Management

The management complexity of Sun Cluster 2.2 is substantially higher than Sun Cluster 3.0 management complexity because each data service relies on a number of disparate commands, for example, haoracle(1M) or hasybase(1M), hadsconfig(1M), rather than the uniform scrgadm(1M) interface in Sun Cluster 3.0. Sun Cluster 2.2 only has limited integration with Sun SyMON, the forerunner of the Sun Management Center.

Summary

Sun Cluster 3.0 corrected the deficiencies of Sun Cluster 2.2—improved failure fencing, cluster membership arbitration, amnesia protection, the ability to automatically boot into an operating cluster, and resource management. Sun Cluster 3.0 also improved the interface to the system management tools and added a wizard for writing agents.

Data Center Guidelines

This appendix contains data center design guidelines that have proved useful for supporting highly available services. This appendix covers these topics:

- Hardware Platform Stability
- Server Consolidation in a Common Rack
- System Component Identification
- AC/DC Power
- System Cooling
- Network Infrastructure
- Security
- System Installation and Configuration Documentation
- Change Control Practices
- Maintenance and Patch Strategy
- Component Spares
- New Release Upgrade Process
- Support Agreement and Associated Response Time
- Backup-and-Restore Testing
- Cluster Recovery Procedures

Hardware Platform Stability

System hardware provides the basis for the operating system and applications and, therefore, must have a solid foundation. A common source of system problems is related to loose mechanical connections resulting in intermittent problems manifested through hard-to-track error messages at both operating system and application levels. Subjecting the hardware platform to mechanical vibration could loosen components and change their electrical characteristics.

All connected components in a system must be correctly fitted and secured to ensure maximum mechanical contact to guarantee that the electrical characteristics remain constant. Memory and CPU components must be fully inserted and secured into sockets. I/O cards must be fully inserted into the self-identifying bus (SBus) or Peripheral Component Interconnect (PCI) connectors, and fully secured. External cables must be fully inserted and secured with the correct strain relief in place to ensure the cable weight does not strain internal components. Cables also have a specified minimum-bend radius that must be maintained. For optical fiber cables, the bend radius is especially important, since a minimum-bend radius violation will result in signal attenuation.

Server Consolidation in a Common Rack

Consolidating multiple servers in a single rack improves accessibility by simplifying system management. Each server in the rack should have independent I/O cabling and an independent power source. These measures can help to remove single points of failure and help to prevent accidental outages when the servers that share the rack are serviced.

System Component Identification

When system components must be replaced, fast and effective repairs greatly improve availability. Accurate system documentation and component identification are an investment that provides you with increased control over existing resources. System documentation allows you to plan future system changes without having to inventory existing resources repeatedly.

Each system platform comprises a large combination of components that may also be connected to network and storage devices. To prevent a technician from removing the wrong part, uniquely label each component, including cables, to ease the identification process. This identification can help ensure that only defective components are replaced. Replacing the wrong components can affect availability.

Solaris Device Labeling

The Solaris operating environment creates controller instances for each device under its control (for example, hme0, qfe1, c3, and so forth). For Sun Cluster systems, it is also useful to note the NAFO group for network devices and the global device ID (DID) for storage devices. A best practice is to identify controller instances on their physical controller ports.

For hard disk devices, the Solaris operating environment creates soft link entries in the /dev/dsk and /dev/rdsk directories. Hard disk devices are also registered as SCSI device (sd) and serial SCSI device (ssd) instances (for details, see the sd(7D) man page and ssd(7D) man page). The Sun Cluster software enables access to these devices as global devices.

The Solaris operating environment displays disk errors by using the controller and sd or ssd instances. The Solaris operating environment identifies tape devices through soft link entries in the /dev/rmt directory (see the st(7D) man page for details).

A best practice is to label storage devices with the controller and sd, ssd, or rmt instances, as well as DID instances at the replacement point to assist identification. These labels are especially important for clusters in which you may be required to service devices while the buses are active.

Interconnection Diagram

A best practice is to make an interconnection diagram that shows all external equipment (for example, storage platforms, routers, hubs, and client machines) of the system platform. Identify physical locations by creating a grid diagram of the data center (FIGURE C-1).

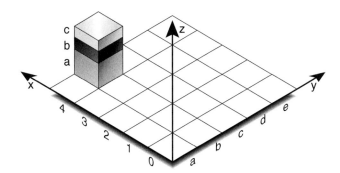

FIGURE C-1 Data Center Floor Plan Grid Diagram—System xyz Is Located at Grid Coordinate b4

The diagram should identify each piece of equipment with unique name labels and its physical location in the data center. The server location identification can have an additional entry to locate system or peripherals placed vertically within a rack. For example, b4c in FIGURE C-1 maps to a peripheral located on the third layer of a rack placed at the b4 coordinate. Ensure that devices on the same vertical layer do not have duplicate port IDs.

Component and Cable Labeling

To minimize service time frames, label cables to reflect their destination location. As an example, one of the private interconnect patch cables has a label of qfe4:b4a on one end to reflect the qfe4 connector located on the first vertical level of a rack placed at the b4 coordinate. The other end of the cable has the hme0:b4b label to reflect the hme0 connector located on the second vertical level of a rack placed at the b4 coordinate. To minimize the service time when a cable needs to be replaced, label each cable to reflect the location of the other end. Using the preceding example, one end of the cable would have the qfe4:b4a-hme0:b4b label; the other end would have the hme0:b4b-qfe4:b4a label. This example shows one method of consistently labeling cables. You are encouraged to use any method that can uniquely identify the cable end points.

AC/DC Power

A reliable power source is a basic requirement of a highly available system. Most computer equipment accepts commercially available alternating current (AC) power. Some equipment is designed to work with direct current (DC) power sources such as those found in telephone company central offices. Power supplies convert the AC or DC power to the DC levels required by the equipment.

In some cases, such as the Sun Enterprise 10000 server, the AC power is converted through bulk power supplies to 48 Volt DC, which is routed throughout the chassis. Programmable DC-to-DC converters are used to change the voltage to the levels required by internal components. Other Sun servers may have slightly different internal power distribution implementations. In all cases, the power and voltage levels should be consistent, reliable, and monitored.

Mission-critical data center devices are commonly equipped with multiple power cords to access alternate AC sources. Systems with high availability requirements should have data center power that comes from different power stations to remove potential SPOF.

Most power outages are brief; therefore, you can fulfill short-term power needs by using an uninterruptible power supply (UPS). The UPS battery should provide sufficient power to the system for a specified time period. Since a UPS converts a battery source to AC, it has the added advantage of smoothing any erratic output from a public utility power source (power conditioning).

Systems with higher availability requirements can use a diesel or natural gas generator to supply power for extended power failures. Since a generator requires time after starting to be fully functional, a UPS is still required to deliver power immediately following a public utility failure.

Position all power cords where they cannot be damaged or tripped over. Securing circuit breakers so that they are not accidentally tripped is critical. Availability can sometimes be enhanced with simple actions such as protecting circuit breakers so that personnel cannot accidentally actuate them and cause a power outage. When protecting exposed circuit breakers, provide enough space to allow free tripping of the breaker during a current overload.

System Cooling

Data center equipment must be operated within a specific temperature range. When cooling is not available in the data center, the only option is to shut down all equipment, since high temperatures can trigger irreversible damage to electronic components. Newer systems and devices generate more heat because they operate at faster clock speeds. Plan to have extra air conditioning units to handle any additional heat output.

Systems with higher availability requirements should have standby or portable air conditioning units on hand to avoid an entire data center shutdown for times when the cooling infrastructure is unavailable.

Network Infrastructure

Network infrastructure (switches, hubs, routers, and bridges) is considered external to the system and is commonly overlooked as being a key component of system availability. The network infrastructure enables communication between peer and client systems at the local area network (LAN) and wide area network (WAN) levels. Therefore, network infrastructure scalability and availability directly affect system availability, even in a clustered environment.

A best practice is to use the network adapter failover (NAFO) software that the Sun Cluster 3.0 infrastructure provides to improve availability of the public network controllers. This improvement is accomplished by switching all network I/O to an alternate controller if the system detects a failure. Most network product vendors are becoming aware of the high availability needs of network infrastructure and are providing switch and router redundancy schemes to improve availability and scalability.

Client connections can improve availability through an alternate WAN link, which uses independent telephone switching stations to avoid SPOFs.

Customers with higher availability requirements should subscribe to the Internet through two different service providers, or at least use separate access points with the same provider to remove another SPOF.

In some cases, the primary network can be a leased line with the backup networks using virtual private network (VPN) connections over the Internet. This enables relatively inexpensive alternate network paths, since the VPN connections can coexist with other network services. If this option is chosen, ensure that the Internet connections access points are, in fact, different from the leased-line connections. Because the quality of service of a VPN is not likely to be guaranteed, the VPN option is not a direct replacement for leased lines in all cases.

Security

In the past, security was mostly required by government and financial sectors. However, the e-commerce revolution is exposing more businesses to the potential of unauthorized access to confidential data and attacks by hackers or viruses.

Malicious hackers attempt to modify business data for the purpose of satisfying their own egos, whereas sophisticated hackers steal business data in an attempt to profit financially. Security breaches can result in partial outages, or even the total demise of an established business.

Denial of service (DoS) attacks involve malicious, repetitive requests into an application with the intention of depleting application and system resources. DoS attacks are less severe, from a security standpoint, than those attacks that interfere with data integrity or privacy. However, since a regular end user is not able to access an expected service during a DoS attack, there is an immediate effect on end-to-end application availability.

If you require Internet access, you should secure external connections by using these designs:

- Secure application architecture with built-in functionality to resolve DoS attacks

- Secure, hardened operating environment with minimized system builds
- Up-to-date security patches
- Chokepoints and proxies where appropriate.

For customers who require higher levels of security, Sun offers the Trusted Solaris™ product. This software supplies security features and assurances supported by the National Computer Security Center (NCSC) and the Defense Intelligence Agency (DIA). Organizations can implement the Trusted Solaris product with their own security-level options, or they can implement full security so users can perform administrative roles on their own workspaces. Currently, Sun Cluster 3.0 is not supported with the Trusted Solaris operating environment.

System Installation and Configuration Documentation

Initially, all system platforms can be accessed only through the OpenBoot™ PROM (OBP) prompt. After the system platform is correctly connected to the tape, disks, networks, and printers, the applications are installed in a series of sequential steps. The Sun Professional Services^{SM} group provides runbook services that produce detailed documentation and include suggested procedures to assist in configuring and managing a system platform.

The simplified system installation sequence is:

1. Install the Solaris operating environment.

2. Install the recommended Solaris operating environment patches.

3. Configure the operating environment tunable parameters in /etc/system.

4. Configure the networks, tape, printers, and disks.

5. Install and configure the volume manager.

6. Install the recommended volume manager patches installation.

7. Configure the system user.

8. Install and configure the software applications.

9. Install the recommended patches for the software applications.

Documenting any discrepancies or irregularities in this process is important because this documentation may prove invaluable as a resource for disaster recovery.

If all of the steps in the application installation are correctly documented, you can use this documentation to regenerate an entire system from scratch if disaster strikes. Additionally, you can use the system documentation to educate system administrators or to provide material for an implementation review.

Note – A documented backup and disaster recovery plan for all critical systems is important. Provide hard copy documentation as a backup to online documentation.

Some system administrators use the script(1) utility to capture the input and output generated during a software installation session. However, the script(1) approach generates excessive text, which can bury important content, and it lacks comments explaining why things must be done a particular way. However, a script(1) output can be edited to create an HTML document with appropriate comments. User responses can be highlighted by an alternate font or text style.

Sun provides the Solaris JumpStart product as an option to install system software and application components from the boot prompt without the risk of errors introduced by human interaction. Originally intended for installing the Solaris operating environment, the JumpStart framework can be extended to include almost any software or local modifications. The Solaris 8 4/01 operating environment release added a feature called Web Start Flash technology. This technology enables a prototype or existing system to be stored as a flash archive (flar) and subsequently installed by an automated JumpStart process. The installation is optimized to minimize the installation time and is significantly faster than installing with the pkgadd facility used for most JumpStart installations. The Web Start Flash technology is ideal for cloning or archiving systems.

Note – A best practice is to have the JumpStart framework automatically regenerate the entire system software infrastructure to enable recovery from any local disaster. You can use the JumpStart Flash technology to easily jump-start a heavily customized Solaris operating environment system.

Change Control Practices

Once the production system platform is stable and all applications are fully operational, any proposed system changes must go through a peer review to identify the impact of the changes and to provide a strategy for implementation.

Rebooting a system immediately after implementing any changes is recommended. This action helps to avoid latent configuration change errors such as typographical errors in the `/etc/system` file. Associating a failed reboot at some future time with previous modifications can be extremely difficult.

Data centers with higher availability requirements should have a production system mirrored by a test system (the mirror could be a scaled-down version of the production system) to implement and evaluate any changes before adoption. In some environments, the development system can also be used as a test system. Take care to isolate systems administration operations on the test system from the real production environment. An example of a system administration operation error: A customer mirroring an SAP manufacturing environment inadvertently generated a test production order, which resulted in the building of a $1.5 million piece of equipment.

Backing up a production system to tape or other persistent storage before you implement any changes is imperative. This backup enables restoration of the original system if the proposed modifications prove detrimental.

Maintenance and Patch Strategy

Sun introduces software patch releases regularly. SunSolve[SM] Online, `http://sunsolve.com`, offers a weekly email Patch Club report service for contract customers to provide a synopsis of current patches. Your local Sun Service provider can suggest additional mail alias subscriptions to notify users of released patches and their contents. You should review the provided patch information to decide if a patch is relevant for a particular production system. For example, some patches might involve I/O interfaces not used by the system or might involve a locality that does not apply.

Sun also provides the PatchPro services available at SunSolve Online. PatchPro services offer two methods for analyzing a system to provide a recommended patch list. The Patch Pro Interactive web site uses an interactive form to obtain a description of the system and then recommends patches. PatchPro Expert software is a Java applet that can be run in a Java-enabled browser to query your system interactively and correlate the configuration to the latest patch database.

You should collect and store all relevant patches, but only apply these patches on a three- or six-month schedule to keep systems current and to minimize any outage impact. Only critical patches that affect the condition of the production system should be applied immediately.

A best practice is to always install all required or recommended patches for:

- Solaris kernel update
- Sun Enterprise 10000 System system service processor (SSP), system controller (SC), lights-out management (LOM and LOMlite), and remote service controller (RSC)
- Sun Cluster software
- Storage management software—Solstice DiskSuite, Solaris Volume Manager, VERTITAS Volume Manager (VxVM), Raid Manager 6.0, and so forth
- Disk controller, disk storage array, disk drive firmware

Data centers with higher availability requirements can benefit from having patches applied to a test system to help analyze their full impact and to assist in a production rollout strategy. Sun Cluster 3.0 offers a limited capability to apply patches to an operational cluster without bringing the cluster down. Contact your local Sun service provider for details.

Component Spares

If spare components are available in the data center, you can reduce the repair time. Sun Microsystems emphasizes the importance of engineering interchangeable components for use with different system platforms. This strategy enables a reduced spare component inventory.

System components have a higher probability of failure in their early and late life periods. Similar to the strategy used by rental car companies, a strategy for customers with higher availability requirements is to take the proactive approach of recycling components that are reaching their wear-out stage, to avoid the exponential frequency of component failures [VargasOL00].

Note – To arrive at a spare component strategy that best matches data center availability needs, you must contact a service representative.

New Release Upgrade Process

Software products evolve over time, with new and enhanced features becoming available with each version release. Similar to the patch evaluation process, your process should be to review and evaluate new software product releases to determine the business impact.

Additionally, as with patches, systems with higher availability requirements can benefit from applying new software releases to a development system to help analyze their benefits and to plan the production rollout strategy.

Data centers with higher availability requirements can also benefit by applying patches to a test system to analyze their full impact and to assist in the rollout strategy. Sun Cluster 3.0 offers a limited capability to apply patches to an operational cluster without bringing down the cluster. Contact your local Sun service provider for details.

Support Agreement and Associated Response Time

Logistics time—the time it takes for your service provider to respond—can have a major impact on a system outage [VargasOL00]. Logistics time on a system has these effects:

- Significant impact on the outage time caused by a single point of failure (SPOF)
- Minimal impact on the outage time caused by additional system failures that occur within the same downtime period
- No impact on outage time caused by system interruptions triggered by automatic system recovery (ASR)
- No impact on outage time caused by maintenance-related events

A service contract is a key element of system availability because it defines the maximum possible time it takes the service organization to assume ownership of a problem. You must understand the service options available in your geographic area to ensure that you select the appropriate service option to meet your business availability requirements. For mission-critical systems, assign a local person to be the central point for gathering information (in both directions).

System availability can be enhanced by being aware of the problem escalation process, which ensures that new bugs and problems are handled appropriately by the service organization. Whenever you discover a problem with product functionality, file a request for enhancement (RFE) document with the service organization to initiate a review process.

Backup-and-Restore Testing

Tape backup of critical systems in a data center is routine. However, tape restores are not a common practice. Often an inadequate backup ends in an incomplete restore process.

Note – A best practice is to routinely schedule tape restore drills to familiarize system administrators with the process and to validate the adequacy of any backup procedure. Tape restore drills help evaluate the time involved to bring mission-critical systems back online—the business impact can be analyzed and reviewed for improvement.

Because the tape medium makes physical contact with the read/write heads on tape drives, it becomes unreliable after a certain number of write cycles. Contact the tape medium manufacturer to determine the best practice for retiring unreliable tapes from the backup pool.

All backup media have an estimated shelf life, which is the time during which the data has a high probability of being reliably readable. This includes all magnetic and optical media, such as disks, tapes, CD-RW, and DVD. For media designed for data archival, the media vendor supplies an estimated lifetime. Typical data archives have very little error recovery capability, and once a small portion of the data is unreadable, the entire archive may be useless. For long-term data storage, the media must be read, verified, and written to new media on a regular schedule.

Cluster Recovery Procedures

The Sun Cluster product infrastructure enables a failover server to execute a mission-critical application if the system detects an application failure. Even though application failover is an automated process, a best practice is to do drills by scheduling a manual failover to enable your system administrator to become familiar with the process. These drills can enable your system administrator to make informed decisions if a real failover occurs.

Summary

Computer hardware, software, people, and processes affect availability. You can optimize availability by using a systematic approach, and by using best practices in the data center to reduce the opportunities for, and to minimize the impact of, human error.

Tools

A number of tools are available to help you analyze and design complex systems. This appendix describes some of these tools and covers the following topics:

- Fault Tree Analysis
- Reliability Block Diagram Analysis
- Failure Modes and Effects Analysis
- Event Tree Analysis

Most of these tools are simple enough that they do not require specialized software; simple spreadsheets will do. Many other tools exist; however, they are beyond the scope of this book For more references and information, you can search the Internet for reliability engineering, high-assurance systems engineering, and the tools mentioned here.

You can classify the analysis and design tools described in this appendix as tools for doing top-down or bottom-up design. In most system designs, a combination of top-down and bottom-up design methods are used as appropriate for different portions of a design.

Top-down tools are:

- Fault tree analysis (FTA)
- Reliability block diagram (RBD)

Bottom-up tools are:

- Failure mode and effects analysis (FMEA)
- Event tree analysis (ETA). Sometimes, you can use ETA for top-down analysis.

You can use most of these tools hierarchically, that is, you can describe a system as a collection of components. You can then describe each component, in turn, as a collection of subcomponents. You can use the same tools and techniques to analyze both low-level components and high-level systems.

Fault Tree Analysis

Fault tree analysis (FTA) is a deductive, top-down method of analyzing system design. It is considered one of the best methods for systematically identifying and graphically displaying the many ways something can go wrong. First, you specify an undesirable top event. Then you identify all of the components in the system that could cause that top event. The components can contribute failure probabilities. You can use Boolean logic to describe the relationship between the components. This method enables you to describe a complex system in much the same way as a digital electronic logic circuit.

Generally, you do FTA graphically by using a Boolean logic structure of AND and OR gates (FIGURE D-1 and FIGURE D-2). To describe very complex systems, you can used additional logic gates. You can also decompose systems into subsystems that use the same logical relationships. This method enables you to analyze very complex systems in a hierarchal manner.

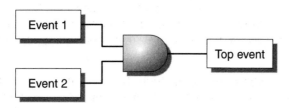

FIGURE D-1   AND Gate Structure Analysis

Logical view: *Top Event = Event1 • Event2*

Probabilistic view: *P(Top Event) = P(Event1) × P(Event2)*

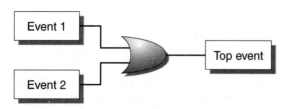

FIGURE D-2   OR Gate Structure Analysis

Logical view: *Top Event = Event1 + Event2*

Probabilistic view: $P(TopEvent) = P(Event1) + P(Event2) - P(Event1 \text{ AND } Event2)$

For convenience, one additional logical grouping, in which the function includes a sum and a conditional, is occasionally used. This grouping is useful when M out of N basic events must occur. An example would be an $N+1$ power supply subsystem. If $N = 2$, there are three total power supplies, but only two must be operational. This logical gate could be constructed out of AND and OR gates, but for more than two inputs, the number of logic gates required to implement the logic becomes tedious, confusing, and error prone. Unfortunately, there is no Boolean logic gate that describes such a function, so a functional block provides clarity (FIGURE D-3).

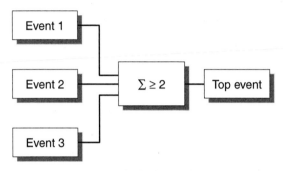

FIGURE D-3 Functional Block Structure Analysis

Logical view: *Top Event = (Event1 • Event2) + (Event1 • Event3) + (Event2 • Event3) + (Event1 • Event2 • Event3)*

The probabilistic view is more complicated. For FTA, we are concerned with minimal cut sets, cut sets that are not a subset of any other cut set. In the logical view (FIGURE D-3), *(Event1 • Event2 • Event3)* is not a minimal cut set. To simplify the expression, the minimal cut sets are:

C1 = Event1 AND *Event2*

C2 = Event1 AND *Event3*

C3 = Event2 AND *Event3*

Probabilistic view: *P(Top Event) = P(C1* OR *C2* OR *C3) = P(C1) + P(C2) + P(C3) − P(C1* AND *C2) − P(C1* AND *C3) − P(C2* AND *C3) + P(C1* AND *C2* AND *C3)*

Obviously, a tool for calculating these probabilities helps to reduce the analysis time.

Building for Analysis

To build a fault tree for analysis:

1. Identify the top event.

   This event can be as simple as a service outage.

2. Identify components that can affect the top event.

   This identification begins the iterative process of examining every component in the architecture that may have a relationship to the top event.

3. Describe the relationships between the components and the top event.

   This description builds the relationships between components into a model that can be analyzed.

FIGURE D-4 is an example of a fault tree for the boot, root, and swap disk subsystem described in "Boot Environment" on page 180.

In this example, the bottom layers represent actual hardware and interconnections. The RAID software manages the presentation of the LUNs to the operating environment. The relationship between the components is clearly shown with dual redundant components feeding into the AND gates. The inputs to the model would be the probability distribution functions for failure of the components. The resulting probability function of the service failure is a complex function, best solved by a modelling program. For simple models, a spreadsheet can be used, but the logical representation is difficult to visualize in a spreadsheet.

Inspecting an FTA

One simple approach to looking at FTA is:

- AND gates represent redundancy and tend to improve system availability.
- OR gates represent dependency and tend to decrease system availability.

However, sometimes the AND gate introduces an OR gate that must be considered. The implied OR gate represents the arbitration and synchronization that is required by active or data components in an architecture.

The example in FIGURE D-4 shows the effects on the system architecture when redundant components are added.

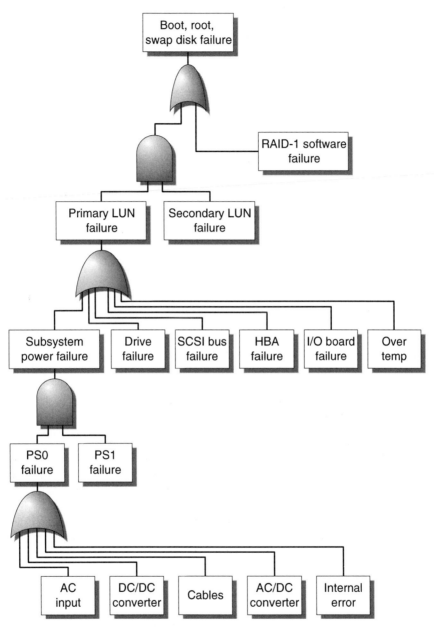

FIGURE D-4 Fault Tree Analysis of Boot, Root, and Swap Disk Subsystem

In FIGURE D-4 the power supplies, PS0 and PS1, are designed to load share. However, no active logic can decide which power supply delivers power to the power subsystem. When both power supplies are functional, each supply shares the load.

When only one power supply is functional, it has enough capacity to supply the required power to the subsystem. In this case, a simple AND gate represents the redundancy. However, this type of load sharing is not properly modelled by FTA, and the mathematics are fairly complicated. Rather, the FTA model for the power supplies is defined as actively redundant. From a practical perspective, the options available to the systems engineer are few, and load-sharing power supplies are a better option for availability than single power supplies. Therefore, it may be more practical to model the power supplies as actively redundant than to create an overly complicated model.

The top-level event requires the use of disk mirroring software to present a single, logical view to the application. This is the role of the logical volume manager (LVM). Failures in the LVM will affect the service. Building a redundant LVM does not work, because some higher level mechanism must provide the arbitration and synchronization between the LVMs. Thus, you must design and build the LVM to be as resilient as possible.

Reliability Block Diagram Analysis

Reliability block diagrams (RBDs) are based on a top-down model similar to FTA. However, instead of the result being a failure, the result is a success. The top event is a successful event such as a service being available. The model depicts the successful components and their relationships to achieve top event success. Removal of a block is equivalent to a loss of the success path represented by that block. The focus is on describing all success paths through the system.

The relationships are mapped as serial and parallel connections of the blocks. Redundant components are shown connected in parallel, similar to the AND gate in the FTA. Dependent components are shown connected serially, similar to the OR gate in the FTA. FIGURE D-5 is an example of an RBD for a mirrored disk example. This example is similar to the FTA shown in FIGURE D-1. The model represents components at the FRU level. More detailed models of each of the components can be used if needed. For example, this model shows a single CPU and memory bank, but the model could be extended to show the multiple CPUs and memory banks used in a multiprocessor computer. The decision on what granularity to use for the model is more likely to be based on the information that is available for the components. At a minimum, the mean time between failure (MTBF) should be measured and known. If the mean time to recover and repair (MTTR) is also known, then an RBD can provide an availability figure.

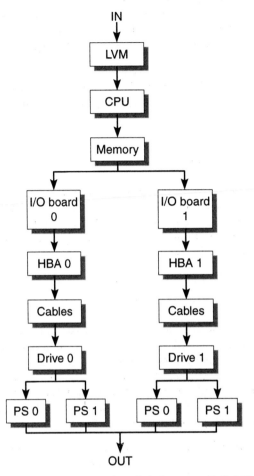

FIGURE D-5 Mirrored Disk Subsystem Reliability Block Diagram

Failure Modes and Effects Analysis

Failure modes and effects analysis (FMEA) is a bottom-up approach to analyzing system design and performance. To begin FMEA, outline the lowest levels of the system. These levels can be the individual components or FRU level in the system. In some cases, a logical component can be used instead of, or in addition to, the physical components. This method enables you to analyze people, process, software, and other failures. For each lowest level, you must generate a list of potential failure modes and determine the effects of each potential failure.

The power of FMEA becomes apparent when you are analyzing large, complex systems. These systems tend to have many failure modes. But not all failure modes have the same effect on the system. The FMEA helps in prioritization, so you can devote the most resources to failure modes that have the largest effects.

You can use FMEA to analyze remedies. If a remedy to a failure mode is found, the analysis of the remedy can be placed in the FMEA to show improvement. Often this is done iteratively, and the resulting tables can become quite large.

Risk Priority Number

The FMEA is basically an exercise in filling out a table. The table can take various forms and different column headings. The example shown in TABLE D-1 is generic. It includes a section for remedies and their effects. The first part identifies the component, its potential failure modes, the potential impact and causes of such a failure, and an initial risk priority number (*RPN*).

The *RPN* is calculated with the following formula:

$$RPN = Severity \times Probability \times Detectability$$

The severity, probability, and detectability values are assigned to a simple scale, such as 1 to 10 (TABLE D-2). These are defined on a project-by-project basis. This scale translates common language into a numerical value. If a numerical scale of 1 to 10 does not fit the common language descriptions, another scale may work better. The calculation of the *RPN* is used for relative differentiation, not for an absolute figure. The scale should fit the problem being solved by the system. For example, the severity may peak at "unsatisfied player" for a card game.

The *RPN* is a weighted value for each failure mode and effect. The goal is to reduce the *RPN*s to a value of 1 (you should not model an *RPN* of zero); however, this is rarely achievable. You can use the *RPN* to prioritize the failure modes or effects to be solved in a complex system. The scale assigned to the severity, probability, and detectability should be nonlinear, to show greater differentiation between each *RPN*. For example, if all of the *RPN*s are in a narrow range, say 20 to 60, the scale may need adjustment to spread the *RPN*s. Engineers tend to try to define or pick the severity, probability, and detectability numbers perfectly. This wastes time and is often counterproductive. It is better to get close on the first pass, observe the *RPN* spread, and determine if higher resolution is required to spread the *RPN* and increase the ease of prioritization.

Another useful feature of the FMEA is that proposed solutions can be examined on the same scale as the original problem. If the proposed solution does not reduce the *RPN*, it is immediately obvious that the solution is ineffective. Competing solutions can be evaluated to see which solution produces the lowest *RPN*.

Item or function	Potential failure mode	Potential effects	Severity	Potential causes	Probability	Current design controls	Detection	RPN	Recommended action	Owner and target completion date	Action taken	Remedy applied			
												Severity	Probability	Detection	RPN
Power supply	Open	Power supply loss	7	See FTA	7	Redundant power supplies	3	147	Dual AC inputs	R. Elling, 09 Sep 05	RTU/RTS added to rack	5	5	3	75
	Short	Service outage	8	Bent pin	1	Fuse	8	64	None	n/a	n/a	-	-	-	-
SCSI cable	Pulled	SCSI bus hang	7	Accidental pull	3	Connector clasps	3	63	Add cable relief	T. Read, 21 Aug 04	Added cable tie-downs	7	1	3	21
	Bent pin	SCSI bus hang	7	Insertion	1	None	6	42	Redesign connector		None	-	-	-	-

TABLE D-2 Key for FMEA Severity, Likelihood, and Detection

Value	Severity	Probability	Detection
1	No impact	< 0.0000001, extremely unlikely	Immediately detected and isolated
2	No noticeable impact	< 0.000001	
3	Minor impact	< 0.00002	Easily detected
4	Slight inconvenience	< 0.0001, rarely occurs	
5	Moderate inconvenience	< 0.005	Likely to be detected
6	Serious inconvenience	< 0.01, occasional failures	
7	Multiple FRUs affected	< 0.05	
8	Does not work	< 0.2	Unlikely to be detected
9	Incorrect service, data corruption	< 0.5	
10	Personnel safety affected	> 0.5, almost inevitable	Impossible to detect

FMEA Process

The FMEA process is:

1. Define the scope and function of the system to be analyzed by means of FMEA.

2. List the system components.

3. List the failure modes for each component.

   The list can be done interactively; it requires the cooperation of the designers and customers of the system with different views of the system.

4. List the effect of each failure mode for each FRU.

   You can use scenario-based analysis and event tree analysis (ETA) to ensure that the impact is well understood.

5. List the causes of each failure.

   If there are multiple causes, each cause should have its own *RPN*.

6. List any controls currently in place that would help reduce the *RPN*.

7. Estimate the values for severity, probability, and detectability according to the agreed-on project guidelines.

   You can use ETA to get more accurate estimates.

8. Calculate the *RPN*.

   The math is simple enough to do by hand, but the row and column structure of spreadsheets enables you to group ideas easily (TABLE D-1).

9. List remedies that can be taken to reduce the *RPN*.

   Without FMEA, the tendency is to reduce the probability of failures. With FMEA, it will be obvious if the severity or detectability could be reduced instead, providing better return on effort than just reducing the probability.

10. Evaluate the remedies by calculating a new *RPN*.

    If the remedies are actually applied, you can use the measured data for the new *RPN*.

11. Iterate by taking the specified actions and re-evaluating the system.

Event Tree Analysis

Event tree analysis (ETA) is a low-level tool that is useful for describing failure sequences. You can use ETA to provide more detail on failure modes or effects for FMEA analysis. ETA occasionally reveals new failure modes within a system.

The ETA develops a model of outcome events based on an initiating event. Many events can be modeled, including automatic system responses and human responses. ETA effectively accounts for the timing, dependence, and domino effects among various contributors that are cumbersome to model in fault trees. If the probability of each event can be measured or predicted, you can also use ETA for risk assessment of service outages.

Because it is limited to one initiating event, ETA is not an exhaustive approach to analyzing failures. Also, you can easily overlook subtle dependencies. For example, common mode errors tend to be hidden. This can lead you to overly optimistic risk estimates.

Terms used in ETA include:

- Initiating event—the first failure in the event tree
- Line of assurance—a redundant system, safeguard, or process that can respond to an event
- Branch point—graphical illustration of two or more potential outcomes when a line of assurance is challenged
- Event scenario—a specific pathway through the event tree from the initiating event to an outcome

ETA Process

The ETA process is:

1. Define the system, component, or activity of interest.

   You should limit the scope of the analysis, because many events may be possible in complex systems. Modeling all of them can be very time consuming.

2. Identify the initiating events of interest.

   For highly available systems, an initiating event could be the failure of one of the redundant components.

3. Identify the lines of assurance and physical phenomena.

Identifying lines of assurance can help mitigate the consequences of the initiating event. These lines of assurance can include physical phenomena such as operator intervention or FRU replacement.

4. Identify the initiating event failure scenarios.

Identifying the possible failures and effects for each initiating event can provide a reference for an FMEA.

5. Analyze the event sequence outcomes.

For each event sequence, determine the possible outcomes and their probabilities.

6. Summarize the results.

The event trees can become quite complex. You can place a summary in a separate table for future reference.

ETA Example

"Boot Environment" on page 180 describes an ETA example in a mirrored boot disk environment in which the hot spare and secondary mirror were attached to the same SCSI bus (FIGURE 6-10 on page 183). This figure shows a failure mode in which a failure in the secondary disk data path follows the primary disk LUN failure. FIGURE D-6 is an example of an ETA that describes the failure modes shown in FIGURE 6-10 on page 183.

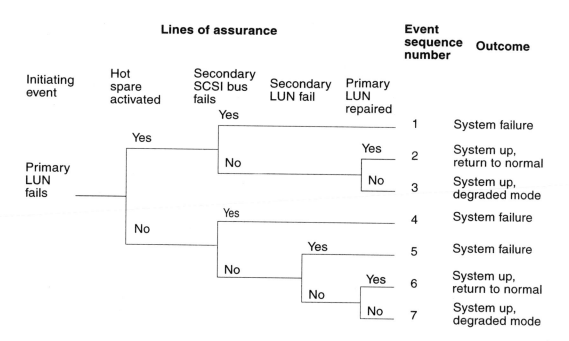

FIGURE D-6 Mirrored Sun StorEdge D240 Media Tray—Event Tree Analysis

Acronyms, Abbreviations, and Glossary

A

AutoFS   automounter file system.

Amnesia   A failure mode in which a node starts with stale cluster configuration information.

Arbitration   The act of deciding.

AP   alternate pathing.

API   application program interface.

ASP   application service provider.

ASR   automatic system recovery.

B

BDC   backup domain controller.

BER   bit error rate.

BSD   Berkeley Standard Distribution.

Blacklist   A feature of the Sun Enterprise server that identifies faulty components. The faulty components are listed in the blacklist.

C

CRM   Customer Relationship Management.

CCD   cluster configuration databases.

CCR	cluster configuration repository.
CC-NUMA	Cache Coherent Non-Uniform Memory Architecture.
CFS	cluster file system.
CGI	Common Gateway interface.
Chokepoints	Filtering routers, flow control devices, and application or packet-filtering fire walls.
CI	The central instance used in the SAP R/3 software.
CIM	Common Information Model.
CIFS	Common Internet File System.
CMM	cluster membership monitor.
CMS	customer management system.
Coherence	The behavior of reads and writes to the same memory location.
Common mode fault	A fault that occurs when a fault in one component causes a fault in another component. This propagation can occur when two components share a common component.
Consistency	The behavior of reads and writes with respect to accesses to other memory locations. Describes the when a read operation returns a written value. Coherency and consistency are complementary.
CORBA	Common Object Request Broker Architecture.
CRM	customer relationship management.
CSMA/CD	carrier sense, multiple access, collision detection.
CTQ	critical-to-quality (issue).
CVM	cluster volume manager; a licensable part of VxVM.
CXS	CORBA executive service.

D

DAG	directed acyclic graph.
DBWR	database writer.
DCS	device configuration system.
Defect	Anything that prevents something, when exercised, from functioning in the intended manner.

DHCP   Dynamic Host Configuration Protocol.

DIA   Defense Intelligence Agency.

DID   device ID.

DLM   distributed lock manager.

DLPI   data link provider interface.

DMP   dynamic multipathing.

DMZ   demilitarized zone.

DNS   domain name service.

DoS   denial of service.

DR   dynamic reconfiguration.

DRAM   Dynamic Random Access Memory.

DRM   distributed resource manager.

DSDL   Data Service Development Library.

DSS   decision support system.

Dynamic reconfiguration   The ability to change the configuration of a running system by putting components online or or taking them offline without disrupting system operation.

E

ECC   error checking and correction.
error checking code.
error correction code.

EDA   electronic design automation.

Error   When a component exhibits unintended behavior.

Error correction   The action taken by a component to correct an error condition without exposing other components to the error.

EMI   electromagnetic interference.

ERP   enterprise resource planning.

ESD   electrostatic discharge.

ETA   event tree analysis.

F

Failfast   Similar to *failstop*, but it also concedes that the stopping may not be instantaneous, and that stopping quickly may be good enough. Sometimes, watchdog timers are employed as a mechanism to achieve failfast behavior.

Failstop   In practice, a component should be internally checking its own correct operation; upon detecting an error in itself, it should stop its execution before it has a chance to corrupt data or propagate errors to other components outside itself. The concept that a component either executes completely correctly or it halts.

Failure fencing   Closely related to failstop and fault containment. A method to ensure that a faulty component cannot propagate errors or failure. Surviving components prevent the defective component from accessing other components or data.

Fault   A defect, but possibly an imprecise error. *See* Error.

Fault containment   A method to prevent a failed component from propagating to other components.

Fault isolation   A method to determine the source of a fault and the component or FRU that requires repair.

Fault isolation zone   A division of a system in which a set of disjointed zones facilitates fault isolation.

Fault propagation   Transmission of a fault to unaffected areas of the system.

Fault recovery zone   An area of the system in which recovery work is performed on a component in that area.

FC-AL   Fibre Channel-Arbitrated Loop.

FIFO   first in, first out.

FMEA   failure modes and effects analysis.

FRU   field-replaceable unit.

FTA   fault tree analysis.

FTP   File Transfer Protocol.

G

GbE   Gigabit Ethernet.

GBIC   Gigabit Interface Converter.

GCS   global cache service.

GFS   global file system. *See* CFS.

GIF	global interface.
GIN	global interface node.
GUI	graphical user interlace.

H

HA	highly available or high availability.
Hardened data center	A data center designed to provide reliable environmental and power sources.
Hardware Diagnostic Suite	A comprehensive, network-savvy diagnostics tool that enhances overall availability by detecting hardware faults before systems are affected and by reducing routine system maintenance through scheduled testing. This tool is an optional agent for the Sun Management Center.
HBA	host bus adapter.
HPC	high-performance computing.
HSFS	High Sierra File System.
HTTP	Hypertext Transfer Protocol.
HWDS	Sun Management Center Hardware Diagnostic Suite.
Hot CPU upgrades	A term applied to upgrades that enable you to install faster CPUs while the Solaris operating environment and applications continue to be available.

I

IAS	iPlanet application server.
IDL	interface definition language.
IIOP	Internet Inter-Orb Protocol.
IP	Internet Protocol.
IPC	interprocess communication.
IPMP	Internet protocol multipathing.
isochronous	Uniform in time; having equal duration or recurring at regular intervals.
ISP	Internet service provider.
ISV	independent software vendors.
IT	Information Technology.
ITO	Information Technology Organization.

IUM   impacted user minutes.

J

JXTA   Stands for *juxtapose*.

K

KAS   administrative server.

KJS   Java server.

KXS   executive server.

L

Latent fault   A fault that is hidden or not detectable. It can manifest itself if conditions permit.

LDAP   Lightweight Directory Access Protocol.

LGWR   log writer.

LMD   Global Enqueue Service daemon.

LMON   Global Enqueue Service monitor.

LOM and LOMlite   lights out management.

LUN   logical unit number.

M

MAC   medium access control.

MII   media independent interface.

MPI   message passing interface.

MMF   multimode filter.

MPxIO   multipath I/O (Sun StorEdge Traffic Manager).

MAC address   The physical address of an Ethernet network expressed as a 48-bit number.

MTBF   mean time between failures.

MTTR   mean time to recover and repair. The average or expected value of the independent and identically distributed downtimes.

Mutex   mutual exclusion (locks).

Metadata Data about data.

N

NAFO network adapter failover.

NAS network attached storage.

NAT network address translation.

NCSC National Computer Security Center.

NFS Network File System.

NIC network interface card.

NIS Network Information Service.

NTFS Microsoft Windows NT file system.

NTP Network Time Protocol.

O

OBP OpenBoot Prom.

OLTP online transaction processing.

OPS Oracle 8*i* Parallel Server.

ORB object request broker.

P

PCI-SCI Peripheral Component Interconnect-Scalable Coherent Interface.

PDC primary domain controller.

PDT packet dispatch table.

PFS parallel file system.

PGR persistent group reservation.

PI past image.

PNM public network monitoring.

PMON process monitor.

Prospect theory A theory by psychologists Amos Tversky and Daniel Kahneman that describes the rational decisions made by people who are risk averse when an opportunity presents a gain and risk-seekers when opportunity presents a loss.

PVM parallel virtual machine.

Q

Quorum The number, usually a majority of officers or members of a body, that when duly assembled is legally competent to transact business.

R

RAC Oracle 9*i* Real Application Cluster.

RAM random access memory.

Reliability An abstract term defined as the probability that a product or system performs its intended function for a specified time period when operating under normal environmental conditions. Reliability differs from availability in that reliability involves only one event, failure, whereas availability takes into account two events: failure and recovery. A system can be highly available yet experience frequent periods of inoperability as long as the length of each period is short.

RBAC role-based access control.

RBD reliability block diagram.

RDBMS relational database management system.

RM-API Resource Management API.

RM replica managers.

RMA replica manager agents.

RMM replica manager manager.

RPN risk priority number.

RSC remote service controller.

RSM Remote Shared Memory.

RTR resource type registration.

RTS redundant transfer switch.

RTU redundant transfer unit.

S

S3L Sun Scalable Scientific Subroutine Library.

SAN storage area network.

SC	system controller.
SCI	Scalable Coherent Interface.
SCN	system change number.
SCSI	Small Computer System Interface.
SCSL	Sun Community Software License.
SGA	system global area.
SLA	service level agreement.
SMAD	switch management agent daemon.
SMB	Now called the Common Intenet File System.
SMON	system monitor.
SMP	symmetric multiprocessor.
SPA	service point architecture.
SPOF	single point of failure.
SRS	Sun Remote Services.
SSP	system service processor.
SVM	Solaris Volume Manager. Formerly known as Solstice DiskSuite.
SQE	software query enable.
Split brain	Condition in which a cluster forms multiple partitions, with each partition forming without knowledge of the existence of any other partition.
SMON	system monitor.
SRAM	static random access memory.
SMP	symmetric multiprocessor.
Systems engineering	The engineering discipline concerned with the design of the whole as distinct from the design of the parts.

T

TC	terminal concentrator.
TCP/IP	Transmission Control Protocol/Internet Protocol.

U

UDP   User Datagram Protocol. Built on top of IP at the transport layer, UDP provides a datagram-based service.

UDLM   UNIX distributed lock manager.

UFS   UNIX file system.

UPS   uninterruptible power supply.

UTC   universal time coordinated.

UTP   unshielded twisted pair.

V

Vote   A usually formal expression of opinion or will in response to a proposed decision.

VPN   virtual private network.

VxFS   VERITAS File System.

VxVM   VERITAS Volume Manager, which includes a licensable CVM.

W

WAN   wide area network.

WBEM   web-based enterprise management.

WERO   write-exclusive, registrants only.

X

XAS   executive application server.

XCS   C++ server.

XJS   executive Java server.

Bibliography

ANOL01	Alex Noordergraaf, "Building a JumpStart Infrastructure," Sun BluePrints Online, April 2001, `http://www.sun.com/blueprints`
Bern98	Peter L. Bernstein, *Against the Gods, the Remarkable Story of Risk*, 1998, ISBN 0-471-29563-9
CORBAhist	*CORBA history*: `http://cgi.omg.org/corba/corbahistory.html`
Dijkstra65	E. W. Dijkstra, "Solution of a Problem in Concurrent Programming Control," *Communications of the ACM*, Vol. 8, 1965
DNS	Domain Name Service: `http://www.polyserve.com/support/whitepapers/wp_load_balancing.html` (DNS round-robin)
Hayes98	John P. Hayes, *Computer Architecture and Organization*, 3rd edition, 1998, ISBN 0-07-027355-3
HPcod2	David A. Patterson and John L. Hennessy, *Computer Organization and Design: The Hardware/Software Interface*, 2nd edition, 1998, ISBN 1-55860-428-6
iMS51	iPlanet Message Server 5.1 manuals: `http://docs.iplanet.com/docs/manuals/messaging/ims51/ig/unix/overview.htm#23546`
JMRM00	Jim Mauro and Richard McDougall, *Solaris Internals Core Kernel Architecture*, Prentice Hall, 2000, ISBN 0-13-022496-0
JHAN01	John S. Howard and Alex Noordergraaf, *JumpStart Technology: Effective Use in the Solaris Operating Environment*, 2001, ISBN 0-13-062154-4
JXTAover	*Project JXTA: A Technology Overview*, by Li Gong, Sun Microsystems (whitepaper)
Lamport74	Leslie Lamport, "A New Solution of Dijkstra's Concurrent Programming Problem," *Communications of the ACM*, 17(8):453-455, August 1974
Laprie85	Jean-Claude Laprie, *Dependable Computing and Fault Tolerance: Concepts and Terminology*, 1985, IEEE 0731-3071/85/0000/0002

Lyu95	Michael R. Lyu, editor, *Handbook of Software Reliability Engineering*, 1995, Tupper and Love/David McKay Company
Madron89	Thomas W. Madron, *LANS: Applications of IEEE/ANSI 802 Standards*, 1989, ISBN 0-471-62049-1
ORBimpl	*ORB Implementations*: `http://www.yy.cs.keio.ac.jp/~suzuki/object/dist_comp.html#corba-r`
PHcaqa2	John L. Hennessy and David A. Patterson, *Computer Architecture: A Quantitative Approach*, 2nd edition, 1996, ISBN 1-55860-329-8
PL01	Peter Lees, "Writing Scalable Service with Sun Cluster 3.0," *Proceedings of the Sun Users Performance Group*, April 2001, `http://www.sun.com/datacenter/superg`
Ramo65	Simon Ramo, "The Design of the Whole—Systems Engineering," in *Listen to Leaders in Engineering*, edited by Albert Love and James Saxon Childers, 1965, Library of Congress Catalog Card Number: 64-23488
SKB00	Stan Stringfellow, Miroslav Klivansky, and Michael Barto, *Backup and Restore Practices for Sun Enterprise Servers*, 2000, ISBN 0-13-089401-X
SunMPG99	*Multithreaded Programming Guide*, Sun Microsystems, Part Number 806-5257-10, `http://docs.sun.com`
SunSCE01	Enrique Vargas, Joesph Bianco, and David Deeths, *Sun Cluster Environment Sun Cluster 2.2*, 2001, ISBN 0-13-041870-6
SunSIG99	*System Interface Guide*, Sun Microsystems, Part Number 806-4750-10, `http://docs.sun.com`
SWuios96	W. David Schwaderer and Andrew W. Wilson, Jr., *Understanding I/O Subsystems*, 1st edition, 1996, ISBN 0-9651911-0-9
Vahalia96	Uresh Vahalia, "Cluster Platform 220/1000 Architecture—A Product from the SunTone Platforms Portfolio," *UNIX Internals: the New Frontiers*, 1996, ISBN 0-13-101908-2
VargasOL00	Enrique Vargas, "High Availability Fundamentals," Sun BluePrints Online, November 2000, `http://www.sun.com/blueprints`
Vargas01	Enrique Vargas, "Cluster Platform 220/1000 Architecture—A Product from the SunTone Platforms Portfolio,"Sun BluePrints Online, August 2001, `http://www.sun.com/blueprints`
VBD01	*Sun™ Cluster Environment: Sun Cluster 2.2, Sun BluePrints™*, 2001, ISBN 0-13-041870-6
Webster87	*Webster's Ninth New Collegiate Dictionary*, 1987, ISBN 0-87779-508-8